6

Paul Dummett

John Hughes

Helen Stephenson

Life Level 6 Student Book

Paul Dummett

John Hughes

Helen Stephenson

Publisher: Sherrise Roehr

Executive Editor: Sarah T. Kenney

Editorial Assistant: Patricia Giunta

Director of Global Marketing: Ian Martin

Senior Product Marketing Manager:
Caitlin Thomas

Director of Content and Media Production:
Michael Burggren

Production Manager: Daisy Sosa

Senior Print Buyer: Mary Beth Hennebury

Cover Designers: Scott Baker and Alex Dull

Cover Image: Michael Melford/National
Geographic Creative

Compositor: MPS Limited

Image credit: Cheoh Wee Keat / Getty Images

Cover Image

The Supertree Grove at twilight. Gardens by
the Bay, Singapore.
Photograph by Cheoh Wee Keat.

Student Book
ISBN-13: 978-1-305-25635-4

Student Book + CD-ROM
ISBN-13: 978-1-305-25638-5

Student Book + Online Workbook
ISBN-13: 978-1-305-26040-5

National Geographic Learning/Cengage Learning
20 Channel Center Street
Boston, MA 02210
USA

Cengage Learning is a leading provider of customized learning solutions
with office locations around the globe, including Singapore, the United
Kingdom, Australia, Mexico, Brazil, and Japan. Locate our local office at
international.cengage.com/region

Cengage Learning products are represented in Canada by Nelson
Education Ltd.

Visit National Geographic Learning online at **NGL.Cengage.com**
Visit our corporate website at **www.cengage.com**

Printed in China
7 8 9 20 19 18

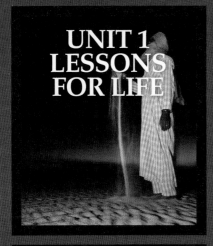

UNIT 1
LESSONS FOR LIFE

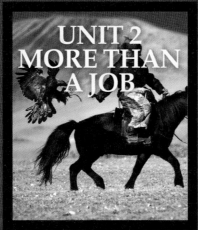

UNIT 2
MORE THAN A JOB

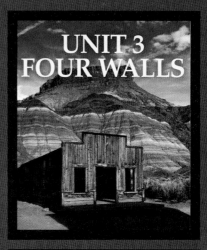

UNIT 3
FOUR WALLS

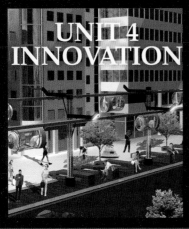

UNIT 4
INNOVATION

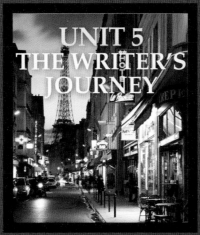

UNIT 5
THE WRITER'S JOURNEY

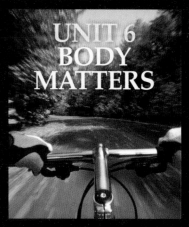

UNIT 6
BODY MATTERS

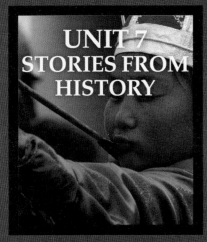

UNIT 7
STORIES FROM HISTORY

UNIT 8
DIGITAL MEDIA

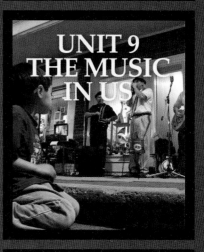

UNIT 9
THE MUSIC IN US

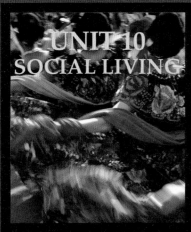

UNIT 10
SOCIAL LIVING

UNIT 11
REASON AND EMOTION

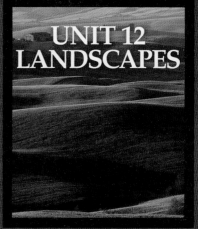

UNIT 12
LANDSCAPES

Contents

LISTENING	READING	CRITICAL THINKING	SPEAKING	WRITING
a talk by a sociologist about defining who you are	an article about the lessons we learn from the past an article about the language of Shakespeare	developing an argument	your favorite saying personality types call my bluff	a cover letter writing skill: fixed expressions
an interview with a woman firefighter	an article about the Moken people of Myanmar an article about rock climbing in Yosemite	using contrasts	work as a way of life health and safety issues your comfort zone	taking notes writing skill: abbreviations
an interview with an architect about small homes	an article about two model towns an article about the architect Zaha Hadid	fact or opinion	your ideal home town planning how spaces affect you	an opinion essay writing skill: linking devices
an interview about the inspiration for inventions	an article about origami engineering an article about a social entrepreneur	finding counter arguments	what you can't live without origami ideas being on the spot	describing how things work writing skill: punctuation
part of a radio show about an extraordinary journey into the Himalayas	an article about the graphic novel a passage from the book *In Patagonia*	analyzing descriptive language	a good read speech bubbles describing impressions	a book review writing skill: descriptive words
an interview with an ultrarunner about sports injuries	an article about different exercise regimes an article about beauty	identifying aims	exercise trends describing an injury does beauty sell?	a formal report writing skill: linking adverbs and adverbial phrases

LISTENING	READING	CRITICAL THINKING	SPEAKING	WRITING
a radio interview about an archaeological find	an article about Herodotus and the story of the Persian invasion of Greece a story about hidden treasure	fact or conjecture	stories from history social history historical irony	describing a past event writing skill: sequencing events
an interview about social media marketing	a photographer's blog about sinkholes an article about a day at a hacker's conference	identifying personal opinions	blogging using social media IT security	an online news report writing skill: cautious language
a talk by a neuroscientist about music therapy	an interview with a musician about music and culture a review of a documentary about Bob Marley	identifying text types	themes of songs mood music a charity concert	a description writing skill: parallel structures
an interview with a sociologist about citizenship education	an article about ant society an article about the Hadza of Tanzania	reading between the lines	civic duties social animals a conservation project	a discursive essay writing skill: critical thinking in writing
an interview with a psychologist about understanding emotions	an article about irrational thinking an article about the new generation of robots	understanding style	modern life mind games technology ethics	an email message writing skill: avoiding misunderstandings
part of a radio show about the Japanese poet Basho	an article about William Allard's American West an article about a camera obscura	identifying aims	special places events in nature explaining a technique	haiku a speculative letter writing skill: persuasive language

Life around the world

Unit 1 Arctic wisdom

Learn how generations pass on their accumulated wisdom in Iqaluit, Canada.

Unit 4 Ethical Ocean

Learn how David Damberger became a social entrepreneur and what his business does.

Unit 3 Denmark bridge

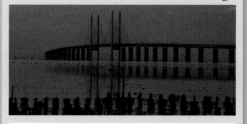

Find out about the challenges behind the construction of the Oresund Bridge, which links Denmark and Sweden.

Unit 8 Talking dictiona

Learn about a project that is helping to preserve dying languages.

Unit 12 Canada oil sands

Find out about the impact of the excavation of the oil sands in Canada.

Canada

Denmark

Russia

UK

USA

Spain

Japan

Palestine

China

Jamaica

Unit 11 Self-teaching robots

Discover how robots are helping themselves to progress.

Unit 2 Climbing Yosemite

Brazil

Find out how Jimmy Chin made a career out of mountaineer photography.

Unit 5 On the road: Andrew McCarthy

Learn how a travel experience changed the life of travel writer Andrew McCarthy.

Unit 7 Collecting the past

Find out how China's cultural heritage is being preserved by shopping.

Unit 9 A biopic

Learn about the inspiration behind the making of the biopic *Marley*.

Unit 10 Initiation with ants

Find out about an unusual ceremony in the Amazonian jungle in Brazil.

Unit 6 Palestinian free running

Discover the liberating influence of free running on teenagers in Gaza.

Unit 1 Lessons for life

A Tuareg tribesman prays at twilight, Libya.
Photograph by Bobby Model

1 Work in pairs. Look at the photo and the Tuareg proverbs. What do these tell you about the Tuareg outlook on life?

Better to walk without knowing where than to sit doing nothing.

In life, it is always possible to reach agreement in the end.

2 Do you know the expressions in bold? Match them to their meaning.

1 Kindess is the **most valuable lesson** anyone has ever taught me.
2 The company's **guiding principle** is customer satisfaction.
3 A good **rule of thumb** is to think before you speak.
4 Try not to worry—I know, **easier said than done!**
5 Try to **make a point** of listening to the other person, even if you disagree with him or her.

a a deliberate effort
b underlying philosophy or goal
c the most important thing learned
d seems simple, but difficult to act on
e basic guideline for behavior

3 Think of an occasion when you learned an important lesson. Describe what happened to your partner. What did you do about it? What principle now guides you?

1a Learning from the past

Reading

1 Work in pairs. Read the quotation. Do you think this is good advice? Is it easy to act on? Discuss with your partner.

> Learn from the mistakes of others. You can't live long enough to make them all yourself.
>
> *Eleanor Roosevelt, Diplomat*

2 Read the article. Match the people with the types of lesson they taught (a–c). There is one extra type of lesson.

  1 Confucius   2 Nelson Mandela

  a a lesson that is difficult to act on
  b a lesson that has been misinterpreted
  c a lesson that had been forgotten

3 Mark the sentences true (T) or false (F).

  1 Sometimes people don't want to understand the lessons of the past.
  2 A lot of Chinese people feel that their society has turned its back on the past.
  3 China's rapid development has begun to slow down.
  4 Nelson Mandela wanted the two sides in South Africa to stop fighting.
  5 Mandela was not opposed to violence in principle.
  6 The writer suggests that most people are too selfish.

4 Find expressions in the article for these definitions.

  1 show the right direction (para 1)
  2 summarizes an idea or approach (para 3)
  3 work hard towards a goal (para 5)
  4 copy someone's behavior (para 5)
  5 paying attention to danger (para 5)

> ▶ **WORDBUILDING suffix -ness**
>
> We can add -ness to the end of an adjective to make nouns describing human qualities.
> *kindness, thoughtfulness, unselfishness*

LEARNING FROM THE PAST

Why do we never seem to learn from the lessons of the past? The actions of others could point the way for us, but we seem either to forget these lessons or deliberately misinterpret them—or knowing them, simply fail to act on them.

Because of the economic boom in China, its government has become worried in recent years about selfish motives overtaking society. Many Chinese have been saying for some time that the traditional values of harmony, respect, and hard work have been lost. So a few years ago, the government focused attention again on the teachings of Confucius, the ancient philosopher.

> "Consideration for others is the basis of a good life, a good society."

Prior to the 1990s, Confucianism had not been fashionable, but now, in a country which is currently developing at a dizzying speed, it offers a sense of stability and order. The Confucian saying that nowadays sums up the government's philosophy is "harmonious society."

Sometimes it is difficult to learn from the past because the "teacher" sets such high standards. This is certainly the case with Nelson Mandela, who preached reconciliation to two sides in South Africa who hated each other deeply. Mandela had always been ideologically committed to peace, and while he was living in prison, he became determined that reconciliation was the only way to unite his divided country.

> "If you want to make peace with your enemy, you have to work with your enemy."

All those who strive for peace know that in the long term they will have to begin this dialogue. Yet few are able to follow the example set by Mandela because it requires such a high degree of unselfishness. It seems that heeding this warning—not to be selfish—may be the hardest lesson of all for people to learn.

> **dizzying** (adj) /ˈdɪziɪŋ/ very fast and confusing
> **reconciliation** (n) /ˌrekənsɪliˈeɪʃən/ making peace and re-establishing relations

Language focus time phrases

5 Look at the article. Identify the verb that accompanies these time phrases and name the tense used in each case.

1 in recent years
2 for some time
3 a few years ago
4 prior to the 1990s
5 currently
6 nowadays
7 while
8 in the long term

> ▶ **TIME PHRASES**
>
> Certain time phrases are commonly (but not always) used with certain tenses.
>
> **Simple present**
> *often, never, every week, generally*
>
> **Present continuous**
> *now, at the moment, this week*
>
> **Simple past**
> *three days ago, last week, at the time*
>
> **Past continuous**
> *while, at the time*
>
> **Present perfect**
> *already, just, recently, so far, over the last two years, how long, for, since, ever, never*
>
> **Present perfect continuous**
> *how long, for, since*
>
> **Past perfect and past perfect continuous**
> *already, before that, up to then*
>
> ***will, going to*, and present continuous for future**
> *next week, in three days, soon, on Friday*
>
> For more information and practice, see page 157.

6 Work in pairs. Choose the correct time phrase below to complete the sentences. Then compare answers. There may be more than one answer.

> at the moment   at the time   before that   ever
> for some time   in the coming years   nowadays   often
> over the last 25 years   50 years ago

a Military service was compulsory in the UK
   ¹ _____ . But ² _____ young people don't
   have to serve. It may change ³ _____ because there
   is a feeling that young people need the discipline that
   military service gives you.
b ⁴ _____ people have definitely become greedier.
   I've been arguing ⁵ _____ that a bank president
   shouldn't earn 150 times what a cashier earns.
c People ⁶ _____ complain that young people don't
   show respect to their elders anymore. I'm having the same
   debate with my daughter ⁷ _____ . She says you
   can't just demand someone's respect; you have to earn it.
d When I was 40, I decided to stop working so hard.
   ⁸ _____ , I was working 60 hours a week and
   I was exhausted. It was the best decision that I have
   ⁹ _____ made. ¹⁰ _____ I had had no time
   to spend with my family or just to enjoy life.

7 Complete the sentences by writing facts about yourself. Then exchange this information with your partner.

1 Currently I…
2 A few years ago, I…
3 I…for several years.
4 Sooner or later I…
5 Generally I…

Currently I'm looking for a new job.

8 Work with a new partner. Tell your new partner two interesting facts you learned about your first partner.

Speaking

9 Match the two parts of these English sayings. Use the time phrases to help you, where necessary.

1 The only easy day was…
2 You always…
3 It will all be OK…
4 No one has ever…
5 Don't sweat…

a …become poor by giving.
b …yesterday.
c …have a choice.
d …the small stuff.
e …in the end.

10 Work in groups. Discuss your favorite sayings. Follow these steps:

- Think of a saying from your country or from English that you like or that has helped you in life.
- Write the saying on a piece of paper.
- Put all the sayings in a pile in the middle.
- Take turns choosing a paper and reading the saying.
- Together, discuss the meaning and guess whose favorite saying it is. Ask the person why they chose it.

"Better late than never!"

I bet Michelle chose that one; she's always late!

1b Who do you think you are?

A Paris painter next to his self-portrait
Photograph by Bruno Schlumberger

Listening

1 Work in pairs. Look carefully at the photo and caption. Discuss the questions.

1 Did the painter want his photo taken?
2 What image of himself is the painter projecting through his self-portrait?

2 Which of the following factors are most important in defining who you are? Discuss with your partner.

a your friends
b your interests/hobbies
c your work
d your cultural background
e your outlook on life
f your beliefs and values
g your life experiences

3 🔊 1 Listen to a talk by a sociologist describing how we define ourselves. Check (✓) the factors in Exercise 2 the sociologist mentions. Which is the most important, according to him?

4 🔊 1 Listen again and choose the correct option (a–c) to complete the sentences.

1 Ana's friends feel…about her commitment to animals.
   a surprised   b angry   c defensive
2 Children are defined by their…qualities.
   a individual   b adult   c shared
3 Teenagers like to define themselves by what….
   a they like.   b their friends like.   c they don't like.
4 For Carlos, the important thing about his job is that it is…
   a comfortable.   b secure.   c independent.
5 Sayah studies bonobo…
   a eating habits.   b society.   c work tasks.
6 Jae finds it difficult to commit to…
   a relationships.   b new environments.   c his work.

Idioms irreversible word pairs

5 Choose the correct irreversible word pairs from the talk.

1 What defines them *foremost and first / first and foremost*…
2 He picks up work *as and when / when and as* he can.
3 He has been doing *pieces and bits / bits and pieces* of carpentry and building work.

6 Work in pairs. Match the irreversible word pairs in bold in the sentences (1–4) with these definitions.

best effort	basic	control of crime	in general
nowadays	objections	small things	a state of calm

1 The builders still have a few **odds and ends** to finish off, but **by and large** they've done a great job.
2 After three days of unrest, **law and order** has been restored and there is **peace and quiet** on the streets again.
3 Sorry, no **ifs, ands, or buts**. We've decided to sell the company. You can't be sentimental **in this day and age**.
4 It's a **rough and ready** movie, made on a small budget, but the director put her **heart and soul** into it.

Language focus the perfect aspect

7 Match the sentences (1–4) with the times they describe (a–d).

1 Sayah **has visited** Central Africa many times.
2 Frank **has been collecting** coins since he was a boy.
3 Jae **will have been** just about everywhere by the time he's 60.
4 Ana **had never even owned** a pet before she joined the Animal Defense League.

a look back from now at something that started in the past and is still continuing
b look back from a point in the future to a completed action
c look back from a point in the past to an earlier event
d look back from now to a completed action at an indefinite time in the past

---

▶ **THE PERFECT ASPECT**

"Aspect" describes not the time of an event, but the speaker's perspective. In the perfect aspect, the important thing is the time the speaker is looking back from.

Present perfect
He hasn't committed to another relationship since they split up.

Present perfect continuous
He has been moving from place to place, doing various jobs.

Past perfect
He had run his own business before he joined Microsoft.

Past perfect continuous
She had been waiting a long time for such an opportunity.

Future perfect
Three years from now, he will have left school.

For more information and practice, see page 157.

---

8 Work in pairs. Look at the language focus box. Then explain the difference in meaning between these pairs of sentences.

1 a I've traveled a lot in my time.
  b I traveled a lot in my 20s.
2 a I've been wondering whether to join the Red Cross.
  b I am wondering whether to join the Red Cross.

3 a By this time next year, I will have retired from teaching.
  b This time next year, I will retire from teaching.
4 a When I left school, I had decided to become an actor.
  b When I left school, I decided to become an actor.

9 Choose the most appropriate option to complete these sentences. Then check your answers with your teacher.

1 Oscar's a dreamer. Each evening he *has been spending / spends* hours reading astronomy magazines, hoping to become an astronaut one day.
2 Kate's a worrier. When I first met her, she *had just left / just left* her job and *has been wondering / was wondering* what to do with her life.
3 Ben's a free spirit. I imagine he *will have settled / will settle* down one day. But he *will have done / will do* a lot more than the rest of us by then.
4 I like to think of myself as a doer. I *have written / wrote* eight books so far and now I *have been working / am working* on my ninth.
5 Pedro is a joker. For a long time *he'd been joking / he was joking* about joining the army, so his friends were shocked to hear he actually had.

Speaking

10 Work in groups. What do the expressions to describe types of people mean?

a chatterbox	a control freak	a doer
a dreamer	a drifter	a fighter
a free spirit	a go-getter	a joker
a planner	an outgoing type	a worrier

11 Which expressions describe you? Give examples of behavior that support this.

People often describe me as a chatterbox because I can't stop talking!

1c Immortal words

Reading

1 Work in pairs. Discuss the questions.

1 Who are the great writers in your country's history? Do you know any famous quotations from their work?
2 Is Shakespeare well-known in your country?
3 What Shakespeare plays do you know the names of? What do you know about them?
4 Do you know any famous quotations from Shakespeare plays?

2 Read the article about the language of Shakespeare. According to the author, why are Shakespeare's plays still so popular today?

3 Read the article again and answer the questions.

1 What adjective describes what England was like in Shakespeare's time? (para 1)
2 What new element did Shakespeare bring to play writing, according to Bloom? (para 2)
3 What two words describe how Shakespeare conveyed his observations about life? (para 2)
4 What expression tells you that Shakespeare created new words and expressions? (para 3)
5 What has happened to the phrase "the be all and end all" over time? (para 4)
6 What two qualities have helped Shakespeare's words to survive? (para 5)

4 Match the phrases listed after paragraph 3 with the definitions (a–h).

a past its best
b show your feelings
c anything is possible
d unimportant
e the result is obvious
f something sad to see
g in one single action
h arriving back at the starting point

Critical thinking **developing an argument**

5 The writer uses the views of others to develop his own arguments. What reasons do these commentators give for Shakespeare's popularity?

a scholars
b Harold Bloom
c Michael Macrone
d Ben Jonson

6 Work in pairs. What does the author think about each of the commentators in Exercise 5?

7 What is the author's own conclusion and which commentator does he agree with most?

Word focus *life*

8 Look at the article again. Find two expressions with *life* that mean the following.

1 realistic
2 to animate or make alive

9 Work in pairs. Look at the expressions in bold with *life* and discuss what they mean.

1 I gave away my records and now they're really collectible. **Story of my life!**
2 He was **larger than life** and would always light up a room with his presence.
3 Work stress is just **a fact of life** these days.
4 There were people from **all walks of life**: writers, students, business people.
5 My daughter didn't want to go to college, but now she's **having the time of her life**.
6 Thanks for driving me to the station; it was a real **life-saver**. I would have missed my train otherwise.

10 Work in groups. Think of a personal example for two of the phrases in Exercise 9.

> *Not doing well on tests has been the story of my life!*

Speaking

11 Work in two groups of three. You are going to play a game called *Call my bluff*. Each group looks at a set of words coined by Shakespeare and follows the steps below.

Group A: Turn to page 153. Look at the words and definitions.

Group B: Turn to page 154. Look at the words and definitions.

- For each word, rewrite the true definition in your own words, then write two more false definitions. For each definition, write an example sentence.
- Group A reads the three definitions and example sentences of the first word to Group B. Group B has to guess the true definition.
- Now it is Group B's turn to read the three definitions of their first word and for Group A to guess the true definition.
- Repeat until all the words have been guessed.

The 16th-century dramatist Ben Jonson generously called his rival Shakespeare a writer "not of an age, but for all time." And so it has proven to be, for Shakespeare's plays are still the most translated and most performed of any playwright's in the world. But if you ask people what accounts for Shakespeare's enduring popularity, you will get a number of different answers. Some will say that he was a great storyteller, others that the magic lies in the beauty of his poetry. Some scholars point out that he was born in a vibrant period of England's history, a time of great national confidence and cultural activity, particularly in the theater. As a consequence, they claim, he was able to produce an extraordinary volume of work.

This last explanation seems a little unsatisfactory. A more interesting answer is put forward, albeit a little over-enthusiastically, by Harold Bloom in his book *Shakespeare: The Invention of the Human*. Bloom argues that Shakespeare gave us something in his writing that the world had not seen in literature before: characters with a strong personality. These lifelike characters give us a real insight into the human condition: Iago, the trusted advisor of Othello, whose jealousy leads him to betray his honest master; Rosalind, the heroine in *As You Like It*, who remains true to her friends and family in spite of the danger to herself. Through the mouths of such characters, we learn truths about life that we can all identify with. These truths are made more moving and more memorable by the way in which they are phrased: succinctly and poetically.

> But love is blind, and lovers cannot see.
> **The Merchant of Venice**
>
> There is nothing either good or bad, but thinking makes it so.
> **Hamlet**
>
> Talking isn't doing. It is a kind of good deed to say well; and yet words are not deeds.
> **Henry VIII**

Shakespeare has been dead almost 400 years, but the words and sayings attributed to him still color the English language today. So whether you are "fashionable" or "sanctimonious," thank Shakespeare, who probably coined the terms. In fact, it is amazing just how great Shakespeare's influence on everyday language has been. Take, for example, these phrases from Michael Macrone's light-hearted book *Brush Up Your Shakespeare*:

foregone conclusion	seen better days
full circle	a sorry sight
at one fell swoop	neither here nor there
wear my heart upon my sleeve	the world is (my) oyster

Macrone is more interested in the Shaksperean language that has survived than the reasons for its popularity. According to his research, some of these sayings have strayed slightly from their original meaning once taken out of the context of the plays in which they first appeared. For example, "the be all and end all" is used today to mean "the most important thing," but in *Macbeth*, it means "the end of the matter."

Regardless of such technicalities, it is still remarkable that so many of Shakespeare's words have survived the large shifts in language between their time and the present day. The beauty of those words is certainly one reason, but as Jonson suggested, it is the humanity and enduring relevance of their message that brings them to life.

albeit (conj) /ɔlˈbiːɪt/ even if it is/was
insight (n) /ˈɪnˌsaɪt/ new understanding
stray (v) /streɪ/ wander

Immortal words

1d Tell me about yourself

Real life presenting yourself

1 Work in pairs. Read the definition of *brand* below and answer the questions.

1. What brands can you think of?
2. Which are your favorite brands and why?

> **brand** (n) /brænd/ *1* a particular name of a product or a manufacturer; *2* a particular set of characteristics to identify a product or manufacturer

2 What do you think a "personal brand" is? Discuss with your partner. Then read the text below and compare your ideas.

Just as a company promotes a consumer brand to customers through advertising, so individuals can promote themselves through their resume, their profile on a social networking site, their own website, and in an interview. This is known as "personal branding." Successful personal branding involves recognizing your particular characteristics and skills, and then shouting about them. Here are five tips for creating your personal brand:

1. Identify your best qualities. They don't have to be spectacular (sociable, a doer).
2. Be yourself. Don't pretend to be something you are not.
3. Show passion. We are all passionate about something (sports, animals, etc.).
4. List your achievements. *You* may not be so interested in your past, but others are.
5. A brand is an image, so present yourself as you would like to see yourself.

3 🎵 **2** Listen to part of a job interview. How well does the candidate follow the guidelines in Exercise 2?

4 Speaking skill keeping going

🎵 **2** Kia paused at one point to think about what she was going to say next. Which phrases below did she use?

> ▶ **KEEPING GOING**
>
> Sorry, let me just look at my notes… Ah, yes…
> Excuse me, I'll just take a sip of water…
>
> Sorry, I lost my train of thought…
> Sorry, I'll begin that again…
>
> Now, where was I? Ah, yes…
> So, as I was saying…

5 What other strategies do you use to keep talking when you feel nervous or under pressure? Discuss with your partner.

6 Pronunciation content words

a 🎵 **3** Look at the first three sentences of Kia's introduction. What are the content words (words that carry the meaning)? Then listen and underline the content words she stresses.

"OK, so I'm Kia. I'm 24 years old and I'm a very active person. I don't just mean that I play a lot of sports, although I do run and go to the gym several times a week. What I mean is that I'm a person who likes to get involved in things."

b Work in pairs. Practice reading the sentences with the same stress and rhythm.

7 Work in pairs. Read the description of the charity and prepare to present yourself as a candidate. Roleplay the interview. Use the notes in Exercise 2 and the phrases in the box to keep going.

River Housing

Passionate about communities | Championing diversity at work

We own and manage over 12,000 properties, providing accommodation and care to vulnerable people: the elderly, disabled, and young.

We have a wide range of career opportunities in housing management and maintenance, marketing, business management, and service provider roles. Interested? Give us a call.

1e An application letter

Writing a cover letter

1 Work in pairs. Read the cover letter and underline the following key elements. Compare your answers.

1 the job applied for
2 where and when it was advertised
3 the candidate's current situation
4 why the writer is a good candidate
5 where and when the candidate can be contacted
6 thanks for their time

2 Using the letter as a model, mark the statements true (T) or false (F).

1 Keep it short. Just refer the reader to your resume.
2 Show interest in the reader and knowledge of the organization you are writing to.
3 Just mention your general suitability for the job. Don't respond to specific requirements.
4 Give a personal touch to your application.

3 Writing skill fixed expressions

The writer follows the conventions of letter writing by using certain fixed expressions. Find words and expressions in the letter with the following meanings.

a I am looking for
b I am sending
c a good person to consider for the job
d I am free to come
e the things you say you need
f I am writing to apply for the job advertised
g please feel free to
h I was interested in the job

4 Write a cover letter to River Housing, the company described on page 16.

Dear Mr. Fairburn:

In response to your advertisement in last Tuesday's newspaper for an assistant accounts manager, please find enclosed my resume. The job stood out to me because it emphasized that your company has great opportunities for people who are eager to learn. I also know that your company is a world leader in the creation of innovative products.

As a recent college graduate, I am well aware that I still have a lot to learn and it is exactly this kind of challenging environment that I am seeking. You will also see from my resume that I am someone who believes in getting results. My two proudest achievements are raising over $25,000 for a local charity and finishing the New York Marathon.

Regarding the other requirements you mention, I think I am a suitable candidate because:

• I have a degree in economics
• I am flexible about where I work
• I have good organizational skills, acquired when I was Treasurer of the Student Social Committee

I am available for an interview at any time. Thank you for considering this application, and please do not hesitate to contact me at any time by phone or in writing if you have questions about any of the above.

I look forward to hearing from you.

Sincerely,

Philip Morrissey

Philip Morrissey

---

5 Exchange letters with your partner. Look at the letter as if you were the employer. Check the following:

• Is it well organized? Does it include all the key points?
• Is it grammatically correct and without spelling mistakes?
• Does it use appropriate fixed expressions?
• Do the skills offered match the needs of the organization?
• Is it interesting and does it have a personal touch?
• Would you call this person for an interview?

The phrase "Respect your elders" is alive and well in Iqaluit.

Nunavut

Kalaallit Nunaat
(Greenland)

Alaska
(USA)

Iqaluit

Atlantic
Ocean

C A N A D A

0   1000 km   U S A

Before you watch

1 Look at the photo and the map. Then choose the options (a or b) that you think best describe this environment as a place to live. Give your reasons.

1 a mild weather conditions
  b harsh weather conditions
2 a calm people
  b stressed people
3 a a traditional way of life
  b a modern way of life
4 a a population that's getting younger
  b an aging population
5 a an isolated area
  b an area with good communication links

2 Work in pairs. In this video, Inuit elders talk about their society and their relationship with the younger generation. Think of three things they might say about modern life and the younger generation.

While you watch

3 Watch the video and check your ideas from Exercise 2.

4 Watch the first part of the video (to 02:24) and answer the questions.

1 What is important about the elders?

2 What phrase is alive in Iqaluit?

3 How did the elders' parents live?

4 How were traditions passed down from generation to generation?

5 Watch the second part of the video (02:24 to 03:40) and complete the summary.

In the past, elders were ¹ _____ for the others in the community. Each one was an ² _____ in a particular area—the weather, the environment, different kinds of ³ _____ —which helped the community to ⁴ _____ . Inuits were happy with the ⁵ _____ . The woman's mother told her daughter that she would see many ⁶ _____ , but she said, "Never ⁷ _____ who you are."

6 Watch the third part of the video (03:40 to end) and answer the questions.

1 What has happened to the Iqaluit population in recent times? Why?

2 Name two things the woman mentions when talking about the key to a happy life.

3 Why does she have a communication problem with the younger generation?

4 What does the narrator say is the key to these people's future?

After you watch

7 Roleplay a meeting of generations

Work in groups.

Imagine you come from a small fishing community in a remote area in northern Canada. An oil company wants to build a refinery near your town. It will employ some local people but also bring in a lot of workers from outside. You have a village meeting to decide if you should oppose this idea or not. Divide into two groups. Think about the effects the new oil refinery will have on your community.

Group A: You are the elders. Think about:

- preserving traditions
- the effect of newcomers on community life
- looking after the older generation
- the effect on the environment

Group B: You are the younger generation. Think about:

- preserving traditions
- job opportunities
- opportunities to meet other people
- the effect on the environment

Act out the meeting to discuss your feelings about this proposal.

8 Work in pairs. Are the advice and wisdom of elders highly respected in your society? Is this as it should be? Why?

---

disproportionate (adj) /ˌdɪsprə'pɔːʃənɪt/ unexpected or out of proportion (to a number or amount)
elders (n) /'eldərz/ the elder or senior members of a community
infant mortality (n) /'ɪnfənt mɔː'tælɪti/ the rate of death among children aged 0–2 years

Iqaluit /ɪ'kæluɪt/ the capital city of the Canadian territory of Nunavut
isolated /'aɪsə,leɪtɪd/ cut off from the rest of the world
pass on (v) /'pɑːs 'ɔn/ transfer from one person to another
self-esteem (n) /self ɪ'stiːm/ the opinion you have of yourself

UNIT 1 REVIEW

Grammar

1 Read the article. What is a griot? What lesson did the writer take away from his visit to Timbuktu?

2 Choose the correct tenses in the article.

3 What stories did you read as a child that told you lessons about life? Describe one to your partner.

Some years ago I ¹ *visited / have visited* Timbuktu in Mali. Generally, people ² *are thinking / think* of Timbuktu as a desert town somewhere at the end of the world. But it ³ *hasn't always been / hadn't always been* this way. Once upon a time, Timbuktu ⁴ *was / has been* a thriving city and key trading post, a place in Africa with a long history, rich with tales.

In the marketplace you get a sense of this: women in brightly colored clothes selling produce of all kinds. But my attention was drawn to a very old man who ⁵ *had sat / was sitting* in a corner. A few others ⁶ *have already gathered / had already gathered* around him, so I joined them. He was a griot, or traditional storyteller. Griots ⁷ *sing / have sung* about kings and magicians, wars and journeys. This is how Malians ⁸ *learned / have learned* about their history for generations. He poured me a glass of tea and then I ⁹ *listened / have listened* to him tell the story of King Mansa and the golden age of Timbuktu, a story he¹⁰ *was telling / had told* countless times before. At the end, the griot ¹¹ *quoted / has quoted* an old Mali saying: "To succeed you need three things: a brazier, time, and friends." The brazier is to heat water for tea. Time and friends are for sharing stories. It's a lesson that ¹² *will stay / will have stayed* with me for a long time.

I CAN	
combine time phrases and tenses	☐
use the perfect aspect to look back at events	☐

Vocabulary

4 Complete these idiomatic expressions.

1 Jackie Chan is a _____-than-life character.
2 There was a great mix at the conference: people from all _____ of life.
3 I had the _____ of my life in college.
4 Being patient is easier said than _____ .
5 If you are annoyed with someone, a good rule of _____ is to speak to them, not write.
6 Stay calm and don't sweat the _____ stuff.

5 Work in pairs. Put the irreversible word pairs in the correct order.

1 soul / and / heart 　　4 quiet / and / peace
2 large / and / by 　　　5 day / and / age
3 first / and / foremost

6 Choose two of the word pairs in Exercise 5 and make sentences about life.

I CAN	
describe lessons in life	☐
use irreversible word pairs	☐

Real life

7 Complete the phrases used to keep going.

a I'll begin that again.
b _____ I was saying,…
c I'll just take a _____ of water.
d I _____ my train of thought.
e _____ me just look at my notes.

8 Match the underlined phrases with a phrase from Exercise 7 that has a similar meaning.

1 Now <u>where was I?</u>…
2 Sorry, <u>I just need to check my facts</u>…
3 Sorry, <u>I forgot what I was about to say</u>…
4 <u>Let me rephrase that</u>.
5 Sorry, <u>I just need to drink something</u>.

9 Work in pairs. Present yourself briefly to each other as if you were answering the question at an interview, "So tell me a little about yourself."

I CAN	
present myself as if at an interview	☐
keep going when I feel under pressure	☐

Speaking

10 Work in pairs. Talk about a successful or unsuccessful interview you've had. Why did it work out that way? What went right or wrong?

Unit 2 More than a job

A golden eagle flies to the call of a Kazakh hunter, Mongolia.
Photograph by Viacheslav Smilyk

FEATURES

1 Work in pairs. Look at the photo and caption. Mongolians are traditionally nomadic people. What do you know about nomads? What do you think this man is doing? In what other countries is this traditional way of hunting still practiced? Do you know of any other nomadic people? Discuss with your partner.

2 Discuss the difference between the phrases in each pair.

1 **a way of life** and **a livelihood**
2 **a career** and **a vocation**
3 **a profession** and **a trade**
4 **an occupation** and **a living**
5 **a job** and **a task**

3 Work in groups. Think of examples of each of the following.

a people who depend on animals for their livelihood
b a traditional occupation that is now dying out
c a task that requires great patience

2a Sea gypsies of Myanmar

Reading

1 Work in pairs. Look at the photo and the title of the article and answer the questions. Then read the article and check your answers.

1 What are "sea gypsies"?
2 What is their livelihood?
3 What skills do they have?

2 Read the article again and answer the questions.

1 Why did the Moken first stay away from the author?
2 What kind of boats are the *kabang*?
3 In what way does the Moken way of life have a low impact on the environment?
4 Why do the Moken move to the land for four months of the year?
5 What is happening to the Moken population?
6 What will be the consequence if they move permanently to land?

3 Work in groups. Discuss the advantages and disadvantages of the Moken way of life.

Sea gypsies of Myanmar

We had been traveling for a few hours when on the horizon we spotted the group of small hand-built boats called *kabang*. The Moken are wary of strangers, so as we approached, I called out some reassuring words in their language. The family elder, Gatcha, was at first reluctant to stop. Outsiders have been harassing the Moken throughout their history and his instinct told him to keep his distance. But after hearing that I had been researching the Moken way of life since 1982, in the end he accepted us into his "home."

Home for this nomadic sea people are the *kabang*, on which they live, eat, and sleep for eight months of the year. In these light craft, they traverse the Mergui Archipelago, 800 islands dotted across the Andaman Sea, off Myanmar, collecting what they need to survive and moving on. They get by only on what they take from the sea and beaches each day: fish, mollusks and sandworms to eat; shells and oysters to trade with Malay and Chinese merchants. They accumulate little and live on land only during the monsoons. But the world is closing in on the Moken way of life.

As divers and beachcombers, they pose no threat to others who share these waters. In spite of this, the authorities are always pressuring them to settle in one place. Ten years ago, 2,500 Moken were still leading a traditional seafaring life, but that population is slowly declining and now stands at around 1,000. If they cease to be sea gypsies, it is feared that their unique understanding of the sea will disappear also. Moken people can dive to 65 feet (20 m) without breathing equipment, and have developed extraordinary underwater vision. They are experts at reading changes in the sea, and it is even said they can anticipate a tsunami.

A day spent fishing and gathering was followed by a night of eating and ritual. The following morning, Gatcha and his family pushed out to sea to continue their journey. The dry season was ending and soon they would be setting up camp on land. But just as the rains come and go, I wonder if the Moken will still be living here when I next return.

Vocabulary phrasal verb *get*

4 Match the phrasal verbs with *get* (1–6) to their correct meanings (a–f).

1 The Moken **get by** on what they take from the sea.
2 They are very content with their simple way of life; **getting ahead** in life is a Western concept.
3 There is often work to **get through** in the day, but it doesn't seem like work to them.
4 While other divers prepare their equipment carefully, the Moken just seem to **get on with** it.
5 It seems some people would like the Moken to **get down to** leading a more conventional life.
6 What the author seems to be **getting at** is that it is important that the Moken way of life survives.

a complete
b implying
c survive
d do the job
e begin
f doing better

5 Work in pairs. Make three sentences about your own experiences using phrasal verbs with *get*.

Language focus the continuous aspect

6 Work in pairs. Match the phrases (1–6) with the descriptions of the continuous form (a–f).

1 We had been traveling for a few hours…
2 Outsiders have been harassing the Moken…
3 …the world is closing in on the Moken.
4 …the authorities are always pressuring them…
5 …the Moken were still leading…
6 I wonder if the Moken will still be living here…

a a present trend
b a continuous action in the past that was interrupted
c an action continuing from a point in the past to now
d an action in progress at a specific point in the past
e (+ *always*) a repetitive action to express annoyance
f an action in progress at a point in the future

7 Look at these pairs of sentences using the continuous and simple aspects. With your partner, explain the difference in meaning in each case.

1 a I'm living on a houseboat.
  b I live on a houseboat.
2 a We were eating when they arrived.
  b We ate when they arrived.
3 a She's been writing a travel book.
  b She's written a travel book.
4 a They had been traveling for days.
  b They had traveled 300 miles.
5 a I will be cooking dinner at eight o'clock.
  b I will cook dinner at eight o'clock.

> ▶ **THE CONTINUOUS ASPECT**
>
> Verbs in the continuous aspect describe incomplete actions that are in progress at a specific time.
>
> **Present continuous**
> *The number of sea gypsies is declining.*
>
> **Past continuous**
> *Ten years ago, many were leading this way of life.*
>
> **Present perfect continuous**
> *Outsiders have been exploiting the Moken for years.*
>
> **Past perfect continuous**
> *I had been researching their way of life for many years before this.*
>
> **Future continuous**
> *I hope they will still be living here in ten years' time.*
>
> For more information and practice, see page 158.

8 Choose the correct form (simple or continuous) to complete the text.

Moken children [1] *are learning / learn* to swim before they can walk. Because of this, the Moken [2] *have been developing / have developed* extraordinary swimming skills. They can hold their breath for twice as long as an average person. Moreover, as one Swedish researcher [3] *was discovering / discovered*, they can shrink their pupils to see more clearly underwater. Sadly, these skills [4] *are being lost / are lost* as more and more Moken settle on the land.

The Moken are experts at reading the ways of the sea. When a tsunami hit the region, some Moken [5] *had already been moving / had already moved* to higher ground. Several minutes before the wave [6] *was arriving / arrived*, they saw that the sea [7] *was receding / receded* and recognized this as a sign of an imminent wave.

Why don't the Moken exploit their skills and knowledge to make more money? What [8] *have they been waiting / have they waited* for? The fact is, they [9] *are not wishing / do not wish* to live complicated lives or accumulate possessions. Left in peace, in 100 years' time, they [10] *will still be leading / will still lead* their simple life.

Speaking

9 Work in groups. Which of these jobs are a way of life for the people who do them? What factors make them more than a job?

banker	coal miner
farmer	firefighter
fisherman/woman	truck driver
physical therapist	teacher

10 Think of another job that is a way of life. Describe the job and your reasons for adding this to the list.

2b Smokejumpers

Listening

1 Work in pairs. Look at the photo and answer the questions about fire.

1 What kind of fire is shown in the photo? How do these fires start? How can they be stopped?
2 What is the difference between a *fireman* and a *firefighter*?
3 What qualities are needed to be a firefighter?

2 🔊 **4** Read the sentences. Then listen to an interview with smokejumper Kerry Franklin. Are the sentences true (T) or false (F)?

1 Smokejumpers are used in places that are difficult to reach.
2 Smokejumpers get their name from their ability to run through forest fires.
3 They evaluate fires, but don't combat them.
4 It's difficult for most men smokejumpers to accept women doing this job.

3 🔊 **4** Listen again and choose the correct option (a–c).

1 It's important for smokejumpers to be the right weight so that they can:
  a land properly.   b carry equipment.
  c wear a protective suit.
2 According to Kerry, a smokejumper's personal safety is:
  a a priority.   b unimportant.
  c not the first consideration.
3 Smokejumpers arrive at the scene of the fire:
  a first.   b to help other crews.
  c if other fire crews have failed.
4 They try to contain the fire by:
  a hosing it with water.   b changing its path.
  c clearing an area in front of it.
5 After their training, men and women smokejumpers treat each other:
  a a little suspiciously.   b as equals.
  c as doing different jobs.

4 What does this statement tell you about Kerry's attitude toward her job? What does she mean by "you either make the grade or you don't"?

> Fire doesn't distinguish between men and women, nor do the trainers at smokejumping school for that matter; you either make the grade or you don't.

▶ **WORDBUILDING phrases with *do***

There are many expressions with *do* in English.
do your best, do someone a favor, do your duty

Language focus present and perfect participles

5 Rewrite the sentences, replacing the participles in bold with a conjunction + pronoun + verb. Choose the correct conjunction below.

after	and in order to do this
with the result that	because (x3)

1 **Weighing** around 160 pounds, women firefighters are well-suited to smokejumping.
  Because they weigh around 160 pounds, women firefighters are well-suited to smokejumping.
2 If you're too heavy, you descend too fast and hit the ground hard, **risking** serious injury.
3 **Not having** a fire engine nearby, you can't fight the fire in the conventional way.
4 **Having located** a firebreak, we do our best to make sure it's going to be effective.
5 We get anything that could burn easily out of the way, **using** controlled burning, if necessary.
6 **Having faced** the same challenges in training, we have a natural respect for each other.

▶ PRESENT AND PERFECT PARTICIPLES

Present participle
Landing near the fire, they quickly assessed the situation.
Not thinking of his own safety, he rushed into the house.

Perfect participle
Having fought fires for 15 years, she is now an expert.
Not having ever been near a forest fire, I can't imagine the heat.

Notes
1 The main clause describes the most important event and the participial clause a secondary event.
2 The subject of a participial clause is the same as the subject of the main clause.
3 We use a perfect participle only to emphasize one thing that happened before another.

For more information and practice, see page 159.

6 Rewrite the sentences with a participial clause.

1 Because I had failed the course twice, I decided not to try again.
2 I burned my hand while I was trying to put the fire out.
3 As I work in forestry, I know the dangers of forest fires very well.
4 He remained calm and got everyone out of the building.
5 When I look back on it, I can see that it was a mistake to leave him in charge.
6 I called the fire department because I thought it was the best thing to do.
7 After the smokejumpers have landed, they search for a firebreak.
8 The smokejumpers work closely together and keep in radio contact.

7 Work in pairs. Look at the second note in the language focus box. In which sentences (1–4) has the speaker not followed this rule?

1 Having called the fire department, we quickly got out of the house.
2 Having finished my main course, the waiter offered to bring me dessert.
3 While waiting for the taxi, a dog came and sat down next to me.
4 Speaking to her, I realized we knew each other.

8 Work in groups. Complete these sentences in a natural way. Then compare your sentences and vote on the best for each item.

1 Having studied English for ten years,…
2 Walking around the center of our town,…
3 Opening the fridge,…
4 Not wanting to make a scene,…

Idioms health and safety

9 Work in pairs. What do you think the idiom in bold used by Kerry, the smokejumper, means?

We're very aware of safety, but at the same time, in this kind of job you can't **wrap** people **in cotton wool**.

10 Use the words below to complete the idioms. Then check your answers with your teacher. Discuss with your partner what you think each idiom means.

book   corners   danger   nature   net
precaution   side

The aim of today's session is to raise awareness of health and safety issues and to ensure they become second ¹ _____ to you all, so that everyone who works here learns to always be on the safe ² _____ . As I'm sure you know, food preparation on this scale is fraught with ³ _____ . There's no safety ⁴ _____ here; mistakes can seriously endanger people's health. So we take every ⁵ _____ to ensure that there's no risk to health. Everything has to be done by the ⁶ _____ ; there's no room for improvisation or for cutting ⁷ _____ .

11 Think of a job where awareness of health and safety is very important. Discuss with your partner what the dangers are of this job and what safety measures can be taken.

Speaking

12 Work in groups. Consider these health and safety issues. Use them to make a list of health and safety rules for a company that supplies office furniture to other companies.

- smoking in delivery vans
- minimum number of breaks for delivery drivers and workers
- minimum number of people to lift and move any piece of furniture
- installation of electrical equipment
- collecting old furniture

2c Daring, defiant, and free

Reading

1 What professional sports can you think of that are particularly dangerous? What motivates people to do this kind of thing?

2 Look at the photo and answer the questions. Then read the article and check your answers.

   1 How do you think this man is able to do this?
   2 How was the picture taken?

3 Read the article again and complete the sentences.

   1 Honnold had nearly reached the top of the rock face when he _____ .
   2 The only equipment needed in this type of climbing is _____ .
   3 Climbing for 2 hours 45 minutes had left Honnold feeling _____ .
   4 When he first visited Yosemite, Jimmy Chin was _____ by it.
   5 When on an expedition with other climbers, the most important thing for Chin is _____ .
   6 Chin wants his photographs to tell _____ .

4 Find the following in the article.

   1 two verbs that mean to hold tightly onto something (para 1)
   2 an expression meaning very focused (para 2)
   3 an adverb meaning perfectly (para 2)
   4 a verb meaning to hesitate between two courses of action (para 3)
   5 a verb that means to recover your strength (para 4)
   6 a verb that means hanging loosely (para 8)

Critical thinking using contrasts

5 The author uses images to describe the extraordinary things these climbers do and simple facts to describe their ordinary backgrounds. Find five images that describe the following.

   1 how flat the rock is (3 images, paras 1 and 2)
   2 how Honnold overcame his doubt (para 4)
   3 Jimmy Chin's athleticism (para 8)

6 Now find other factual information which contrasts with the descriptions in Exercise 5.

   1 two statements about Honnold's and Chin's ordinary backgrounds (paras 4 and 6)
   2 two quotations which show that they think their achievements are ordinary (paras 4 and 7)

7 Work in pairs. Compare your answers from Exercises 5 and 6 with your partner's. What is the impact of these contrasts? Which of the sentences made the strongest impression on you? Why?

Word focus *foot*

8 Work in pairs. Find two words in the article built from the root word *foot*. Discuss with your partner what they mean.

9 Look at these other expressions with *foot* and discuss what each one means.

   1 It's difficult to get a job with a newspaper. If you can **get your foot in the door** by getting one article published, you stand a better chance.
   2 It's an expensive repair and I don't see why I have to **foot the bill** for something that is clearly the garage's fault.
   3 When she told the interviewer that money wasn't important to her, she really **shot herself in the foot**.
   4 You **put your foot in your mouth** when you asked Jim about his job; he was fired last week.
   5 She's **followed in her mother's footsteps** and become a dentist.
   6 You've got to **put your foot down**. Tell them you mean what you say.

10 Make two questions using two of the expressions with *foot*. Then ask and answer the questions with your partner.

Speaking

11 Work in pairs. Climbers like to live at the limits of their comfort zone. Do the quiz on page 153 to find out what your comfort zone is.

12 Work in groups. Which of the following motivates people, including yourself, most to stay in their comfort zone and why?

- fear of failure
- general dislike of being in the spotlight
- fear that success will bring more challenges and responsibilities
- fear of physical discomfort
- fear for your personal safety
- fear of confrontation

DARING, DEFIANT, AND FREE

On a bright September morning in 2008, a young man is clinging to the face of Half Dome, a sheer 2,130-foot wall of granite in the heart of Yosemite Valley. He's alone, so high off the ground that perhaps only the eagles take notice. Hanging on by his fingertips to an edge of rock as thin as a coin, shoes resting on mere ripples in the rock, professional climber Alex Honnold is attempting something no one has ever tried before: to climb the Northwest Face of Half Dome without a rope. In many ways, it's another day at the office for Honnold, but less than a hundred feet from the summit, something potentially disastrous occurs: he loses the smallest measure of confidence.

For two hours and 45 minutes, Honnold has been in the zone, flawlessly performing one precise athletic move after another, and not once has he hesitated. In the sport of free soloing, which means climbing with only a chalk bag and rock shoes—no rope, no gear, nothing to keep you stuck to the stone but your own belief and ability—doubt is dangerous. If Honnold merely believes his fingertips can't hold, he will fall to his death. Now, with mental fatigue and the glass-slick slab in front of him, he's paralyzed, out of his comfort zone.

"My foot will never stay on that," Honnold says to himself, staring at a greasy bump

on the rock face. He hadn't felt that way two days before, when he'd raced up the same route with a rope. Now, clinging to the granite, Honnold vacillates, delicately chalking one hand, then the other, carefully adjusting his feet on invisibly small footholds. Then abruptly he's in motion again, stepping up, smearing his shoe on the slick stone. It sticks. He moves his hand to another hold and within minutes he's at the top.

"I rallied because there was nothing else I could do," Honnold tells me later, releasing a boyish laugh. "I stepped up and trusted that foothold and was freed of the prison where I'd stood silently for five minutes." Word of his three-hour free solo of Half Dome flashes around the world. Climbers are stunned and bloggers buzz. On this warm fall day in 2008, the shy 23-year-old from the suburbs has just set a new record in climbing's big league.

This is the magic of Yosemite: it forges heroes. One such is Jimmy Chin. He is no less accomplished a mountaineer; in fact, in some ways his achievements are greater, for in addition to climbing, Chin takes photographs as he does it.

Chin had a traditional upbringing from his Chinese-American parents in the flat countryside of southern Minnesota. Rock climbing has been his passion

since Glacier National Park first "blew his mind" as a boy on a family vacation. Photography came later, when an outdoor clothing company bought one of the photos he had taken on an expedition. Encouraged, he bought his own camera and hasn't looked back.

He thanks his parents, who taught him Chinese calligraphy, for his sense of composition. "When I started shooting photos I didn't really think too much about it." Combining this with his mountaineering skills, he has become the ultimate practitioner of what has been called "participatory photography." Chin is able to carry a camera where few dare to go, at the same time remaining a solid and reliable member of the climbing team, which is always his priority.

"Photographing an expedition is like building a film; it's storytelling." His favorite photo moment was on an expedition to China's Chang Tang Plateau with the late Galen Rowell. Climbing a nearby mountain, Chin's team had to chop a hole through a snow cornice just below the summit. "I put my head through the hole," says Chin, "looked down and saw Galen climbing toward me." Dangling like a spider, there was only one thing on his mind. "I should have found a more secure footing, but I knew the moment would be lost, so hanging on by one arm I squeezed out three shots."

chalk (n) /tʃɔk/ soft white stone (formed from limestone)
cornice (n) /ˈkɔrnɪs/ a horizontal projection (usually at the top edge of a building)
late (adj) /leɪt/ no longer living
ripple (n) /ˈrɪpəl/ a very small wave on the surface (usually of water)
slab (n) /slæb/ a large, thick, flat piece of stone

2d In my experience

Real life giving a talk

1 Work in pairs. Think about when you started a job, college, or a training program. Answer the questions.

1 Before you started, how did you find out what it was going to be like?
2 What introduction or orientation did the employer or organization offer?

2 🔊 **5** Listen to a speech from an orientation day and answer the questions. Discuss your answers with your partner.

1 Who is the orientation day for?
2 Who is the speaker?
3 What does he advise his audience to do?
4 What did he do when he was in their situation and how did it help him?

3 Speaking skill keeping people's attention

🔊 **5** The speaker used certain techniques to keep people's attention: stressing the main message; telling stories from personal experience; and using rhetorical questions. Listen again and check (✓) the phrases in the box that he used.

> ▶ KEEPING PEOPLE'S ATTENTION
>
> **Stressing the main message**
> I'd just like to say one thing…
> If there's one thing I'd like you to take away from this talk it's…
> So that's really my message to you today.
> That's the key thing.
>
> **Telling stories from personal experience**
> Just the other day I was…
> I remember when I first…
> I'll just give you an example of something that happened to me.
>
> **Using rhetorical questions**
> So, why should that be important? Well,…
> How many of you actually…?
> So what does that tell us?

4 Work in groups. What other techniques can you think of for keeping your audience's attention? Are they appropriate in all situations? Why?

5 Pronunciation checking specific words

a 🔊 **6** Work in pairs. When preparing to give a talk, you should always check the pronunciation of difficult words (those words where the relationship between spelling and pronunciation is not always obvious). Think about the pronunciation of the underlined words in the opening part of the talk. Then listen and check.

"Hello, everyone. I hope you're enjoying your first day. I <u>imagine</u> you're feeling pretty <u>overwhelmed</u> by <u>everything</u> you've had to take in, and I don't want to keep you long. I've been <u>brought</u> back as someone who's been <u>through</u> the system and come out the other side, so the college asked me to <u>talk</u> to you as one of you and give a <u>student's</u> side of the story."

b Work in groups. Practice saying the paragraph yourselves.

6 Prepare to give a short informal talk to people who are new to your college, company, or organization. Decide on your main message and build your talk around this. Use the language in the box and these points to help you.

• KISS: **k**eep **i**t **s**hort and **s**imple
• make the aim of your talk clear
• introduce what you're going to say; then say it; then at the end, remind the audience of what you've said
• talk to your audience directly, using "you"
• use rhetorical questions
• begin and end powerfully

2e Your first day

Writing taking notes

1 🔊 **7** Look at the notes taken by a student at a university orientation day for international students. Then listen to part of the talk and complete the information marked ??? in points 1 and 2 that the student was not sure about.

> Talk by president to new students → or ???
>
> 1 Course reg Mon 10 a.m. – (3 p.m.) in main coll hall
>   – mandatory.
>
> 2 Overseas students i.e., all except US,
>   → (room number ???)
>   must take docs to (Admissions office) – incl.
>   H.S. transcripts, student visas + bank account
>   details – by end of next week.
>
> 3 Coll has "buddy" system (a 2nd year student)
>   to help int sts know where things are and what
>   to do.
>
> 4 Most courses approx. 9–12 contact hrs p.w.; plan
>   study time carefully. Lots of places to work,
>   e.g., faculty library, main library, IT center.
>
> 5 If worried about study or sthg else, see
>   student counselor. NB each group has native
>   speaker counselor.
>
> 6 Extra academic writing skills instruction
>   available for 1st year students – details in
>   student handbook (times, level, etc.)

2 Work in pairs. Discuss what other information the speaker gave that isn't in points 1 and 2.

3 🔊 **7** Listen again and check your answers. Why do you think this information wasn't included?

4 Writing skill abbreviations

a Work in pairs. How many different abbreviations can you find in the notes? What does each one mean?

b Compare your answers in Exercise 4a with another pair. Which abbreviations have the following meanings?

a including   d that is to say
b roughly   e please note
c for example   f and so on

c The use of abbreviations is acceptable in semi-formal writing and when writing in note form. It is not considered good style in more formal contexts. In which of the following could abbreviations be used?

1 an academic essay
2 the footnotes to an academic essay
3 a letter of complaint to a hospital
4 an internal memo to a colleague

d Look at this memo and rewrite it in note form. Then compare notes with your partner.

> Please note that the meeting with Ellis & Company will be tomorrow, Tuesday May 12 at three o'clock. Please send me any information you have about them, including financial details, names of directors, and so on.

5 🔊 **8** Listen to a talk and take notes. Remember to include only the relevant points and to use abbreviations where necessary.

6 Exchange notes. Did your partner:

- include the same relevant points?
- leave out unnecessary information?
- use abbreviations correctly?

You have to be able to control the fear.

Before you watch

1 Look at the photo taken by the photographer Jimmy Chin. How was he able to take it?

2 How would you describe this kind of activity/job? Choose from these adjectives.

cerebral	difficult	methodical	monotonous
rewarding	scary	slow	thrilling

While you watch

3 Watch the first part of the video (to 01:04). Say which of the adjectives in Exercise 2 Jimmy Chin used to describe his work. Did his use of any of these adjectives surprise you?

4 Read these sentences about Jimmy Chin's career. Then watch the second part of the video (01:05 to end). Are the sentences true (T) or false (F)?

1 Jimmy Chin's parents hoped he would follow a professional career.
2 Chin realized right away that climbing was something he wanted to do permanently.
3 Chin felt very at home in Yosemite.
4 Chin's real ambition was to be a photographer.

5 Watch the second part of the video again (01:05 to end) and complete the notes about Jimmy Chin's career. Use one word in each space.

1 In college, Chin was part of the _____ team.
2 After college he went to the Bay Area to find a job in the _____ realm.
3 Not finding a job, he decided to take a _____ off and _____ and ski full time.
4 Seven years later Chin was still living in the back of his _____ and doing odd jobs, like _____ tables.
5 He spent most of his time in Yosemite, where he found his _____ .
6 Here he lived the _____ life.
7 After some time in Yosemite, Chin decided he would like to visit the greater _____ of the world.
8 He took a photo which a friend sold for $_____ and which helped him _____ what he was doing.

---

awesome (adj) /ˈɔsəm/ amazing, incredible
cerebral (adj) /səˈribrəl/ involving a lot of thought and concentration
cringe (v) /krɪndʒ/ shrink back in fear or embarrassment
free soloing (n) /ˈfri ˈsouloʊɪŋ/ climbing without any ropes
realm (n) /relm/ a particular sphere or world
shovel (v) /ˈʃʌvəl/ move earth or snow with a spade
wait tables (v) /ˈweɪt ˈteɪbəlz/ work as a waiter

---

6 Work in pairs. Look at the phrases that Jimmy Chin used. Discuss with your partner what he was referring to and what he meant in each case.

1 "I couldn't get myself excited about it."

2 "I've got to get it out of my system."

3 "I've got to do it for me."

4 "I was just doing odds and ends for jobs."

5 "I was going to throw myself at climbing and skiing."

After you watch

7 Roleplay an interview with an adventure photographer

Work in pairs.

Student A: Imagine you are a journalist from a photography magazine. You are going to interview an adventure photographer. Look at the points below and prepare a list of questions.

Student B: Imagine you are an adventure photographer: someone who combines an extreme sport—climbing, scuba diving, exploring—with photography. Look at the points below and think about what you are going to say to the journalist.

- how you became involved with this activity
- where you do it
- what it typically involves and what the dangers are
- why you are passionate about it

Act out the interview, then change roles.

8 Work in pairs. Think about your own life and interests. Then ask and answer the questions.

1 Did your parents have an ambition for you that you couldn't get excited about?
2 Is there something—a job or hobby or adventure—that you would still like to get out of your system? Why?
3 If you could take a year off, what would you do?
4 Is there something—a job or hobby or adventure—that you would like to do "for you"? What is it and why do you feel this?
5 What odd jobs have you done in your life? Which was the best? What was the worst?

UNIT 2 REVIEW

Grammar

1 Complete the article about an unusual job. Put the verbs into the correct tense or participle form.

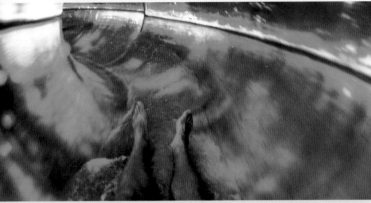

Tommy Lynch has found his dream job. A few years ago he [1] _____ (work) as a waiter in a restaurant, but now he [2] _____ (travels) around the world [3] _____ (test) water slides at vacation resorts. [4] _____ (work) for the travel agency *First Choice*, Lynch must find the best water parks to put into the company's vacation brochure. Lynch [5] _____ (do) this for the last 18 months and [6] _____ (test) over 50 water slides and pools.

[7] _____ (create) their own selection of "Splash Resorts," the company realized they needed someone to control the quality. A spokesperson for the company said, "[8] _____ (understand) how important swimming pools are to families, we knew that to offer the best we would have to appoint a full-time tester. Tommy [9] _____ (take) his job very seriously and [10] _____ (succeed) in finding some of the world's best pools."

[11] _____ (beat) hundreds of other applicants for the job, Tommy says, "I [12] _____ (have) the time of my life. It's not all fun, though. I [13] _____ (have) a lot of paperwork, but I hope I [14] _____ (still / do) this in five years' time!"

2 Answer the questions.

1 What does Tommy's job involve?
2 Why was this job created?
3 What are the less enjoyable parts of the job?

3 Work in pairs. What would be your dream job? Why? Discuss with your partner.

I CAN	
describe actions that are/were in progress (continuous aspect)	
use present and perfect participles to connect ideas	

Vocabulary

4 Complete the questions about work with the correct words.

1 What do you consider a reasonable monthly salary to get _____ on?
2 In the area you want to work in, is it difficult to get your foot _____ the door?
3 How much work correspondence—letters, emails—do you have to get _____ each day?
4 In your work, have you followed _____ either of your parents' footsteps?
5 Is getting _____ in life and moving up the career ladder important to you?
6 Would you rather do a job that really challenged you or stay _____ the safe side?

5 In pairs, ask and answer the questions above.

I CAN	
talk about jobs and careers	
use phrasal verbs with *get*	
use health and safety idioms	

Real life

6 Complete this part of a training talk using these phrases (a–d).

a I remember when I first started
b So that's really my message to you today
c So what does that tell us
d That's the key thing

Always check at the end of each call that the customers feel they have gotten an answer to their questions. [1] _____ . I know it sounds obvious, but [2] _____ , I was so conscious of trying to sell the customers some extra product or service that I would fail to deal properly with their questions. Last month our call center had a 97% customer satisfaction rating. [3] _____ ? That our operators are giving customers the right answers. We would like to keep it that way. [4] _____ : always put yourself in the customer's shoes.

7 Work in pairs. Give a short talk to some new students about to start an English language course. What key point would you like to make? What advice from your own experience can you give?

I CAN	
give a talk about a certain subject	
keep people's attention when giving a talk	

Speaking

8 Work in pairs. Which person in Unit 2 do you admire the most for the work that they do? Why?

Unit 3 Four walls

Grand Staircase, Escalante National Monument, Utah
Photograph by Cook/Jenshel

FEATURES

1 Work in pairs. Look at the photo and caption and answer the questions.

   1 What type of building is this? What does it remind you of?
   2 How old do you think it is?
   3 What do you think it is used for these days?

2 Read the sentences about the building below. Then replace the words in bold with a synonym from the box.

blends in	false	modest	ornate	plain	wood

   1 This is a picture of an **ordinary**, **timber**, Old West style shop; nothing fancy about it.
   2 It **fits** in very naturally with its surroundings.
   3 One interesting aspect is the **fake** front on the building.
   4 Many building had these fronts, which were bigger and more **elaborate** than the **simple** structure behind it.

3 Put these words describing buildings into four categories: material, period/style, impression, and type.

1960s	brick	characterless	colonial	concrete
cottage	elegant	futuristic	glass	imposing
modern	office block	plain	shack	steel
striking	tower	traditional	warehouse	wooden

4 Work in groups. Think of a building that you know. Describe it to your group, saying what you like or dislike about it.

3a Compact spaces

Listening

1 Work in pairs. Ask and answer the questions.

1 How many different rooms are there in your home?
2 Do any of the rooms have more than one function?
3 If you had more space, what would you use it for?

2 🔵 **9** Look at the photos and listen to an interview with an architect who specializes in compact designs. Answer the questions.

1 Where are these two homes?
2 Why is he inspired by them?

A

B

3 🔵 **9** Read the sentences. Then listen to the interview again and choose the best option to complete the sentences.

1 Jonas Wilfstrand is a specialist in *small vacation homes / the efficient use of space*.
2 An increasing number of people *would like to own / are curious about* smaller homes.
3 Dolgan homes consist of *one room / a communal space and a bedroom*.
4 The Dolgan need to be able to move easily because of *the weather / their animals*.
5 In Gary Chang's apartment, you can *move / fold away* the walls.
6 The interviewer *dislikes / has mixed feelings about* Chang's apartment.

4 Do either of the homes the architect describes appeal to you? Why?

Language focus intensifying adverbs

5 For each sentence (1–8), identify the intensifying adverb, the word it intensifies, and if it's an adjective, verb, or adverb.

intensifying adverb

1 We're <u>changing</u> focus (completely) today and looking at small homes.
The word it intensifies = changing (verb)

2 I'm very pleased to welcome Swedish architect Jonas Wilfstrand.
3 Some of them are absolutely stunning.
4 People are either incredibly short on space or they simply can't afford a bigger house.
5 The Dolgan move houses, quite literally.
6 They're just so simple.
7 As you probably know, Hong Kong is a really overcrowded city.
8 He entirely rethought the way we arrange living space.

6 Look at the words *stunning* and *short* in Exercise 5. Which of these adjectives can vary in intensity (gradable)? Which has a meaning that is already intense (ungradable)?

7 Work in pairs. Look at these adjectives. Which are gradable? Which are ungradable?

brilliant	difficult	filthy	freezing	huge
innovative	perfect	plain	simple	strong

▶ INTENSIFYING ADVERBS

extremely, incredibly, very (+ gradable adjective)
They are extremely basic.

absolutely, utterly (+ ungradable adjective or ungradable verb)
The designs are absolutely wonderful.
I utterly detest that building.

really (+ gradable/ungradable adjective or gradable/ungradable verb)
I would really like to go.

completely, entirely, totally (+ ungradable adjective or verb)
It was completely empty.
I accept the blame entirely.

quite (+ ungradable adverb or adjective)
They quite literally built it by hand.
I am quite sure it's the best thing to do.

so (+ gradable or ungradable adjective)
We're so happy in our new house.

Notes
1 *Utterly* is usually used with ungradable adjectives with a negative meaning.
2 *So* is like *very, really,* etc.

For more information and practice, see page 159.

8 Look at the language focus box. Then choose the correct adverb to complete the sentences.

1 Our house is *so / utterly* cold at the moment. The heat broke last week.
2 It's *completely / extremely* sad that so many people live in just a single room.
3 The elevator stopped *absolutely / quite* suddenly on the way to the apartment.
4 I agree with you *extremely / completely* about the color of the walls.
5 The price of houses in New York City is *utterly / incredibly* ridiculous.
6 It's an *entirely / absolutely* beautiful apartment.
7 I *really / completely* want to live in a penthouse apartment downtown.
8 The design of the house is *very / totally* clever.

9 Pronunciation stress in intensifying adverbs

a 🎧 **10** Listen to the sentences with intensifiers and underline the syllables which are stressed.

1 You're absolutely right.
2 That's really kind of you.
3 I'd be very grateful.
4 It's completely out of the question.
5 Yes, I'm quite certain.
6 That's so typical.

b Work in pairs. Make two-line conversations using the expressions in Exercise 9a. Then act out your conversations using the correct stress.

Vocabulary adverb and adjective collocations

10 Look at this example of an adverb + adjective. What does *distinctly* mean here: *very* or *a little*?

Studio apartments are a **distinctly** urban type of housing.

11 Look at these other adverb + adjective collocations. Find the two collocations in which the adverb does <u>not</u> mean *very* or *absolutely*.

deadly serious
desperately unlucky
hopelessly wrong
mildly amused
painfully slow
blatantly obvious
perfectly reasonable
simply unacceptable
vaguely familiar
wildly optimistic

12 Work in pairs. Think of examples that fit the descriptions (1–5). Then discuss them with another pair.

1 a process which is painfully slow
2 a prediction that seems wildly optimistic
3 a statement that is blatantly obvious
4 a sports game in which someone was desperately unlucky
5 an employee's perfectly reasonable demand

Speaking

13 Work in pairs. The architect in the interview had designed a timber and glass vacation house with a built-in sauna. Look at these rooms and features in a home. Discuss what each one is. Which are the most desirable features in a home in your country?

garden	courtyard
game room	garage/workshop
gym	home theater
roof garden	sauna
terrace	walk-in closet

14 Work in groups. Describe what your ideal home would be and what rooms and features it would contain.

3b Old new towns

Vocabulary towns

1 Work in pairs. Match the collocations with the definitions (1–8).

sprawling metropolis	vibrant city
historic neighborhood	bedroom community
commercial district	quiet town
housing development	leafy suburb

1 famous for its old buildings
2 attracts shoppers
3 a concentration of affordable residential homes
4 a large lively city
5 lots of commuters live here
6 nothing much happens here
7 a rich green residential area outside the center
8 an area that keeps growing outwards

2 Use the collocations in Exercise 1 to describe where you live.

Reading

3 Look at the photos. Where do you think these towns are? What makes you say this? Read the article and check your answers.

4 Read the article again and answer the questions.

1 What do Poundbury and Thames Town have in common?
2 For what reasons was each town built?
3 Are they successful?

5 Work in pairs. Find examples of the following:

1 two things that characterized town planning in Britain in the 1960s
2 two types of buildings found in Poundbury
3 two buildings found in Thames Town
4 two examples of good town planning ideas in Poundbury

O L D   N E W   T O W N S

Where would you look for inspiration if you were planning a new town? If you are Prince Charles or the Shanghai Planning Commission, the past would seem to be the answer; or to be more precise, the English past. The town of Poundbury in the south of England, designed by Prince Charles, is an answer to what he calls the "heartless urban planning" of the 1960s. It offers an alternative to "ugly" high-rise apartment blocks, large housing projects, and zoned planning, where industry, stores, and homes are separated into different areas.

Poundbury's buildings imitate the cottages and grander houses of 18th-century Dorset. "What I was trying to do," the prince said, "was remind people that it is pointless to throw away the knowledge and experience of what has gone before."

If you find such reproductions of the past artificial, then you will certainly not enjoy Thames Town, a new development just outside Shanghai. Rarely do you find nostalgia taken to such extremes. But this is not nostalgia for traditional Chinese living. Thames Town is modeled on the English town of Dorchester, not far from Poundbury, and is part of a plan to create a new suburbia for Shanghai's richer classes. It boasts a pub, a fish and chips shop, and a 19th-century church. Nine such replica towns are planned around Shanghai, each based on a different Western style: Italian, Austrian, etc.

But are these model towns a success? As far as friendly urban planning goes, Poundbury does seem to work. Businesses are placed close to residential buildings, enabling residents to walk to work. A third of the houses are "affordable housing," giving the town a social and economic mix. They have small gardens, but there is plenty of communal green space, making it easy to get to know your neighbors.

Unfortunately, the same cannot be said for Thames Town. It is popular with day visitors and Chinese couples planning Western-style weddings, but, going there, you get the distinct feeling you are in a museum, not a town.

affordable housing (n) /əˈfɔrdəbəl ˈhaʊzɪŋ/ homes for people with low incomes
quaint (adj) /kweɪnt/ attractively old-fashioned or unusual
take root (v) /ˈteɪk ˈrut/ become settled

6 Do you like the idea of recreating old towns?
Do you think it is a realistic model for other
towns? Why? Discuss with your partner.

Language focus emphatic structures

7 Work in pairs. Look at the sentences (1–4)
and pair them with similar sentences in the
text. Then answer the questions (a–c).

1 He could offer an alternative here to
"ugly" high-rise apartment blocks…
2 I was trying to remind people that it is
pointless to throw away the knowledge…
3 You rarely find nostalgia taken to such
extremes.
4 As far as friendly urban planning goes,
Poundbury seems to work.

a Which sentence in each pair has more
emphasis?
b What idea in each case is being
emphasized?
c What changes have been made to the
sentence to add this emphasis?

8 Look at the language focus box. Rewrite these sentences
with more emphasis.

1 I love the human scale of Poundbury.
What I _____.
2 You rarely need a car to go shopping.
Rarely _____.
3 The architects wanted to encourage people to mix, so
they included communal green spaces in the design
of the town.
The thing the architects _____.
4 Children socialize in these public spaces.
It's in these _____.
5 It isn't surprising that Poundbury has cost a lot of
money to build.
What _____.
6 The developers didn't once opt for cheaper materials
like concrete when they were building Poundbury.
Not once _____.
7 The developers admitted that they expected Thames
Town to be more popular.
When asked, the developers _____.
8 They think, however, that the Italian and Austrian
towns will be popular.
They _____.

9 Work in pairs. Which three sentences use an emphatic
structure when the context does not really justify it?

1 I've traveled a lot, but never have I been to England.
2 It's in big cities that we really need to address the
problems of bad town planning.
3 What's normal is that I get up at 7:30 a.m. Then I
have my breakfast.
4 It's in the cafeteria that we usually eat our lunch, but
sometimes we go out.
5 How can she possibly argue that? Never have I
heard such nonsense!
6 It's a wonderful town. What's unusual is that there
aren't more towns like this.

Speaking

10 Work in groups. Look at the following choices in town
planning and discuss the advantages and disadvantages
of each choice for society and the environment.

1 Mixing residential, commercial, and industrial areas
OR keeping them separate.
2 Mixing expensive and affordable housing OR
keeping them separate.
3 Allowing cars downtown OR banning them.
4 Having dense residential areas OR creating space
around each home.

3c The paper architect

Reading

1 Work in pairs. Why do you think this woman is called "the paper architect"? Discuss.

2 Read the article about architect Zaha Hadid. Which statement best summarizes her goal?

    a   to create unusual buildings
    b   to be a successful woman architect
    c   to create buildings people like to be in

3 Read the article again and answer the questions.

    1   Why was Hadid called "the paper architect"?
    2   Why do many female architects in Britain not stay in the profession?
    3   What did her professor mean when he called her "a planet in her own orbit"?
    4   What characterizes the buildings designed by Hadid's contemporaries?
    5   What kind of buildings does Hadid like to work on?
    6   Why did Hadid try to create a feeling of space in Evelyn Grace Academy?
    7   How do visitors to the MAXXI Rome feel when they are inside the museum?
    8   What does Hadid say her designs are influenced by?

Critical thinking fact or opinion

4 Work in pairs. Find evidence in the article to support the following statements. Compare answers with your partner.

    1   There are not many women architects in Britain compared to men.
    2   Hadid's style is in the same spirit as some of her contemporaries' styles.
    3   She is interested in designing public buildings.
    4   People are captivated by the spaces she creates within buildings.
    5   She is interested in giving people the experience of a journey within her buildings.
    6   Architecture would be more human if there were more architects like Hadid.

5 Mark each statement in Exercise 4 according to whether it is a fact (F) or the author's opinion (O).

6 Use the facts to write a short summary of what you now know about Zaha Hadid and her work.

Word focus *wall*

7 Find these expressions with *wall* in the article and choose the correct meaning.

    1 **bang your head against a brick wall**
       a fail to persuade others after trying repeatedly
       b fail to achieve a goal due to a mistake
    2 **off-the-wall**
       a strange or eccentric
       b unstable and dangerous

8 Work in pairs. What do these other expressions with *wall* mean? Discuss with your partner.

    1   Can you ask Manuel to stop practicing on his drums? The noise is **driving me up the wall**.
    2   The supermarket is closed now, but you can get a few things from that **hole in the wall**.
    3   Architecture firms **were up against the wall** during the slowdown in construction.
    4   **The writing is on the wall**. Unless we improve, we'll be shut down.
    5   I wish I could have been **a fly on the wall** when Jen had her meeting with the boss.
    6   I was making progress, but now **I've hit a wall**.

9 Think of examples of the following. Discuss your examples with your partner.

    1   something that drives you up the wall
    2   a situation where you would have liked to be a fly on the wall
    3   a company that is up against the wall

Speaking

10 Some of the public spaces mentioned in the article can have bad associations for people, for example, schools and hospitals. Look at these places which people in a survey said they didn't like being in. How do you feel in each of them? Why?

    1   a dentist's office
    2   an elevator
    3   an airport departure lounge
    4   a classroom or lecture hall
    5   a large open-plan office

11 Work in groups of three or four. Choose one of the public spaces in Exercise 10 and discuss how its design could be improved to make people feel more comfortable. Think about the following.

- shape and size of the space
- lighting
- arrangement of furniture
- other additions (music, plants, etc.)

THE PAPER ARCHITECT

For a long time, Zaha Hadid was known as "the paper architect," someone whose grand designs never left the page to become real buildings. But in recent years her buildings have sprouted up like mushrooms all over the world: the Guangzhou Opera House in China, a car factory in Germany, a contemporary art museum in Rome, a transportation museum in Scotland, and the Aquatics Center for the 2012 Olympics in London.

Hadid is now one of the most sought-after architects of our age. She is also one of the few women to have made it in a profession still dominated by men. In Britain, where Hadid lives (she was born in Iraq in 1950), fewer than 15 percent of working architects are women. A lot more than that enter the profession, but either because of the difficulty in getting recognized or because of the deep conservatism surrounding most British architecture, over half of them leave. But being a woman in a man's world seems to have given Hadid extra strength. At times she felt she was banging her head against a wall trying to get her designs accepted, but she persevered. Famous for her fierce independence, she was called "a planet in her own orbit" by a former tutor.

Pinning down her individual style is difficult. Certainly she has been influenced by the modern trend in architecture that likes to play with the traditional shape of buildings and fragment them, creating unpredictable angles and surfaces. Working in this way, she and her fellow architects have produced some off-the-wall, spaceship-like structures that seem to defy the normal laws of engineering, but which have intrigued and excited the public.

But while the visual impact of her designs is clearly important to her, Hadid maintains that the key consideration for her is people's well-being. In other words, how they will feel inside the spaces she creates. This has drawn her increasingly to public projects, such as housing, schools, and hospitals. Recently she won the RIBA Stirling Prize for her design of a school complex in Brixton, south London.

Shaped as a zig-zag, the steel and glass structure of Evelyn Grace Academy takes up only 150,000 square feet compared to 860,000 square feet for a typical high school. To compensate for the lack of internal space, Hadid designed a building with lots of natural light and dramatic angles, so that students view the activity of other students from different perspectives within the structure. The masterstroke is the insertion of a 100-m running track right in the middle of the site between buildings to celebrate the school's emphasis on sports.

This idea of offering the viewer multiple perspectives from within the building is a theme that runs through Hadid's work. Her most famous building, MAXXI—a museum for the 21st century—in Rome, is a great example. It is a complex and spectacular structure of interlocking concrete shapes. Inside spaces interconnect "like winding streets," so that the visitor is surprised and charmed at each turn. The Rosenthal Center in Cincinnati produces a similar effect. Like an extension of the street it sits on, it draws you in, with walkways directing you this way and that, and windows inviting you to sample the view. "It's about promenading," says Hadid, "being able to pause, to look out, look above, look sideways."

So what inspires someone like Hadid to produce such radically different buildings? She speaks in complimentary terms about the work of her contemporaries. She also cites the natural landscape and organic geological patterns as an influence. But it is not a question that she seems too concerned with and nor perhaps should we be. Hadid is an artist, sharing with us her vision of what buildings should be like and always, as she does so, trying to keep human interests—our interests as users and viewers—at heart. Perhaps we could do with more architects like her.

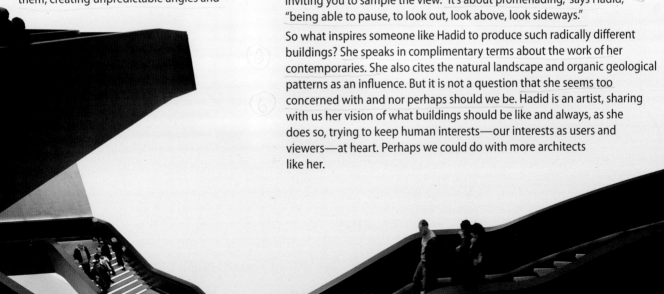

3d A public project

Real life making recommendations

1 Work in pairs. Think about a public work of art in your town or area. Describe it to your partner, saying what you like or dislike about it.

2 Look at the photo and caption and discuss the questions.

1 Do you like this public work of art? Why?
2 What benefits do you think the city authorities hoped it would bring (to both the locals and visitors)?

3 🔊 **11** Listen to part of a debate about a proposal for a public work of art in a city. Answer the questions.

1 What piece of art is being proposed?
2 Is the speaker in favor of or against it?
3 What are the main arguments he puts forward to support his view?

4 Speaking skill making a case

a 🔊 **11** Listen again and complete the sentences below.

A girl plays in the Crown Fountain in Millennium Park, Chicago.

> ▶ **MAKING A CASE**
>
> I have to say, ¹ _____ .
> It has ² _____ to recommend it.
> First of all, it seems ³ _____ .
> What I mean is ⁴ _____ .
> I think everyone should ⁵ _____ .
> Also, the fact that ⁶ _____
> will give it popular appeal.
> It's a clever touch, I think.
> Third, and I don't think we should
> underestimate this, ⁷ _____ .
> I think this is important, given
> ⁸ _____ .
> And the idea that ⁹ _____
> also really appeals to me.

b Look at the phrases in the box.

1 Which are always positive (P)?
2 Which give extra emphasis (E) to the point the speaker makes?

5 Pronunciation linking

a 🔊 **12** Work in pairs. Which words are linked in these phrases? How do words that end in a vowel link to ones that begin with a vowel? Listen and check.

1 "What I mean is, it's not too intellectual…"
What_I mean_is,_it's not too_intellectual…
/w/
2 "The idea that it could be a tourist destination…"
3 "The water and the area in front of the fountain…"

b Practice saying the sentences aloud.

6 Read the guidelines for a proposal for a public work of art in a downtown park. What are the city authorities hoping to do with the park and why?

> The city would like to commission a public work of art for its central park, which is used mainly by joggers and office workers on their lunch breaks. The city feels it has the potential to attract many more visitors. The successful proposal will add to the park without taking anything away from its natural beauty, and will respect environmental considerations. It is also hoped the proposal will make reference to the traditions of our public-spirited city.

7 Work in pairs. You are each going to make a proposal for a public work of art for the city's central park.

Student A: Turn to page 153 and look at the proposal.

Student B: Turn to page 155 and look at the proposal.

Prepare to make the case in favor of your proposal. Look at the guidelines in Exercise 6 and the language in the box in Exercise 4 to help you. Then take turns presenting your proposal. Decide which proposal you find most convincing.

3e Old and new

Writing an opinion essay

1 Look at the photo. Do these two buildings complement each other? Why?

2 Read the essay question and the essay. Answer the questions.

  1 What is the writer's opinion?
  2 How does he support it?

3 Look at the essay again and underline examples of the writer:

  1 examining other people's arguments
  2 trying to be reasonable when giving his opinion
  3 making his point more forcefully (final paragraph)

4 Look at the four key elements of an opinion essay. Find each element in the essay. What is the correct order?

  a make your conclusion
  b give your opinion and present the arguments supporting it
  c evaluate counter arguments
  d analyze the question and set your terms of reference

5 Writing skill **linking devices**

a The writer uses linking and adverbial phrases to connect and balance his ideas. Answer the questions using these words.

admittedly	although
but	even though
however	in fact
so	therefore

  1 Which words link two contrasting ideas?
  2 Which word balances an argument by accepting there is some evidence against it?
  3 Which word reinforces an idea by giving further evidence?
  4 Which words make a conclusion?

Should we allow modern buildings to be built next to older buildings in historic areas?

To answer this question, we must first examine whether people really want to preserve the historic feel of an area. Not all historic buildings are attractive. However, there may be other, perhaps economic, reasons for preserving them. So, let us assume that the historical buildings are both attractive and important. What should we do, then, if a new building is needed?

In my view, new architectural styles can exist perfectly well alongside an older style. In fact, there are many examples in my own hometown of Boston where radical modern designs have been placed very successfully next to old buildings. As long as the building in question is pleasing and does not dominate its surroundings too much, it often enhances the attractiveness of the area.

Admittedly, there are examples of new buildings which have spoiled the area they are in. But the same can be said of some old buildings, too. Yet people still object to new buildings in historic areas. I think this is simply because people are naturally conservative and do not like change.

Although we have to respect people's feelings as fellow users and viewers of the buildings, I believe that it is the duty of the architect and planner to move things forward. If we constantly reproduced what was there before, we would still be living in caves. Therefore, I would argue against building imitations. Choose something fresh and different, even though that might be the riskier option.

b Work in pairs. Use linking devices from Exercise 5a to complete this text.

Buildings that imitate previous styles of architecture do not always work. [1] _____, they can often look cheap. Yet some local authorities will insist on building in a "traditional" style, [2] _____ there may be much more attractive modern designs to choose from. [3] _____, choosing the right modern design is not easy. [4] _____, the rewards for getting it right are much greater. [5] _____, we should encourage authorities to be more adventurous in their choices of designs.

6 Write an opinion essay about this question (250–300 words).

Should we create more socially mixed residential areas, where rich people live next to poorer people, instead of in separate communities?

7 Exchange essays with your partner. Check the following:

  • Is the opinion clear and are the arguments balanced?
  • Does the structure follow the one in Exercise 4?
  • Are linking devices used correctly to connect ideas?

3f Denmark bridge
Video

Enter the Oresund Bridge.

Before you watch

1 Work in pairs. Look at the photo of the bridge and discuss the questions.

   1 What kind of bridge is it?
   2 What difficulties do you think the architects faced in its construction?
   3 What are the alternatives to joining two pieces of land separated by sea?

While you watch

2 Watch the video and answer the questions.

   1 What were the obstacles to joining Sweden to Denmark?

   2 What solution did the architects come up with?

3 Watch the first part of the video (to 01:54) and complete the table.

1	Width of the Oresund Strait	
2	Weather in this region	
3	Needs of Copenhagen	
4	Needs of Malmö	
5	What the bridge carries	
6	Height above the sea	
7	Height of support towers	

4 Watch the second part of the video (01:55 to end). Then answer the questions.

   1 How did the architects know it would be dangerous to build a bridge close to the Danish shoreline?

   2 What would the result of building a lower bridge have been?

   3 What two adjectives does the project director use to describe the tunnel solution?

   4 What was the problem with the part-bridge, part-tunnel solution?

   5 How did the architects get around it?

5 Complete the summary using one word in each space. Then watch the video again to check.

The Oresund Bridge was built to connect Denmark and Sweden over the Oresund [1] _____ in the Baltic Sea. The idea was to merge Malmö and Copenhagen to create one large [2] _____ with economic benefits for all.
The two countries signed a(n) [3] _____ and a [4] _____ was formed to carry out the work. But the project faced a lot of technical difficulties because of [5] _____ and sea traffic. A tunnel would have been the ideal solution but it was too [6] _____ . So they decided to build part tunnel and part [7] _____ . The result is one of the [8] _____ cable-stayed bridges in the world.

After you watch

6 Roleplay a debate about local communications

Work in groups.

Imagine you live in a city built around the base of a hill. At the moment people have to drive around the hill to get from the north side, where most of the residential areas are, to the south side, where most of the commercial and industrial activity is. The local population want to connect the two sides more easily. Look at these options and think about the benefits and drawbacks of each.

- a three-mile tunnel through the hill
- a new six-lane highway ring road running through the city and around the hill
- a new high-speed rail line around the hill
- something else

Debate which you think is the best solution.

7 Work in groups and discuss the questions.

   1 Why are good transportation links important in big cities?
   2 How do you rate the transportation links in your own city? How could they be improved?

---

cable-stayed (adj) /ˈkeɪbəl ˌsteɪd/ a way of supporting a deck or road by attaching cables to a tall column
consortium (n) /kənˈsɔːrʃəm/ a number of companies which join together to work on a project
converge (v) /kənˈvɜːrdʒ/ come together
dangle (v) /ˈdæŋgəl/ hang in the air
lousy (adj) /ˈlaʊzi/ bad or poor quality
pact (n) /pækt/ an agreement
setback (n) /ˈsetˌbæk/ something which stops or reverses your progress
soar (v) /sɔːr/ rise or fly very high
strait (n) /streɪt/ a narrow strip of water between two pieces of land

UNIT 3 REVIEW

Grammar

1 Look at the photo. What do you think this building is for? Read the text and check your answers.

2 Choose the correct option to complete the text.

I ¹*really / so* love the London Olympics Aquatics Center. It's a great example of architect Zaha Hadid's ability to design large public buildings that work. It's rare for design and function to come together as successfully as this. It's both practical and ²*extremely / absolutely* stunning to look at. I like the way that she has made the roof look like moving water. From the outside, it's been compared to a(n) ³*very / absolutely* large turtle with its flippers outstretched. The "flippers" are, in fact, rectangular structures at each side of the building which were put there to accommodate 15,000 spectators. Hadid ⁴*really / completely* wanted the whole structure to be under one undulating roof, but the organizers were ⁵*quite / incredibly* certain about the necessary seating capacity. After the Olympics, most of the seats were removed and the seating capacity reduced to 2,500. Inside the center, the bare concrete sweeps this way and that in beautiful curves; the diving boards seeming to grow out of the floor. The whole effect is ⁶*utterly / incredibly* dramatic.

3 Rewrite these three sentences from the text to make them more emphatic. Use the words given.

1 ...Zaha Hadid's ability to design large public buildings that work. (do)
2 It's rare for design and function to come together as successfully as this. (rarely)
3 I like the way that she has made the roof look like moving water. (what)

4 Work in pairs. What's your favorite sports building or stadium? Why do you like it?

I CAN	
use adverbs to intensify meaning	
give emphasis to statements	

Vocabulary

5 Complete the definitions of buildings and places.

characterless	bedroom	leafy
metropolis	wooden	quiet

1 A _____ shack is a very basic structure, often with just one room.
2 A _____ suburb is a pleasant, green residential area.
3 A _____ building is one that is plain and has no special features.
4 A vibrant _____ is a very large and lively city, like New York.
5 A _____ community is an area where people who commute into the city for work live.
6 A _____ town is a town where very little happens.

6 Work in pairs. Describe examples of buildings and places in Exercise 5 that you know.

I CAN	
describe buildings	
talk about places	

Real life

7 Choose the correct options to complete the text.

I ¹*ought / have* to say, I really like Helen's idea of creating a water park. It has lots of things to ²*recommend / suggest* it. First of all, we don't have many water features in the center of the city. Second, it will attract a lot of birds and other wildlife. Third, and I don't think we should ³*overestimate / underestimate* this, it will attract children. And I ⁴*think / say* that's important, because right now families don't come downtown much. And that's what ⁵*appealed / called* to me about the idea. Also, the idea of having a café and boats for rent is a clever ⁶*touch / point*, because over time it will help us to recoup some of the cost.

8 Work in groups. Make a short proposal for a new recreation feature like a small zoo, a museum, or gallery downtown. Present your ideas to your group using language to support the proposal.

I CAN	
propose an idea	
use expressions to make a case	

Speaking

9 Work in pairs. Look at the photos of the different buildings in Unit 3. Are there any you would like to live in or visit? Give your reasons.

Unit 4 Innovation

An artist's impression of the Shweeb urban transport system of the future

FEATURES

1 Work in pairs. Look at the picture and caption. Then complete the summary of the Shweeb urban transportation system using one word in each space.

above	amusement	fun	Google
pedal	rails	smoothly	

The Shweeb transportation system is a combination of a monorail and a bike. The original idea for putting a bicycle on ¹ _____ so that it could run more ² _____ appeared in the 1800s. The idea was updated by a company called Shweeb for an ³ _____ park. ⁴ _____ has now invested money to develop it into an urban transportation system. Drivers sit in pods hanging from a monorail, and ⁵ _____ while almost lying down. They travel ⁶ _____ the traffic. It is a solution with many advantages: it is green, convenient, cheap, and ⁷ _____ .

2 Match the halves of the collocations. What do they mean?

1	have	a	a need
2	make	b	a breakthrough
3	spot	c	(an idea) one stage further
4	take	d	a bright idea
5	fill	e	the wheel
6	reinvent	f	a trend

3 Work in groups. Each describe an innovation or invention from the last 100 years. Which innovation had the most impact?

4a The mother of invention

Listening

1 Work in pairs. Look at the saying below. Discuss what it means. Is it always true?

"Necessity is the mother of invention."

2 Look at the photo and the caption. What adjectives would you use to describe this invention? What other inventions have you seen that fit that description?

3 🎵 **13** Listen to an interview and choose the statement that best summarizes the speaker's view.

  a Most inventions are an answer to an urgent need.
  b Most inventions are things that we didn't imagine we needed until we became used to them.
  c Most inventions come from companies who want to make a commercial profit.

4 🎵 **13** Choose the correct option to complete the sentences.

  1 People in their teens or twenties probably can't imagine *doing research / following the news* without the Internet.
  2 Martha Kay is *a businesswoman / an academic.*
  3 A British parliamentary committee said the telephone was *too expensive / of little use.*
  4 The presenter uses the telephone as an example of a case where a need *was filled / didn't exist before.*
  5 Most innovations make our lives *richer / easier.*
  6 The presenter suggests that women in the 1960s liked *going out to shop / staying in the house.*
  7 The cell phone and the computer are examples of innovations that were *very expensive at first / seen as unnecessary.*
  8 *Literary Digest* predicted that the automobile would *remain a luxury / go out of fashion.*

5 What fact or point of view did you find most interesting? Why? Discuss with your partner.

Charles Steinlauf's invention: a four-position bicycle that also contains a built-in sewing machine

Vocabulary phrasal verb *come*

6 Look at the sentences (1–6), which use phrasal verbs with *come*. Choose the correct meaning (a–c).

  1 But how do such inventions **come about**?
    a succeed   b happen   c work
  2 Entrepreneurs often **come up with** ideas that will make our lives a little more convenient…
    a think of   b ignore   c search for
  3 What it **comes down to** is wants rather than needs.
    a relies on   b emphasizes   c is a question of
  4 A researcher **came across** the material for Post-it notes while looking for a new kind of glue.
    a thought of   b found by chance   c stole
  5 Early experiments with flying didn't really **come off**.
    a succeed   b get noticed   c fail
  6 Perrelet was so respected that when other watchmakers **came up against** a problem, they would consult him.
    a solved   b encountered   c analyzed

7 Work in pairs. Write three sentences using the phrasal verbs in Exercise 6. Then read your sentences to your partner omitting the verb and see if they can guess the missing verb.

Language focus past modals

8 Match each sentence (1–4) with the function of the modal verb (a–d).

1 It's difficult to imagine what life **must have been** like before the invention of certain things.
2 In 1878, a British parliamentary committee **had to comment** on the usefulness of the telephone.
3 Maybe they **should have been** more open-minded.
4 But in 1878, people **didn't need to have** phones.

a to talk about obligation
b to talk about necessity / lack of necessity
c to speculate about the past
d to say what was advisable/inadvisable

> ▶ **PAST MODALS**
>
> **Obligation**
> *They had to patent the product before trying to sell it.*
>
> **Necessity**
> *They needed to have a way to communicate more quickly.*
> *They didn't need to / have to make the instructions so complicated.*
>
> **Speculation**
> *He must have realized it was an important discovery.*
> *He may/might/could have wanted to keep it a secret.*
> *It can't/couldn't have been easy to convince people of the idea.*
>
> **Advisability**
> *They should have included more safety features.*
> *They ought to have tested it first.*
>
> For more information and practice, see page 160.

9 Look at the language focus box and complete the sentences using past modals. Sometimes more than one answer is possible.

1 Before cars were invented, it _____ (not / be) easy to take your family for a weekend outing.
2 In the 1940s, people _____ (not / own) a television, because they could get news and shows on their radios.
3 Before satellite navigation in cars, people _____ (depend) on a passenger for directions.
4 Some people _____ (drive) with the steering wheel in one hand and a map in the other.
5 I _____ (buy) this microwave oven. I never use it.
6 Before we all had digital cameras, it _____ (be) expensive to keep buying film for your camera.
7 The electric spaghetti fork is a useless invention. The inventor really _____ (bother).
8 The inventors of "cat's eyes"—reflectors in the road— _____ (be given) a medal, they have saved so many lives.
9 When James Watt invented the steam engine, he _____ (realize) that the railway locomotive would follow.
10 Who knows what inventions people like Leonardo da Vinci _____ (come) up with using modern technology!

10 Pronunciation weak forms

a 🔊 14 Underline the weak forms (not stressed) in these phrases using past modals. Then listen and check.

1 You should have told me.
2 Did you have to wait?
3 He must have forgotten.
4 You shouldn't have worried.
5 She may have left already.
6 I didn't need to be there.

b 🔊 15 Work in pairs. Listen to the pronunciation and underline the stressed words. How is the meaning different in each one?

1 a You might have told me.
  b You might have told me.
2 a You shouldn't have waited.
  b Flowers? Oh, you shouldn't have!

11 Work in groups. Use past modals to speculate on the answers to these questions.

How did people:
• wake up on time before there were alarm clocks?
• keep money safe before banks existed?
• amuse themselves in the evenings without electricity?
• deal with aches and pains without medicine?
• contact each other in an emergency without telephones?
• light candles before matches were invented?
• find out if bones were broken before x-rays existed?

Speaking

12 Work in pairs. Think of two commonly used inventions: one that you couldn't live without and one that you find unnecessary. Discuss the inventions with your partner and the reasons why you chose them.

4b Fold everything

Reading

1 Look at the picture of a horse made using origami, the traditional Japanese art of paper folding. Answer the questions.

    1 Do you do any kind of hand crafts? What are they?
    2 Have you ever tried origami? What did you make?

2 Work in pairs. What are the basic principles of origami? Are these sentences true (T) or false (F)? Read the first paragraph of the article and check your answers.

    1 You need more than one piece of paper.
    2 The paper should be square.
    3 You shouldn't use scissors.
    4 Sometimes you need to use glue.

3 Read the rest of the article and find the following.

    1 two things used in space exploration that are folded using origami techniques
    2 two origami-inspired devices that help to save lives
    3 a use of origami that seems like a fantasy
    4 a use of origami that can make machines more powerful

Fold EVERYTHING

At one time or another in your life you have probably done origami, even if it was just making a paper airplane or something more sophisticated like a paper crane. The chances are that as you did it, you reflected on how ingenious this traditional Japanese art is. Animals, boxes, flowers, boats: it all can be created from a single square or rectangular sheet of paper simply by folding it. No cutting, no pasting.

But did you ever stop to think how the same techniques might be applied to engineering? Equipment that could be of real practical use? Origami meets the demand for things that need to be small when transported and large when they arrive, like the everyday umbrella. In fact, origami-inspired creations have already flown in space; in 1995, Japanese engineers launched a satellite with solar panels that folded like a map. And very soon origami engineering may well be seen in a host of other applications.

"It's now mathematically proven that you can pretty much fold anything," says physicist Robert J. Lang, who quit his engineering job eight years ago to fold things full time. Lang, an origami enthusiast since age six, advised a well-known car manufacturer on the best way to fold an airbag into a dashboard. He is currently working on a space telescope lens that, if all goes according to plan, should be able to unfold to the size of a football field.

At the other end of the scale, researchers are also working on tiny folding devices that could lead to breakthroughs in medicine and computing. These include origami stents that are inserted into arteries and open up to keep the blood flowing.

There's no doubt that saving space has become important in our world, as the search for ever smaller electronic components shows. Computers of the future may contain tiny, folded motors or capacitors for faster processing and better memory.

Applications for origami engineering go further than many of us might imagine. "Some day," says MIT's* Erik Demaine, "we'll build reconfigurable robots that can fold on their own from one thing into another," like Transformers. Too much iike science fiction to be true? Maybe—though you certainly wouldn't want to bet against it.

* MIT = Massachusetts Institute of Technology

crane (n) /kreɪn/ a large bird with long legs
ingenious (adj) /ɪnˈdʒinjəs/ very clever
stent (n) /stent/ a thin tube used in medicine

4 Work in pairs. Explain the following terms and expressions from the article.

1 How is a paper crane "more sophisticated" than an airplane? (para 1)
2 What "plan" is referred to in the phrase "if all goes according to plan"? (para 3)
3 What scale is referred to in the phrase "At the other end of the scale"? (para 4)
4 What does "it" mean in the phrase "you wouldn't want to bet against it"? (para 6)

> ▶ **WORDBUILDING past participles as adjectives**
>
> We often use past participles as adjectives.
> a well-**known** car manufacturer, tiny **folded** motors
> In a few cases, the adjective form is different from the past participle.
> It has been **proved**.   A **proven** method.

Idioms partitives

5 Compare these two expressions. Which expression means "some" or "a piece of" and which means "a small piece"?

1 **a sheet** of paper   2 **a scrap** of paper

6 Which of the partitive expressions in bold mean "some" and which "a small piece or amount"?

1 I'm really thirsty. I haven't had **a drop** of water all day.
2 It was **a stroke** of luck getting those tickets. They were the last two available.
3 There's not **a shred** of evidence to suggest that there is life on other planets.
4 The latest figures offer **a glimmer** of hope that the recession is coming to an end.
5 She had **a flash** of inspiration. Why not use the principles of origami to make foldable furniture?
6 There was **a hint** of disappointment in his voice, but he took the news very well.

Language focus probability

7 Work in pairs. How many phrases can you find in the article that say something is:

1 possible   3 more or less
2 probable   certain

Example:
1 ...you have probably done origami... (paragraph 1)
Compare your answers.

8 Look at the sentences and say whether they use a verb, an adverb, an adjective, or a noun phrase to express probability. Is there any difference in meaning or register between them?

1 He probably won't come with us.
2 It's unlikely that he'll come with us.
3 He may not come with us.
4 The chances are that he won't come with us.

> ▶ **PROBABILITY**
>
> **Modal verbs**
> may/could/might; should
> Origami may be the answer.
> The telescope should help us to explore the universe.
>
> **Adverbs**
> perhaps; maybe; probably; almost certainly
> Perhaps one day they will invent foldable robots.
>
> **The adjective (un)likely**
> It's (un)likely that this technology will be used in computers.
> This technology is (un)likely to be used in computers.
>
> **Noun phrases**
> The likelihood is; The chances are; There is a good chance
> The chances are that it will be used in robot design.
>
> Note: should is not used for the probability of something bad happening.
>
> For more information and practice, see page 161.

9 Rewrite the paragraphs using the words given.

The grocery bag of the future [1] *will perhaps be made of steel* (could). Invented by Dr. Zhong You from Oxford University, it [2] *will probably inspire other packaging solutions too* (likely to). Flat-pack boxes used by the industry have to be folded at the bottom. But with Dr. You's origami design [3] *you can make boxes with a fixed base* (possible). [4] *This is likely to save industry a lot of time and money* (should).

Dr. You thinks that if this process works for steel, [5] *it will probably work for a range of other materials* (the chances). Origami engineers hope that [6] *one day perhaps it will be possible to build houses from flat-pack materials* (might). In ten years' time, [7] *it's very possible that we will be folding away our kitchen counters or table* (may well). [8] *The likelihood is that we won't have foldable TVs or cars* (unlikely), but who knows?

Speaking

10 Work in pairs. Think of three more ideas for how origami methods could be used to help save space in the modern home. Then present your ideas to another pair.

4c The shoe giver

Reading

1 Read the definition of *social entrepreneurship* and say which of the organizations (a–c) fit the definition and why. How would you describe the others?

Social entrepreneurship is the art of creating a socially responsible business that aims to generate profit while solving social and environmental problems.

a   An organization which collects food near its sell-by date from supermarkets and distributes it free to homeless people.
b   An organization which sells gardening services to companies. The people it employs are all long-term unemployed people who get training, work experience, and a small salary.
c   An organization that collects old clothes that people are throwing out and recycles the material to make new clothes which it sells.

2 Read the article on page 51. In what ways does TOMS fit the definition of social entrepreneurship?

3 Read the article again. Are the sentences true (T) or false (F)?

1   Mycoskie's early career was characterized by establishing and then selling companies.
2   Mycoskie immediately saw the children's shoe problem as another business challenge.
3   The main advantage of the one-for-one scheme is that each child is given one pair of shoes.
4   Podoconiosis is a disease that affects children in developed countries as much as in developing countries.
5   The author suggests that, in business, energy and enthusiasm are as important as knowledge.
6   Any business could profit from making a similar one-for-one offer to its customers.

Critical thinking **finding counter arguments**

4 The author presents a positive picture of TOMS, but there are suggestions of arguments against the initiative. Find possible criticisms in the text in these areas.

a   the price and quality of the product
b   buying shoes as a way of giving to charity
c   the business model

5 Work in pairs. Compare your answers from Exercise 4. Then write some questions to challenge Mycoskie on those points.

Word focus *give*

6 Work in pairs. Find these expressions with *give* in the article and discuss what they mean.

give it a break   give it some thought

7 Complete the expressions with *give* using these words. Discuss what each expression means.

best   break   shot   go-ahead   thought   time

1   There's no need to tell me your answer now. **Give it some** _____ and then let me know.
2   Don't worry if you don't win, just **give it your** _____ .
3   I wasn't actually expecting him to like our business proposal, but he **gave us the** _____ .
4   **Give him a** _____ . He's new and can't be expected to know everything.
5   It's hard when you're new, but **give it some** _____ and you'll feel more at home.
6   The only way to find out if you can fix it yourself is to **give it a** _____ .

8 Match these expressions with a similar expression from Exercise 7.

a chance   consideration   the green light
a try   a while   your all

Speaking

9 Work in pairs. You are going to act out an interview between a reporter for an ecology magazine and Blake Mycoskie. Take turns playing the roles of interviewer (the reporter) and interviewee (Blake Mycoskie). Think about the questions that were raised about the shoe-giving initiative in Exercise 5.

Student A: You are the reporter. Focus on the possible problems with the one-for-one shoe-giving business and ask questions that challenge Mycoskie to defend it.

Student B: You are Blake Mycoskie. Defend your business and its philosophy.

Blake Mycoskie is a self-confessed serial entrepreneur. He set up his first business, EZ Laundry, a door-to-door laundry service for students, when he was still in college. Having grown the company to service seven colleges in the southwestern US, he sold his share to his business partner and moved on to a media advertising business in Nashville. This he sold to Clear Channel, one of the industry's leading companies.

Three more businesses later, still only 29 years old, and feeling somewhat burned out, Mycoskie decided to give it a break for a while and head down to Argentina for some rest and relaxation. But resting wasn't really in his nature, and it wasn't long before Mycoskie had hit upon an idea that would come to define him as a social entrepreneur.

On a visit to a village outside Buenos Aires, he was shocked to see that many of the children didn't have any shoes or, if they did, the shoes were worn out and didn't fit. Since shoes, particularly the local farmers' canvas shoe, the alpargata, can be bought relatively cheaply in Argentina, Mycoskie's first instinct was to set up a charity to donate shoes to the children. But after giving it some thought, he realized that this was not a model that would work. One pair of shoes per child would not make that much difference because they wear out. And if he asked people to donate repeatedly, sympathy for the cause might also wear out pretty quickly.

Instead he came up with the idea of TOMS One for One Shoes. He would take the alpargata to America, manufacture it and sell it as a high-end fashion item at around $50 a pair. (A pair of similar shoes with a well-known brand name costs around $30.) For each pair he sold, he would donate another to shoeless children, guaranteeing a continual supply. Also, rather than running a charity, something he had no real experience in, he could run the project as a business.

Several years later, the business is thriving, supplying shoes not only to children in Argentina but also other parts of the world where foot diseases are a problem. In southern Ethiopia, a high concentration of silicone in the soil can cause podoconiosis, a disease which severely swells the feet. The shocking appearance of the disease means sufferers are often ostracized. There are 300,000 affected people in Ethiopia simply because they have no shoes. The same silicone-rich soil exists in parts of France and Hawaii, but people have shoes and are not affected.

Mycoskie had no manufacturing experience and understood that he had to learn fast. For the first eighteen months, by his own admission, he made "a poor job of making shoes," but since then he has brought in help from experienced industry people. The vital element that Mycoskie added was his passion—a passion he wants others to share. One criticism of initiatives like TOMS is that the money spent by customers might otherwise have gone directly to charities. So Mycoskie encourages his customers to become more involved with TOMS by volunteering to hand-deliver the shoes to children in need. It's an intimate giving experience and he hopes it might inspire some of the volunteers to develop similar projects.

But can the one-for-one model be repeated with other products? Mycoskie is doubtful. TOMS is a for-profit business, but does not yet make a profit. He says one-for-one is not an offer that you can just add to your existing business model; you have to build it in from the beginning.

Some would also argue that the charity aspect is just a marketing tool, but does it matter? TOMS is making a real difference to poor children all over the world and Mycoskie is enjoying being an entrepreneur more than ever.

The shoe giver

ostracize (v) /ˈɒstrəˌsaɪz/ to refuse to allow someone to take part in a social group
self-confessed (adj) /ˈself kənˈfest/ the person admits this themselves
swell (v) /swel/ to grow larger

Changing a life begins with a single step

4d An elevator pitch

Real life making a short pitch

1 Work in pairs. Look at the advice about public speaking. Discuss with your partner what it means.

> Be sincere, be brief, be seated.
> *Franklin D. Roosevelt, former US president*

2 Do you know what an "elevator pitch" is? Read the text quickly. Then cover the page and summarize the key points.

An elevator pitch is like a TV commercial. You're trying to sell an idea to someone whose attention you have for a very short time: 30 seconds to a minute before they get out of the elevator. Just as with a TV commercial, the idea is to get the person in front of you interested in coming back and taking another look. So the key things to convey are:

- the problem that your idea solves
- the uniqueness or freshness of your idea

That's it. You're not selling yourself, talking about your own achievements and experience, and you're not criticizing the competition.

3 You are going to listen to a business proposal based on the idea of doing volunteer work in the local community. Before you do, discuss these questions with your partner.

1 What motivates people to do volunteer work?
2 What kind of things might people volunteer to do?

4 🔊 16 Listen to the proposal and answer the questions.

1 What is the unique idea that the speaker describes?
2 What problem(s) does it solve?
3 What phrases does the speaker repeat often?

5 Speaking skill using rhetorical questions

🔊 16 The speaker used rhetorical questions. Listen again and check (✓) the phrases you hear.

▶ USING RHETORICAL QUESTIONS	
What is it?	"So what?" I hear you say.
How does it work?	Isn't it going to be expensive?
Why is it necessary?	So, how do we achieve this?
What does it do exactly?	What's our ambition for…?

6 Pronunciation long and short vowels

a 🔊 17 Work in pairs. Listen to the questions in the box and say if the stressed syllables in these words contain a long or short vowel sound. Then practice saying them.

is   work   necessary   do   what   expensive   achieve   ambition

b Underline the word in each pair that contains a long vowel sound. Then practice saying the words.

1 look   loop
2 scheme   skim
3 training treasure
4 bottle   both

7 Work in groups of three. You are each going to present your own elevator pitch for a new social enterprise.

Student A: Turn to page 153 and read the notes.

Student B: Turn to page 154 and read the notes.

Student C: Turn to page 155 and read the notes.

- Prepare your pitch carefully. Use the guidelines in Exercise 2 and the language in the box to help with the structure.
- Speak for no more than a minute.
- Write down the main message of each pitch and at the end compare your answers.
- Vote on who you think gave the most persuasive pitch.

4e Volunteer planner

Writing describing how things work

1 Work in pairs. Read the description of the "Volunteer Planner" phone app, then answer the questions.

1 Who is this description written for?
2 Which adjective best describes this piece of writing?
a friendly   b factual   c technical   d analytical

Volunteer Planner

Overview

Volunteer Planner is an easy-to-use tool that makes volunteering simpler. The application can be downloaded from www.volunteero.com and set up in five minutes or less. It consists of two main components: a database of volunteers and organizations and the planner itself.

The database

For each geographical area, there is a registry or database of both volunteers and organizations.

For each volunteer, the database provides information on:

- their general availability (like afternoons per week)
- their contact number
- a brief description of their qualifications (such as driver's license) and skills

For each organization, the database lists:

- the type of activity and skills needed
- any special conditions relating to the work
- its precise location

The planner

The planner allows volunteers and organizations to fill slots in a real-time calendar using their smartphones. When a volunteer enters their name in a slot, the organization is alerted by text message, inviting them to confirm the offer. By selecting "accept" on the calendar, the organization sends the volunteer confirmation. To cancel at a later date, the volunteer selects "cancel" on the calendar. A message is then sent automatically to the organization; it is also sent to other eligible volunteers, inviting them to fill the slot.

---

2 How is the description organized to make it easier for the reader to follow? Did you find these features helpful?

3 Writing skill punctuation

a Find examples of these punctuation marks in the description:

a colon :
b semicolon ;
c dash —
d bullet ●

b Match the punctuation marks in Exercise 3a with their uses (1–5).

1 to separate items in lists where commas would be confusing
2 to explain the idea in a preceding clause or sentence
3 in place of parentheses ( ) to give extra information
4 to introduce a list
5 to separate two very strongly connected ideas

c Punctuate this passage with a colon, two semicolons, and two dashes.

> The three good reasons to use the Volunteer Planner are to help you plan your volunteering to help the organization and this is our sincere hope to increase the number of volunteers.

4 Write a description of how something works for a potential investor. Use the idea that you presented in Exercise 7 on page 52 or another idea. Remember to organize your description using subheadings and bullet points.

5 Exchange descriptions with your partner. Check that you each have:

- written a clear, factual description.
- organized the text under subheadings and bullet points.
- used punctuation correctly.

4f Ethical Ocean
Video

Ethical Ocean, a social enterprise

own
WHAT'S
good

Before you watch

1 Work in pairs. What does a *social entrepreneur* do? Discuss with your partner.

2 David Damberger is a social entrepreneur and winner of a scholarship from the Skoll Center for Social Entrepreneurship. Look at the photo. What kind of activities do you think *Ethical Ocean* is involved with? Discuss with your partner.

While you watch

3 Read these sentences about David Damberger's background. Then watch the first part of the video (to 01:23) and choose the correct option to complete the sentences.

1 David Damberger is from *Canada / Colorado*.
2 He helped start an enterprise called Engineers *Without Borders / With Ideas*.
3 Their idea was to help people in poor countries to improve *walls / wells* or bridges.
4 They realized that the problem was not a lack of technology or *engineers / politics*.
5 The problem was *too much bureaucracy / a lack of business ability*.

4 Watch the second part of the video (01:24 to 02:06). Complete the table about Ethical Ocean.

1	Type of business:	An e-_____ for ethical goods
2	Description:	A one-_____ shop for everything ethical
3	Categories of goods:	_____, fair trade, _____ friendly, sweatshop-labor _____
4	Product range:	clothing, _____, home _____ products

5 Watch the third part of the video (02:07 to 03:12). Look at these words and listen to how Ethical Ocean ensures the companies on the site are ethical. Then summarize this to your partner.

1 certification   2 story   3 vote

6 Watch the fourth part of the video (03:13 to end) and answer the questions.

1 What category do the majority of products on the website fall into?

2 What particularly successful product does David Damberger mention?

3 What are the advantages of this product?

After you watch

7 Work in groups. Discuss what you think of David Damberger's social enterprise idea, Ethical Ocean.

8 Work in pairs. Look at these products and the list of ethical criteria (a–g). Which criteria are relevant to each product? Which do you actually consider when buying these products?

car	electronic equipment	furniture	stationery
toys	fruit and vegetables	cosmetics	clothes

a Are the materials used from sustainable sources?
b Was a lot of energy consumed to make this product?
c Where has it been transported from?
d Did the maker have good working conditions?
e Did the maker receive a fair proportion of the selling price?
f If it is a food product, is it organic (grown without the use of chemicals)?
g Will the product biodegrade or be recycled when it is no longer used?

9 Roleplay a product pitch

Work in pairs.

Student A: Imagine you are a representative from a company who is going to pitch a product for Ethical Ocean to sell through their website. Look at these points and prepare your pitch.
• think what your product is
• think about what its ethical credentials are
• prepare to sell its benefits

Student B: Imagine you are a representative from Ethical Ocean. Prepare questions about price, ethical criteria, product benefits, etc.

Act out the conversation. Then change roles and act out the conversation again with a different product.

accessory (n) /æk'sesəri/ an extra, supplementary item
bunch (n) /bʌntʃ/ a group
credentials (n) /krɪ'denʃəlz/ qualifications, proof of a thing's suitability
detergent (n) /dɪ'tɜrdʒənt/ powder or liquid used to clean clothes or dishes
naively (adv) /naɪ'ivli/ making a judgment that's too simple because you lack experience
sweatshop (n) /'swet,ʃɑp/ a workplace where people work for very low wages under poor conditions

UNIT 4 REVIEW

Grammar

1 Read the article and complete it with these words.

chances	could	likelihood	likely	might
must	need	probably	should	unlikely

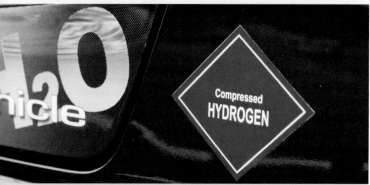

What is the ¹_____ that in fifteen years' time we will still be burning fossil fuels and driving gas-powered cars? Looking at the progress that has been made with alternative forms of energy, the ²_____ are pretty high. The problem with green innovation is that each time you think you ³_____ have found the answer, you also find a catch. Wind turbines only work when the wind blows. The inventors ⁴_____ have realized that, surely? Hydrogen is a clean alternative to gasoline, but it is highly explosive and when the first accident happens, there is ⁵_____ to be a strong public reaction against it. The real innovation in energy ⁶_____ will not come from a new means of power generation, but in how the energy grid is organized. Advances in IT mean that, in the future, homes, factories, and public buildings ⁷_____ be able to generate small amounts of energy, which they ⁸_____ either use themselves or put back into the grid for others to use. The question is: can we make that change? Some say that because it is not in the interest of big business, it is ⁹_____ to happen any time soon. But look what happened to the music business. We didn't ¹⁰_____ to change from a system of buying CDs to sharing music online. But that is what happened.

2 Answer the questions according to the author.

1 What is the problem with most innovations?
2 What is the answer to our future energy needs?
3 Is the writer optimistic or pessimistic about finding alternative ways of generating power?

3 Work in pairs. Are you optimistic about finding a different way to manage our energy needs? Why?

I CAN	
express obligation and necessity, speculate and give advice in the past (past modals)	☐
talk about the probability of things happening	☐

Vocabulary

4 Complete the idiomatic expressions. The first letter has been given for you.

1 Just play with the idea and see what you come u_____ with.
2 There's not a s_____ of evidence to suggest that this is going to work, but you can give it a t_____ anyway.
3 I came a_____ some old plans for an extension to the house. It was a real s_____ of luck, because I was about to hire an architect to do some drawings.
4 For a long time they were making no progress. Then Natalia had a f_____ of inspiration and suggested using hydrogen. It was then that they made a b_____ in the engine's design.
5 I don't really understand how the invention of the television came a_____ .

5 Work in pairs. Have you ever experienced any of the following? Discuss with your partner.

- an idea which needed some thought
- a flash of inspiration
- a stroke of luck
- an invention that didn't fill a particular need

I CAN	
use idioms	☐
talk about inventions and innovations	☐

Real life

6 Look at the statements from a short product pitch. Write a rhetorical question before each one.

1 _____ ? It's a vacuum cleaner that can clean any type of floor surface.
2 _____ ? Because there's no other machine that can perform all these functions.
3 _____ ? At the base, there's a rotary brush which cleans as it sucks up the dirt.
4 _____ ? Despite its sophistication, we're hoping to keep the cost down.
5 _____ ? By making it in China, where manufacturing costs are much lower.

7 Work in pairs. Think of a product that you use frequently. Present it to your partner as if it was a new product. Use at least three rhetorical questions.

I CAN	
give a short presentation for a new product	☐
use rhetorical questions in a presentation	☐

Speaking

8 Work in pairs. Discuss what device or technological gadget would most improve your life.

Unit 5 The writer's journey

A street at sunset in one of the world's most famous cities
Photograph by Fred Derwal

FEATURES

1 Work in pairs. Look at the photo. Discuss where it was taken and what you know about this place (its character, its landmarks, its people).

2 Look at the questions and discuss them with your partner.

1 What different factors influence how we experience a place when we travel?
2 What makes a good travel writer?

3 Look at these adjectives. Which ones normally describe people (P), places (PL), or both (B)?

romantic	cozy	officious
affable	wary	grand
lazy	lively	elegant

4 Work in groups. Use adjectives to describe the following places. Use words from Exercise 3 if helpful.

- the city or town you are living in now
- one of your favorite cities

5a *Where the Indus Is Young*

Listening

1 Work in groups. Discuss the questions.

    1 Do you read any travel writing? What kind: travel guides, travel blogs, travel fiction, adventure stories, accounts of expeditions?

    2 What well-known books (nonfiction or novels) have been written about your country? Do they give a true picture?

2 🔊 **18** Listen to part of a radio show, *The Book Club*, where a guest talks about and recommends a book. Then complete the table.

1	Type of book	
2	Setting (time and place)	
3	Subject of book	
4	Adjectives used to describe it	w................, g................

3 🔊 **18** Listen again and choose the best option (a or b) to answer the questions.

    1 Why did Shyla choose this book?
       a the writing is incredible
       b it's an amazing story

    2 Who is the real hero of the book?
       a the mother
       b the daughter

    3 What is frightening about the descent they make on horseback?
       a there is a deep drop on one side
       b the path is very steep

    4 Why did this particular section sum up the Himalayas for the writer?
       a they make people seem insignificant
       b they are so beautiful

    5 What does the writer blame for new diseases coming to this area?
       a Western tourism
       b modern technology

    6 What is Shyla suspicious about?
       a the author's political motives
       b Western travelers who want places to remain untouched by Western civilization

> **WORDBUILDING** *-ing* adjectives
>
> We form *-ing* adjectives from verbs and we use them in descriptive writing to convey a dynamic feeling.
> *falling, gripping, raging*

4 Should such a young child have been taken on such a dangerous trip? Discuss with your partner.

Vocabulary roads and ways

5 Work in pairs. Find the following words in the audioscript on page 177: *ascent*, *path*, and *track*. Discuss what each word means. Then answer the questions about each pair of related words.

    1 **ascent** and **descent**   Which is up and which down?

    2 **path** and **track**   Which could not be for cars?

    3 **way** and **course**   Which describes the route of a river?

    4 **trail** and **route**   Which is only an overland way?

    5 **road** and **street**   Which is only in a city, town, or village?

Language focus substitution

6 Work in pairs. Look at the highlighted words in the audioscript on page 177. What does each of the following substitutions refer to?

    a the girl   *the daughter*   g that
    b This   h others
    c one   i the former
    d to do so   j the same thing
    e does   k not
    f this

Substituting words
It was a rough track, a path made of uneven stones.

Substituting nouns
It was a brave action, but not a smart one.
Tea and coffee both contain caffeine, the former even more than the latter.

Substituting verbs and verb phrases
I love traveling in dangerous places, but Sophie doesn't.
I want to take a vacation, but to do so means taking time off.

Substituting clauses
Not many people know this region.   Yes I'm aware of that.
The road was blocked. This meant we had to find another route.

Ellipsis (omitting words)
She wasn't the first person to write about this region, but she still wanted to.

For more information and practice, see page 162.

7 Substitute the underlined phrases in the review with the words and punctuation below.

a lot	doesn't	it	one	others	this
to do so	a trip	—			

Some people go out of their way to make travel convenient and comfortable. Dervla Murphy [1] *doesn't go out of her way*. Since she began writing, Murphy has shown a passion for eccentric travel. Lucky for us, she is also keen to share [2] *her travel passion* with us in her writing. Her first book, *Full Tilt*, describes her journey from Ireland to India on a bicycle. This was [3] *a journey* that she had been planning since she was ten years old. Where [4] *other travelers* might not have attracted so much attention, Murphy, being a lone woman on a bicycle, attracted [5] *a lot of attention*. She took a revolver for protection and had to use [6] *the revolver* twice: once to scare off wolves in Bulgaria and once [7] *to scare off* people in Persia. To tell a story in an interesting way is one thing, but [8] *to tell a story* in such a humorous and good-natured way is another. As an example of good travel writing, I can't think of a better [9] *example*.

Full Tilt
Ireland to India with a Bicycle
DERVLA MURPHY

8 Pronunciation intonation in short responses

a Work in pairs. We often use substitution in spoken exchanges. Complete the answers to each question using one word in each case.

1 You have to be careful not to get lost.
  Yes, I know _____ .
2 Would you like to drive?
  No, I'd rather you _____ .
3 Did he take warm clothes with him?
  I hope _____ .
4 Do you mind traveling alone?
  No, I actually prefer _____ .
5 Are there guidebooks about La Paz?
  Well, there are _____ .
6 Do you have an up-to-date map of Russia?
  No, but I have an old _____ .

b 🔊 **19** Listen and check your answers. Pay attention to the stress and intonation in the responses. Read the exchanges aloud.

Vocabulary and speaking
a good read

9 Rewrite the phrases describing books using a noun in place of each word in bold.

1 It is **set** in…
  The _____ for the story is…
2 It **describes** a journey to…
  It's a _____ of a journey to…
3 What **appealed** to me about it was…
  Its _____ for me was…
4 The author **is commenting** on…
  It's a _____ on…
5 It's **about** two people who…
  It's a _____ of two people who…
6 It **deals with the subject of**…
  The main _____ is…

10 Work in groups of three roleplaying an edition of *The Book Club* radio show.

Student A and Student B: You are the guests. Each choose a book to talk about and include these points: the genre of book, the author's name, the setting, the theme or basic plot, and what you liked about it.

Student C: You are the radio host. Prepare to ask your guests questions about their choices: what was different about the book, the style of writing, what they thought about the main characters, etc.

5b The adventures of Hergé

Reading

1 Work in pairs. Discuss the comics or cartoons you read as a child. Do you still read any?

2 Read the article and answer the questions.

1 What is a graphic novel?
2 Why did readers particularly like Hergé's stories when they were first published?
3 What makes Hergé special among graphic novel writers?

3 Read the article again. Are the sentences true (T) or false (F)?

1 Cartoons are a good medium for readers today.
2 The idea of publishing whole books of Tintin's adventures came after Hergé's death.
3 Hergé's stories are not entirely serious.
4 Hergé's account of a journey to the Moon was based only on his intuition and instinct.

4 Why do you think Hergé's books are so successful? What interests you about them, having read this article? Discuss with your partner.

★ THE ADVENTURES OF HERGÉ ★

Cartoons suit the way we like information to be presented these days: graphically and in small chunks. We are used to cartoons and comic strips that take a wry look at modern life or provide a bit of escapism. But recently we have seen an increase in the number of graphic novels: book-length comics with a single, continuous narrative. Historically, graphic novels were not popular outside France, Belgium, Japan, and the US. The exception is the worldwide popularity of a young reporter-detective from Belgium, Tintin.

The creation of the Belgian cartoonist Hergé, *The Adventures of Tintin* first appeared in a Belgian newspaper in 1929. Each story appeared as a cartoon strip week by week, but soon after was republished in book form. One of the main attractions for readers was that they were taken to parts of the world they had never seen and probably never would: Russia, the Congo, America. Hergé himself only traveled outside Belgium later in life, but his passion was educating his readers about other cultures and places.

Two things set Hergé apart as a graphic novelist. The first was his technical drawing skills: with just a few simple lines he could communicate a particular facial expression or movement. The second was the careful research he put into his stories. In *The Crab with the Golden Claws*, Tintin follows an opium-smuggling ring to North Africa; in *King Ottakar's Scepter*, he foils an attempt at a military coup in a central European country. While telling these stories, Hergé also steered a fine line between serious topics and humor.

Tintin had more than his fair share of adventures, but perhaps the greatest is his journey to the Moon, told in *Destination Moon* and *Explorers on the Moon*. Written in 1953, sixteen years before the first Moon landing, the stories show a remarkable eye for technical detail and feeling for the nature of space travel. In the early 1950s, few could imagine what it was like to be looking down at our planet from outer space. And that is Hergé's true gift: to understand what a place was like without ever having been there.

---

foil (v) /fɔɪl/ stop a plot or crime
military coup (n) /ˈmɪlɪteri ˌku/ a takeover of the rule of a country by the army
wry (adj) /raɪ/ humorous, making fun of something

Idioms rhyming expressions

5 Work in pairs. In a rhyming expression, two words with the same sound are put together, for example, "snail mail" for letters sent by mail, not email. Look at these expressions. Find two in the article. Discuss what they all mean. Which expressions truly rhyme and which just sound similar?

fair share	fine line	ill will	nitty-gritty*
no-go	real deal*	telltale	wishy-washy*

more colloquial

6 Complete these sentences using an expression from Exercise 5.

1 He got the job and I didn't, but there's no _____ between us.
2 Sneezing and feeling hot and cold are _____ symptoms of the flu.
3 It's a _____ ; the negotiations fell apart and we don't have a contract.
4 "It's OK" is a pretty _____ answer.
5 We need to get down to the _____ : the exact price, quantity, and delivery date.
6 As an example of a sportsman who never gives up, Rafael Nadal is the _____ .

Language focus nominalization

7 Look at the pairs of sentences below (1–3). Answer the questions (a–d).

1 a Putting collections of cartoons into book form is <u>fashionable</u> now.
  b There is now <u>a fashion for</u> putting collections of cartoons into book form.
2 a The number of graphic novels <u>has increased</u>.
  b We have seen <u>an increase in</u> the number of graphic novels.
3 a Historically, graphic novels, <u>except</u> *Tintin*, were appreciated only in France, Belgium, Japan, and the US.
  b Historically, graphic novels were appreciated only in France, Belgium, Japan, and the US. <u>The exception</u> to this is *Tintin*.

a What part of speech has been changed to make a noun in each case?
b What part of speech follows the noun in these sentences?
c Is there any difference in meaning between the sentences in each pair?
d Which of the sentences (a or b) do you think is less conversational in tone?

▶ **NOMINALIZATION**

Verb → noun nominalization
Hergé recognized that his readers wanted to see the world.
Hergé recognized his readers' desire to see the world.

Adjective → noun nominalization
The characters are original, which is one reason for the books' success.
The originality of the characters is one reason for the books' success.

Other types of nominalization
The funny characters are partly why the books are so successful.
The funny characters are one reason (why) the books are so successful.

For more information and practice, see page 163.

8 Look at the language focus box. Find nominalizations in the article which mean:

1 how popular Tintin has been.
2 he was created by the Belgian cartoonist Hergé.
3 the thing that attracts readers mainly.
4 when the army tried to stage a coup.
5 what space travel is like.

9 Rewrite these sentences using nominalization. Note that sometimes (as in items 4 and 5 in Exercise 8) you have to find a noun which isn't from the same root as the verb or adjective.

1 Hergé was inspired partly by Chinese drawings.
  One of Hergé's _____ .
2 He admired them because they were so simple.
  He admired _____ .
3 In later life, Hergé started collecting modern art enthusiastically.
  In later life, Hergé became _____ .
4 Pop art interested him in particular.
  He had _____ .
5 Although they sometimes refer to the politics of the time, the books are not political.
  Despite _____ , the books are not political.
6 Hergé has been recognized for all that he achieved in a museum in Belgium.
  A museum in Belgium recognizes _____ .

Speaking and writing speech bubbles

10 Work in pairs. Look at the cartoon strip on page 156. Discuss what you think the story is and complete the speech bubbles accordingly. Then work with another pair and read the dialogues to each other. Were your stories similar or very different?

5c In Patagonia

Reading and speaking

1 Work in pairs. You have two minutes to get an impression of Patagonia.

Student A: Look at the map and the photo.

Student B: Look at the fact file.

Then close your books and tell each other what you know.

2 The author Bruce Chatwin traveled through Patagonia in the 1970s and wrote a book about it, *In Patagonia*. Read the excerpt and say which sentence (a–c) is true.

a Living in Patagonia enables the poet to produce lots of poetry in peace and quiet.
b The poet's environment is harsh and he finds life a constant struggle.
c The poet is passionate about the nature and history of Patagonia.

3 Correct the underlined words.

1 The poet had lived in Patagonia for <u>a few</u> years.
2 Strangely, he kept <u>sheep</u> as pets.
3 <u>Every surface</u> was covered with Patagonian objects.
4 He obviously liked to eat <u>seafood</u> while writing.
5 One of his poems celebrated a <u>glacier</u> being <u>formed</u>.
6 He was relaxed about his work and wrote <u>a large number of</u> poems.

Critical thinking analyzing descriptive language

4 The writer uses descriptive language to paint a picture of the place and the person (the poet). Find the adjectives that describe the following.

1 the location   3 the poet
2 the house itself   4 the poet's work

5 Work in pairs. Putting the adjectives you found in Exercise 4 together, state your overall impression of this man and where he lives. Compare your answers with your partner's.

6 What other descriptions in the passage also contribute to your impression?

PATAGONIA FACTS

Land area: 300,000 mi² (France is 260,000 mi²)

Population density: < 5 people per mi²

Industry: sheep farming, whaling, oil and mineral mining

Geography: plains and lakes in the east; Andes Mountains in the west

Climate: cool and dry, wet in the west

Ethnic groups: Welsh, Spanish, other European, indigenous people

Attractions: dramatic landscape, rich in fossil remains

Word focus *cast*

7 *Cast* is a literary word meaning "throw." Find an expression with *cast* in the excerpt. What did the poet use it to describe?

8 Work in pairs. Complete these other phrases with *cast* using the words given. Then discuss their meaning with your partner.

doubt	eye	mind	net	shadow	vote

1 I'd like you to cast your _____ back to when you first traveled abroad.
2 They have cast the _____ wide by not asking job applicants for specific qualifications.
3 Cast your _____ over this speech I've written.
4 New video evidence has cast _____ on the defendant's claim.
5 You should cast your _____ for the best candidate.
6 Getting food poisoning cast a _____ over the rest of our vacation.

Speaking

9 Work in groups. Take turns describing a meeting with someone during a journey and how that meeting affected your perception of the place. Include:

- a description of the place you were visiting and what you were doing there
- how the meeting came about
- a description of the person and the impression that they made on you

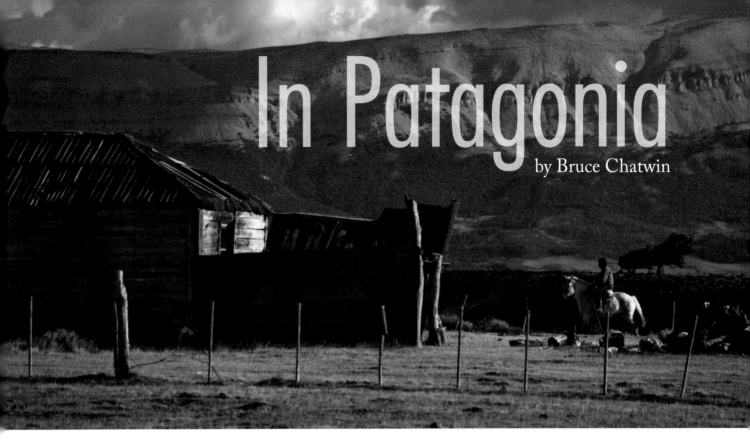

In Patagonia

by Bruce Chatwin

The poet lived along a lonely stretch of river, in overgrown orchards of apricots, alone in a two-roomed hut. He had been a teacher of literature in Buenos Aires. He came down to Patagonia forty years back and stayed.

I knocked on the door and he woke. It was drizzling and while he dressed, I sheltered under the porch and watched his colony of pet toads.

His fingers gripped my arm. He fixed me with an intense and luminous stare. "Patagonia!" he cried. "She is a hard mistress. She casts her spell. An enchantress! She folds you in her arms and never lets go."

The rain drummed on the tin roof. For the next two hours he was my Patagonia. The room was dark and dusty. At the back, shelves made of planks and packing cases bent under the weight of books, mineral specimens, Indian artifacts, and fossil oysters. On the walls were a cuckoo clock, a lithograph of pampas Indians, and another of the Gaucho Martin Fierro.

"The Indians rode better than the Gauchos," he said. "Brown limbs! Naked on horseback! Their children learned to ride before they walked. They were one with their horses. *Ah! Mi Indio!*"

His desk was littered with broken almond shells and his favorite books; Ovid's *Tristia*, the *Georgics, Walden*, Pigafetta's *Voyage of Magellan, Leaves of Grass, The Poem of Martin Fierro, The Purple Land,* and Blake's *Songs of Innocence,* of which he was especially fond. Smacking it free of dust, he gave me a copy of his *Canto on the Last Flooding of the Chubut River,* privately printed in Trelew, which combined, in Alexandrines, his vision of the Deluge and a paean of praise for the engineers of the new dam. He had published two volumes of poetry in his life, *Voices of the Earth* and *Rolling Stones,* the last named after the layer of glacier-rolled pebbles that cover the Patagonian pampas. The scope of his verse was cosmic; technically, it was astonishing. He managed to squeeze the extinction of the dinosaurs into rhymed couplets, using Spanish and Linnaean Latin.

> "Patagonia!" he cried. "She is a hard mistress…! She folds you in her arms and never lets go."

He gave me a sticky aperitif of his own manufacture, sat me in a chair, and read, with gestures and clattering of false teeth, weighty stanzas that described the geological transformations of Patagonia. I asked him what he was writing at present. He cackled humorously. "My production is limited. As T.S. Eliot once said: 'the poem can wait.'"

It stopped raining and I came to leave. Bees hummed around the poet's hives. His apricots were ripening, the color of a pale sun. Clouds of thistledown drifted across the view and in a field there were some fleecy white sheep.

---

aperitif (n) /ə‚perɪˈtif/ a drink taken before a meal
artifacts (n) /ˈɑrtɪ‚fækts/ objects of cultural interest
couplet (n) /ˈkʌplɪt/ two lines of a poem that go together
drizzle (n) /ˈdrɪzəl/ light rain
gaucho (n) /ˈgaʊtʃoʊ/ an Argentinian cowboy
hive (n) /haɪv/ a house for bees to live in
lithograph (n) /ˈlɪθə‚græf/ a print made from a drawing on a flat sheet of metal
oyster (n) /ˈɔɪstər/ type of shellfish
pampas (n) /ˈpæmpəs/ the plains of Argentina
pebble (n) /ˈpebəl/ a small round stone
stanza (n) /ˈstænzə/ one verse of a poem

5d I'd like to read

Real life reading aloud

1 Work in pairs. Have you ever had to do any of these things? Tell your partner and then discuss the questions (1–4).

a read an essay at school or college
b recite a poem
c give a presentation from notes
d read at a book group
e read stories to children
f read a formal speech

1 When did you last listen to someone reading aloud? What did they read?
2 When did you last read something aloud to others? Where? What? Why? Do you think you did a good job?
3 Have you ever read aloud in English?
4 What tips would you give someone who has to read aloud?

2 **Speaking skill** engaging your audience

Look at the tips. Then complete the sentences with these words.

background	dialogue	enthusiasm
enunciate	pause	volume

> ▶ **ENGAGING YOUR AUDIENCE**
>
> 1 If you are reading from a book, prepare your audience by giving some _____ to the story or its author.
> 2 Read at a moderate pace and _____ the words clearly.
> 3 _____ from time to time to give the reader time to digest the information.
> 4 Vary your _____ , speaking more quietly for calm passages and more loudly to stress words or when the action heats up.
> 5 When reading speech or _____ , try to give different speakers a different voice.
> 6 Always read with expression and _____ .

3 🔊 **20** Listen to someone reading a passage from a book and answer the questions.

1 What type of book is the passage from?
2 What writing technique is the reader trying to illustrate with this passage?
3 Who does the character, Martins, think he sees in the shadows? Who is it in reality?

4 🔊 **21** Listen to the last part of the passage again, following the reader's notes. Practice reading it to each other.

"… he began to believe that the whole thing was <u>an illusion</u> [stress] caused by shadow. He called sharply. 'Do you want anything?' [pause] and there was no reply. He called again. 'Answer, can't you?' [express urgency] and an answer came, for a window curtain was drawn petulantly back by some sleeper he had awakened and [build volume here] the light fell straight across the narrow street and lit up the features… [pause] of Harry Lime."

5 Work in pairs. You are each going to read a passage from Bill Bryson's *Neither Here nor There*, about an American's first visit to Europe in the 1970s. Follow the instructions.

Student A: Turn to page 153.

Student B: Turn to page 156.

- First read the passage carefully and think about how you will introduce it and read it.
- Make notes on the text to help you read it, following the tips for engaging your audience.
- Read the passages to each other.
- Then read your passages again to another pair and compare the way each was read. Which reading did you prefer? Why?

5e Book of the month

Writing a book review

1 Work in pairs. How do you normally choose what books to read? Discuss your answers.

a personal recommendation
b a book review in the newspaper
c the blurb on the back cover
d seeing the movie version of the book

2 Read the book review. What is the reviewer's opinion of the book? How does she justify this?

Book of the month

THE BRIDGE OF SAN LUIS REY
by Thornton Wilder

In 1714, a rope suspension bridge in Peru snaps and five people fall to their deaths. Brother Juniper, a Franciscan monk, witnesses this tragedy. He is not only troubled by what he has seen but also by why it happened. Why at this precise moment? Why these five people? Accordingly, he sets out to find out about their lives and make sense of the tragedy.

This short novel (only 124 pages long) is a beautiful reflection on the subject of destiny. It is not a true story, but some of the characters are based on real people. Written in elegant prose, each chapter describes the life of one of the five people on the bridge: from the aristocratic Marquesa de Montemayor, who longs to be back in her native Spain, to the wise Uncle Pio, whose lifelong ambition to make a star of a young actress is in the end frustrated. Our interest is not kept alive by the mystery of their deaths, but by the compelling characters that Wilder has drawn so vividly: eccentric in their own way, and each very human in their virtues and in their faults.

I cannot recommend this thought-provoking book highly enough.

3 Read the review again and answer the questions.

1 What type of book is it?
2 What is the topic?
3 What tense is used to describe the plot?
4 What words describe the style of writing?

4 Which ways to begin a book review (a–e) are most effective? Why? Which does the reviewer use?

a give your opinion about the book directly
b talk about the writer's background
c describe the opening of the story
d give a short summary of the whole story
e discuss the topic of the book

5 Writing skill **descriptive words**

a Underline the adjectives and adverbs in paragraphs 2 and 3 of the review. What does each describe? Which two are compound adjectives?

b Complete these compound adjectives. One item will not be used.

fetched	going	paced	packed
provoking	willed	written	wrenching

1 a thought-_____ essay
2 a far-_____ plot
3 a well-_____ article
4 an action-_____ adventure
5 a heart-_____ ending
6 a fast-_____ story
7 a strong-_____ character

c Match the opposites with the correct compound adjective from Exercise 5b.

convincing	happy	indecisive
poorly written	slow-moving	uneventful
uninspiring		

6 Write a review of a novel you have read (200–250 words). Follow this plan.

• Describe the setting and summarize the plot.
• Say what the theme of the book is.
• Describe the style of writing.
• Give your opinion or recommendation.

7 Exchange reviews with your partner. Check if:

• the review is organized into clear paragraphs.
• it does NOT reveal the whole story.
• you are persuaded by the recommendation.

5f On the road: Andrew McCarthy

That trip changed my life.

Before you watch

1 Look at the photo and answer the questions.

   1 Where do you think this is?
   2 What kind of trip are these travelers on?

2 Work in pairs. Discuss the most memorable trip you have been on. What made it so special?

While you watch

3 You are going to watch an interview with travel writer Andrew McCarthy. Watch the video and answer the questions.

   1 What was the trip that changed his life?

   2 In what way did it change him?

4 Work in pairs. Watch the first part of the interview (to 02:09), where McCarthy describes how he became interested in this trip. Look at the words (a–e) and note why they are significant in the story. Then, with your partner, reconstruct the story.

   a a bookstore
   b a plane
   c the Internet
   d *Harper's* magazine
   e a home phone number

5 Watch the second part of the interview (02:10 to 03:09) and answer the questions.

   1 What adjectives does McCarthy use to describe:
    a this travel experience?

    b his feelings while on the trip?
    c what the experience was not?
    d what he felt for the first time?
   2 What was the reason for the trip that he didn't know at the time but now realizes?

6 Watch the third part of the interview (03:10 to end) and answer the questions.

   1 What makes him unsure about going again?

   2 How long was the trip?

   3 Where did he stay?

   4 Complete this description of himself: "a _____ pilgrim." What does he mean?

   5 How did he justify being this kind of traveler?

7 Complete the summary of Andrew McCarthy's story using one word in each space.

About eighteen years ago, I was in a [1] _____ and I picked up a book by a guy who had [2] _____ the Camino de Santiago in [3] _____. It sat on my bookshelf for months and one day I [4] _____ it when I was looking for something to read on the plane. Having read it, I decided I wanted to do that. There was no [5] _____ to research places in those days so I called the [6] _____ up and I asked him questions about how to go about doing this trip.

I went to Spain for a month and I had a [7] _____ experience. I felt [8] _____ and frightened but then something happened that [9] _____ my life. And for the first time I felt [10] _____ in the world. I stayed in little pilgrim [11] _____ and justified it by saying that this is the way to meet the [12] _____ .

After you watch

8 Roleplay an interview with a traveler

Work in pairs.

Student A: Imagine you are a traveler who went to a place that you have always wanted to visit. Look at the points below and make notes.

Student B: Imagine you are a reporter who is going to interview the traveler. Look at the points below and prepare questions.

- what the place was like
- a significant event that happened while you were traveling there
- the effect that the trip had on you

Act out the interview. Then change roles and act out the interview again with a different place.

9 Work in groups. Make a list of five things that make people nervous about travel. Which ones make *you* anxious? Then discuss the items and how you deal with each one.

---

backpack (n) /ˈbækˌpæk/ a large bag carried on the back
bunk bed (n) /bʌŋk ˌbed/ a pair of beds, one over the other
grab (v) /græb/ take hold of something strongly and suddenly
Moors (n) /mʊərz/ the Muslim peoples of northwest Africa
pilgrim (n) /ˈpɪlgrɪm/ a person who makes a journey to a religious destination

UNIT 5 REVIEW

Grammar

1 Read a travel writer's description of the Fiji islands in the South Pacific. Answer the questions.

1 In what ways is Fiji an exclusive destination? In what ways is it not?
2 What impression do you get of the locals?
3 What is the real Fiji?

Fiji is a collection of over a hundred inhabited islands in the South Pacific; most are the image of what a perfect desert island should be like. So it's no surprise to find a lot of upmarket hotels and beach cabanas catering to rich tourists. I went there hoping to experience this paradise more simply and wondering if it was possible to do so on a limited budget.

I shouldn't have worried about it. The Fijians' long experience of dealing with the needs of different types of tourists means they have provided for this by offering less expensive accommodations for backpackers like me in places like Yasawa. Here, charming and hospitable locals will invite you to see their fishing villages and coral gardens, even taking you fishing with them, if you want to.

But beautiful and relaxing though these islands are, the feeling of being a tourist remains. It's not an uncomfortable sensation, but if, like me, your wish is to see a country's true way of life, then you should visit the main island of Viti Levu. This is the cultural hub of Fiji, where three-quarters of its population live and where you can experience real Fijian culture.

2 What words or phrases have the following words from the article been substituted for?

a most (para 1)   e this (para 2)
b paradise (para 1)   f here (para 2)
c do so (para 1)   g want to (para 2)
d it (para 2)   h sensation (para 3)

3 Look at the sentences (1–4). Find similar sentences in the description and underline the part of each sentence that has been nominalized.

1 It's not surprising that you find a lot of upmarket hotels.
2 The Fijians are very experienced in dealing with the needs of tourists…
3 … you still feel as if you are a tourist.
4 … if you want to see how people really live in a country…

I CAN	
use substitution to avoid repetition and write more naturally	
use nominalization to adjust register	

Vocabulary

4 Complete the sentences about travel and travel writing. The first and last letters have been given.

1 We walked along a dirt t_____l.
2 The flight was canceled so the trip is a n_____-_____o.
3 This part of the country was the s_____g for the novel *Rebecca* by Daphne du Maurier.
4 We felt a little w_____y about trusting him.
5 The main t_____e of the book is the advantages of traveling alone.

5 Work in pairs. Describe a journey that you particularly enjoyed. What did you like about it?

I CAN	
describe places and journeys	
talk about travel writing	

Real life

6 Work in pairs. Discuss the best way to read this passage aloud. Then practice reading it to each other.

"Martins stood there, twenty yards away, staring at the silent motionless figure in the dark side-street who stared back at him. A police spy, perhaps, or an agent of those other men, those men who had corrupted Harry first and then killed him: even possibly the third man?"

7 Work with a different partner. Read the passage aloud to each other and compare your reading.

I CAN	
read a passage aloud with dramatic effect	
read in such a way as to engage an audience	

Speaking

8 Work in pairs. Tell each other about a place you visited that was not as you had expected it to be. What was surprising? Did you like the place? Why?

Unit 6 Body matters

FEATURES

1 Work in pairs. Write a short caption to accompany the photo. Compare your caption with another pair.

2 Look at the expressions about exercise and health. Write in the words that are missing from four of them. Then check your answers with your teacher.

1 stay _____ healthy
2 keep _____ shape
3 watch _____ your weight
4 work _____ at the gym
5 go _____ a walk/run/ride
6 stretch _____ your legs
7 go _____ a diet
8 stay _____ active

3 Work in groups. Ask each other questions about your fitness using the expressions in Exercise 2.

> A: What do you do to stay in shape?

> B: I walk a lot and I go swimming a couple of times a week.

> C: Don't you find swimming boring?

> B: Just doing laps is a little dull, but it keeps me in reasonable shape.

6a Exercise around the world

Reading

1 Look at this quotation by the professional swimmer David Walters. What point was he making about exercise? Do you agree?

> An hour of basketball feels like fifteen minutes. An hour on a treadmill feels like a weekend in traffic school.

David Walters, swimmer

2 Quickly read the article and match the sentences to the exercise they describe: Radio Taiso (RT), swogging (S), or yoga (Y). There is sometimes more than one possibility.

1 It's a trendy form of exercise.
2 It benefits the mind and the body.
3 It is not a strenuous form of exercise.
4 Your body feels as if it is under attack.
5 People have been doing this form of exercise for centuries.
6 It's an enjoyable way to exercise.

3 Work in pairs. Write a suitable heading for each paragraph.

4 Work in groups. Discuss the main benefit of each exercise. Do you do anything similar? Do any of them appeal to you? Why?

> ► **WORDBUILDING** *off* and *up*
>
> There are certain phrasal verbs that use *off* and *up* to mean doing something completely or to the end. *dry off, eat up, finish off*

EXERCISE
AROUND THE WORLD

Here are a few of our readers' experiences.

KEVIN

Not many people outside Japan have come across Radio Taiso. Each morning at 6:30 you hear this tinkly piano sound coming out of the radio and everywhere people start doing calisthenics (gentle warm-up exercises) to get ready for the day ahead. They're group exercises that everyone can join in with, at home or in the park. That group ethic is very Japanese. People say the idea was copied from US factories in the 1920s. It's fun and they're simple movements that anyone can do, old or young. They get the brain working, too.

JO

I do something called "swogging," a mixture of jogging and swimming. The inspiration came from a book about people in the Caucasus mountains who can live to well over a hundred and remain mentally and physically fit. For generations they've been walking down steep slopes each day to swim in cold mountain streams. The idea of freezing cold water might put a lot of people off, but it's scientifically proven to help your circulation and boost your immune system, because it triggers your body's self-defense mechanisms. Then they dry off and climb back up the mountain. I do the same thing in North Wales where I live, but I jog two miles to a lake. It's exhilarating, but I've got a little way to go before I reach a hundred!

RASHMI

To an outside observer, yoga doesn't look hard; it's just slow stretching and holding certain positions. Yoga practitioners came up with their own version of the saying "Don't just sit there, do something," which is "Don't just do something, sit there." But actually, it's a very good workout. Like a lot of Eastern exercise regimes, it offers a more holistic approach to health by combining physical fitness with mental well-being. The idea is to concentrate on your breathing to make movement easier and reduce tension. Although it started out in India, only a small proportion of the population there practice yoga seriously. Recently more Indians have taken it up, partly because they've seen it become trendy in the West.

Language focus phrasal verbs

5 Look at the verb + preposition(s) combinations and answer the questions.

> come across   come out of   join in with

a Which one(s) are not phrasal verbs; they simply combine the meanings of the verb and the preposition to give a more literal meaning (like *go into* a room)?
b Which one(s) are phrasal verbs? They have a meaning that is different from the separate meanings of the verb and preposition and is more metaphorical or idiomatic.

6 Look at the sentences (1–3) about yoga and answer the questions (a–b).

1 It started out in India.
2 In recent years, a lot of Westerners have gotten into it.
3 Recently more Indians have taken it up.

a Which phrasal verbs have an object?
b What do you notice about the position(s) of the object?

▶ **PHRASAL VERBS**

Intransitive phrasal verbs
We get along very well.

Separable phrasal verbs
I don't want to put off the appointment.
I don't want to put the appointment off.

Inseparable phrasal verbs
I came across a book on Tai Chi at the library.
I came across it at the library.

Three-part phrasal verbs
Yoga practitioners came up with their own version.
Yoga practitioners came up with it.

Three-part phrasal verbs with two objects
He took us up on the invitation.

For more information and practice, see page 163.

---

7 Put the objects of each phrasal verb in the correct position below.

8 What do the phrasal verbs in bold in Exercise 7 mean? Discuss with your partner.

9 Put the words in sentence order.

1 I'm thinking / of / up / Pilates / taking
2 I hurt my back playing tennis. It took / it / me / over/ forever / to get
3 My friend has his own dance school. He / up / set / last year / it
4 At school we had to exercise twice a week. We / of / it / get / couldn't / out
5 The doctor / out / some tests / is going / to carry / on my knee
6 How / hit / that idea / did you / on?
7 Don't / away! / that / throw /
8 It takes / back / my childhood / to / me

Speaking

10 Work in pairs. Check the meanings of the phrasal verbs, then interview your partner using the questionnaire.

1 How much time do you **set aside** for exercise each week?
2 What kind of exercise do you **go in for**?
3 Have you **taken up** any new forms of exercise in the last twelve months?
4 Do you **keep up with** exercise trends?
5 Do you prefer to exercise alone or to **join in with** others?
6 What do you **put off** more: exercising or cleaning?

11 Compare your findings with another pair. What are their attitudes to exercise?

Sickness as a child left Joseph Pilates, born in Germany in 1880, frail and weak. To [1] *get over* (this), he developed a series of exercises to build core muscle strength. Some of his early students then opened studios using his methods, [2] *setting up* (them) in various cities. Pilates is now practiced by millions all over the world.

The idea for Zumba *came about* in Colombia in the 1990s. Alberto Perez [3] *hit on* (it) when he was teaching an aerobics class in his native Colombia. Having forgotten his usual music for an aerobics class, he [4] *fell back on* (some Salsa music) he had with him. Zumba, a routine combining aerobics with Latin dance moves, was born. Since then it has *taken off* and become an international exercise craze.

Most people think Tai Chi is a form of meditation. In fact, it's an old Chinese martial art based on the idea of [5] *getting out of* (dangerous situations) by turning an attacker's force against him. The most common form of Tai Chi today is a routine of slow movements. You often see people [6] *carrying out* (them) in parks and public spaces.

6b No pain, no gain

Ultrarunner on the 100-mi *Ultra-Trail du Mont-Blanc* annual race, France

Vocabulary injuries

1 Work in pairs. Look at the photo and caption. What injuries do you think this runner risks?

2 Choose the best noun to complete these collocations to describe injuries.

1 graze your *knee / voice / rib*
2 bump your *tooth / head / toe*
3 pull a *back / muscle / knee*
4 lose your *ankle / voice / back*
5 stub your *toe / ribs / knee*
6 sprain your *ankle / ribs / toe*
7 strain your *head / wrist / back*
8 chip a *tooth / voice / knee*
9 bruise your *head / ribs / muscle*
10 break your *knee / muscle / arm*

3 Work in groups. Put the injuries in Exercise 2 in order according to the following criteria.

a most/least painful
b most/least annoying
c most/least common

Listening

4 🔊 **22** Listen to an interview with ultrarunner Ben Newborn talking about sports injuries. Answer the questions.

1 How does Newborn define ultrarunning?
2 What was his biggest fear about doing the Ultra-Trail du Mont-Blanc?
3 What mistake do many athletes make?
4 What is his answer to sports injuries?

5 🔊 **22** Listen again and complete the sentences.

1 He had to overcome _____ and the things that make you feel _____ .
2 A lot of athletes try to ignore small _____ or _____ in a joint.
3 Minor problems can develop into more _____ injuries.
4 His exercises have prevented him from getting ankle _____ , lower _____ pain, and _____ knee.

Idioms health

6 Work in pairs. What do you think this idiom means?

"I'm not talking about when they**'re in a** really **bad way**."

7 Complete these idioms using the prepositions below. Discuss their meaning with your partner and check your answers with your instructor.

down   in   off   on   out   under   up

1 A: I heard Sarah fell off her bicycle. Is she _____ **a bad way**?
   B: Luckily she didn't break anything; she was pretty **shaken** _____ though.
2 A: Is it true that Jack nearly cut his finger off?
   B: Yes, he practically **passed** _____ when he saw what he'd done. It was a pretty deep cut, but he's _____ **the mend** now, I think.
3 A: You look a little _____ **color**. Are you feeling _____ **the weather**?
   B: No, I'm not sick. I'm just **run** _____ from working too much.

8 Match these words with the correct idioms from Exercise 7.

> distressed   fainted   getting better
> lacking in energy   pale   suffering
> unwell

Language focus verb patterns

9 Work in pairs. Match the verbs (1–6) with the verb patterns (a–f) that follow them. Then look at the highlighted verbs in the audioscript on pages 177–8 and check your answers.

1	involve	a	to do
2	require	b	someone to do
3	worry	c	someone do
4	make	d	doing
5	tend	e	about doing
6	discourage	f	someone from doing

10 Find one more example of each type of verb pattern in the audioscript on pages 177–8.

> ▶ **VERB PATTERNS**
>
> **Verb + *to* + infinitive**
> *Accidents seem to happen most when people are tired.*
>
> **Verb + object + *to* + infinitive**
> *The fallen tree caused the driver to stop suddenly.*
>
> **Verb + object + infinitive**
> *Drinking lots of water helps people feel less nauseous.*
>
> **Verb + *-ing***
> *I don't recommend riding a bike without a helmet.*
>
> **Verb + preposition + *-ing***
> *If you think about getting injured, it's more likely that you will.*
>
> **Verb + object + preposition + *-ing***
> *She accused him of not paying attention.*
>
> For more information and practice, see page 164.

11 Look at the language focus box. Complete the sentences about sports injuries using the correct verb patterns. You need to add prepositions in some of the sentences.

1 These people often complain _____ (suffer) from "pink eye" from the chlorine in the water. They also tend _____ (be) susceptible to shoulder problems.

2 These people risk _____ (damage) the joints in their legs. But they can avoid _____ (get) long-term injuries by wearing the right shoes.

3 Since their sport relies so heavily _____ (use) the arm, these people tend _____ (have) problems with their elbows and forearms.

4 Because these people pull muscles so often, they are encouraged _____ (warm) up properly before a match to prevent such injuries _____ (occur).

5 Neck pain is common among these people because they insist _____ (bend) low over the handlebars, forcing them _____ (raise) their heads to see ahead.

12 Which of these athletes are being referred to in the sentences in Exercise 11? Discuss with your partner.

> cyclists   runners   soccer players   swimmers
> tennis players

13 Often verbs that express a similar idea are followed by the same verb pattern. Look at the sentences (1–8). Choose a verb from the box that could replace the verbs in bold without changing the verb pattern.

appear	blame	convince	decide
expect	mean	postpone	stop

1 We can't **prevent** people from having accidents.
2 The organizers were **criticized** for not having paid enough attention to track safety.
3 If the job **involves** straining my back in any way, I'm afraid I can't risk it.
4 I've **made up my mind** to get in shape.
5 She **seemed** to pull a muscle as she stretched to reach the ball.
6 Don't **delay** going to the doctor. If you do, it'll take longer to recover from the injury.
7 I **hope** to be playing again in a few weeks.
8 The doctor **persuaded** him to take it easy for a while.

Speaking

14 Work in pairs. Choose one of the following incidents and describe what happened.

1 A time when you or a friend were injured doing a sport or in some other situation.
2 A time when you or a friend narrowly escaped being injured.

> *I was playing tennis one time and I got hit in the head with a ball and passed out!*

> *Oh no! Did anyone take you to a hospital?*

6c The enigma of beauty

Reading

1 Work in groups. Check (✓) the faces that you think are beautiful or handsome. Can you explain why? How many do you agree on? Discuss your findings.

2 Look at the sentences and discuss if you think each one is true or not. Then read the article and find out the author's views.

1 There are no universal characteristics of human beauty.
2 Perceptions of a person's beauty can be connected to their social position.
3 Your character can have an influence on whether people think you are beautiful or not.
4 The search for beauty is superficial and vain.

3 Read the article again. Choose the meaning (a or b) that best matches the phrases from the text.

1 *meets the question with a composed reply* (para 1) means:
   a has a ready answer   b is calm
2 *we may as well dissect a soap bubble* (para 2) means:
   a delicate   b impossible
3 *aesthetic* (para 2) means:
   a looking nice   b being healthy
4 *a shallow quest* (para 5) means the search is:
   a pointless   b trivial
5 *fussed over* (para 6) means:
   a made to feel special   b discussed a lot

Critical thinking **identifying aims**

4 Work in pairs. Look at this list of purposes for writing an article and discuss which best fits the article *The enigma of beauty*. Underline the parts of the article that support this view.

1 to persuade using objective or scientific facts
2 to persuade using subjective argument and anecdotal evidence
3 to inform and teach the reader something new
4 to inform and invite reflection on particular issues
5 to entertain by telling stories about real or imaginary characters

5 Compare your answers from Exercise 4 with another pair. Discuss your conclusions.

Word focus *face*

6 Find two expressions with *face* in paragraphs 1 and 6 of the article which mean the following.

a to be honest   b sad looks

7 Choose the meaning that *face* has in sentences (1–6). Then explain the meaning of the expressions.

attitude/expression	confront
credibility	surface

1 He couldn't admit he was wrong. He didn't want to **lose face** in front of us.
2 I'm sure she was disappointed not to win, but she **put a brave face on** it.
3 I took her offer to help **at face value**. I don't think she had any hidden motive.
4 The actors had trouble **keeping a straight face** when Jon fell off the stage.
5 You should tell her that you scratched her car, because sooner or later you will have to **face the music**.
6 **On the face of it,** it seems like a good idea, but I wouldn't rush into making a decision.

Speaking

8 Work in pairs. You are planning an advertising campaign for a face cream that your company is launching. Read your role cards and prepare ideas for the campaign. Decide on the name of your product, then act out the meeting to agree on the ads that will run.

Student A: Turn to page 155.

Student B: Turn to page 156.

Sheli Jeffry is searching for beauty. As a scout for Ford, one of the world's top modeling agencies, Jeffry scans up to 200 young women every Thursday afternoon. They line up and one by one the line diminishes. Tears roll and there are long faces as the refrain "You're not what we're looking for right now" extinguishes the conversation—and hope. Faced with rejection, one hopeful asks: "What *are* you looking for?" Jeffry meets the question with a composed reply. "I know it when I see it."

Define beauty? Some say we may as well dissect a soap bubble; that beauty is only in the eye of the beholder. Yet it does seem that across different cultures we can agree on certain points. Psychologists have proven this by testing the attractiveness of different faces on children. Symmetry is one characteristic that meets with general approval; averageness is another: we seem to prefer features that are not extreme. Things that speak of strength and good health, such as a glowing complexion and full lips in women or a strong jaw in men, are also universal qualities. Scientists maintain that this is the true definition of beauty, because for them we are influenced not by aesthetic but by biological considerations: the need to produce healthy children.

But there are also cultural differences in how beauty is defined. The women of the Padaung tribe in Myanmar put brass coils around their necks to extend them because in their culture very long necks are considered beautiful. In China and Japan, small feet are admired in women, though thankfully the ancient practice of foot-binding has long since disappeared. In cultures where people's skin is dark, it is often seen as desirable to have fair skin. Conversely, in the northern hemisphere, fair-skinned people put value on having a tan.

Perceptions of beauty also change over time. Historically in northern Europe and the US, tanned skin belonged to those who had to work outside (agricultural workers or other poorer members of society) and so a white skin was a symbol of status and beauty. Now a tan reflects status of a different kind: those that can afford a beach vacation in the Mediterranean or the Caribbean. Our idea of the perfect body shape is also different from 200 years ago. In almost all cultures, a little fat was a positive trait, a sign of wealth and well-being. Nowadays a very different image stares out at us from the pages of fashion magazines: that of a long-limbed, impossibly thin figure. Whatever the perception of ideal beauty may be, the search for it has preoccupied people of all cultures for centuries, from ancient Egypt to modern China.

Is it a shallow quest? We all like to think that beauty is not only skin deep; that personality and charm contribute as much, if not more, to attractiveness as superficial beauty. Certainly, as we grow older, the more generous our definition of beauty seems to become. Experience teaches us to look for the beauty within, rather than what is on the outside.

But let's face it, most of us still care how we look. Until she was a hundred years old, my grandmother had a regular appointment at the beauty salon down the street. A month before she died, I took her there in my car. I stayed and watched as she was still being greeted and fussed over by the hairdresser and manicurist. Afterwards, in the nursing home, she radiated happiness. She is not alone in getting satisfaction from looking nice. It seems the quest for beauty goes deeper than vanity; maybe it fulfills a deep human need in all of us.

glowing (adj) /ˈɡloʊɪŋ/ bright and healthy looking
limb (n) /lɪm/ an arm or a leg
manicurist (n) /ˈmænɪˌkjʊrɪst/ someone who cleans, cuts, and polishes fingernails
scout (n) /skaʊt/ someone whose job is to search for people with certain qualities or talents

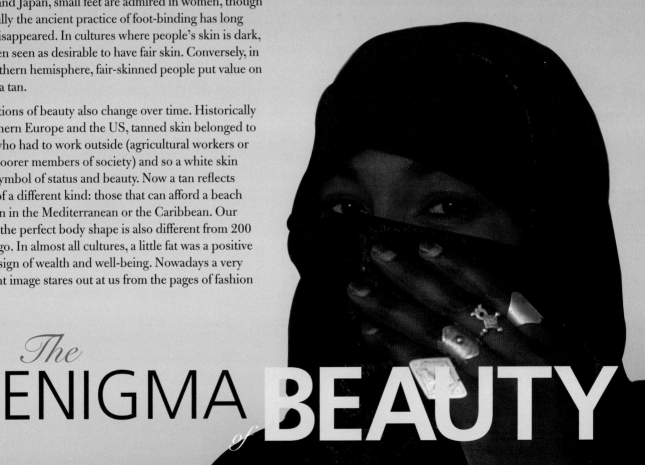

The ENIGMA *of* BEAUTY

6d A bold initiative

Real life discussing proposals

1 Work in pairs. Read how some governments around the world encourage their populations to get in shape and stay healthy. Answer the questions.

1 What are the pros and cons of each idea?
2 Which initiative would work best ? Why?
3 Are there any similar initiatives in your country?

1 JAPAN: Broadcast a daily morning exercise routine on national radio.

2 WASHINGTON STATE, US: Make it compulsory for fast food chains to show the calorie count for each item on the menu.

3 QATAR: Encourage companies to install gyms in the workplace so that workers can exercise on breaks.

4 UK: Use public health campaigns to promote exercise activities that are quick and easy to do.

5 SOUTH KOREA: Make getting a good grade in physical education at school count toward college acceptance.

6 PHILIPPINES: In school, promote sports like karate that combine exercise with self-defense skills.

2 🔊 **23** Listen to the discussion between a group of human resources managers at a large company about ideas to promote health and fitness among their employees. Answer the questions.

1 Why is promoting fitness important to the company?
2 What different ideas are proposed?
3 Were any of them like those in Exercise 1?
4 Which idea got approval? Which idea was rejected?

3 Speaking skill conceding a point

🔊 **23** The speakers tried to anticipate objections to each proposal. Look at the phrases in the box for conceding a point. Then listen again and complete the phrases.

> ▶ **CONCEDING A POINT**
>
> I realize that [1] _____ .
> Admittedly, [2] _____ .
> It's not (a) particularly [3] _____ , I'll grant you, but _____ .
> I know [4] _____ , but _____ .
> I'm just thinking off the top of my head.
> I haven't worked this out exactly, but…
> I haven't thought through [5] _____ , but _____ .
> It wouldn't be so [6] _____ , but _____ .

4 Pronunciation toning down negative statements

a 🔊 **24** Listen to these two statements where the speaker tries to reduce the impact of a negative statement. Underline the words which are most strongly stressed in each sentence.

1 It's not a particularly original idea…
2 It wouldn't be so easy to monitor…

b 🔊 **25** Work in pairs. Practice saying these sentences where a negative sentiment has been toned down. Then listen and compare your pronunciation.

1 I know it's not a very practical solution.
2 It wouldn't be that simple to convince people.
3 I'm not actually sure of the exact numbers.

5 Work in groups. Each think of another idea to promote the health of company employees. Then present and discuss your ideas. Try to anticipate arguments against your proposal.

6e A controversial plan

Writing a formal report

1 Work in pairs. Have you ever had to write a formal report? Who was it for and what was it about? Discuss with your partner.

2 Read the internal report about a public health initiative and look at the questions. Underline the answers in the report.

1 What is the aim of the report?
2 What are the main findings?
3 What action is proposed?

3 Read the description below and say which of the features in bold appear in the report.

> Formal reports present the **findings** of an investigation and make **a recommendation** based on these findings. The important thing is for the reader to be able to scan the document quickly for key information, so **bullet points**, **subheadings**, and **short paragraphs** are all useful. Reports present **objective** facts, but internal reports between colleagues can also offer more **subjective** comments.

4 Writing skill linking adverbs and adverbial phrases

a Find the adverb or adverbial phrase in the report that has the same meaning as the phrases below. Which introduce more subjective comments?

> as might be expected
> clearly
> in view of this
> on the face of it
> on the other hand
> whatever the justification

PROPOSED INITIATIVE

Over 100 people of different ages and social backgrounds were interviewed to decide on the viability of a public health initiative.

The initiative examined was a proposal for smokers to pay higher health insurance premiums. *Ostensibly*, the proposal is logical since insurance is based on the evaluation of risk. *Evidently*, if a person smokes, the risk of disease is increased.

PUBLIC REACTION

Thirty percent of the interviewees objected on the grounds that the initiative was discriminatory. A common argument was that, by this principle, higher premiums should also be paid by people who overeat. *Right or wrong*, these critics view smoking and overeating not as a question of personal choice, but as something beyond an individual's control.

Not surprisingly, 55 percent took the opposite view: that smokers ought to pay for the consequences of their behavior. However, when interviewees were asked if people should be helped to quit smoking, the response was 90 percent positive.

RECOMMENDATION

Accordingly, we recommend setting up a pilot program giving smokers free help from their insurance company to stop smoking over a six-month period. During this time, they will be offered various solutions to stop smoking. If they succeed, they will be rewarded with a discount of 5 percent on their insurance premiums for as long as they remain non-smokers. *Conversely*, if they fail, their insurance premiums will increase by 20 percent.

b Work in pairs. Replace the expressions in bold in the sentences (1–6) with these adverbs.

alternatively	apparently	interestingly
overall	specifically	ultimately

1 **It seems that** this idea has already been tested in the US.
2 **It was worth noting that** 15 percent had no opinion.
3 **To be exact**, smokers objected to higher premiums.
4 **On the whole**, the response to the idea of a trial was positive.
5 **In the end**, it will be the insurance companies who decide.
6 **Either that or** the government will take some other measures.

5 Write a short internal report for a company's health initiatives. You can use the ideas you discussed in Exercise 5 on page 76. Write between 200 and 250 words.

6 Exchange reports with your partner. Answer the questions.

- Have they presented their aims, findings, and recommendations?
- Have they divided the summary into clear sections?
- Have they been objective but at the same time presented a clear argument for the next step?
- Have they made use of linking adverbs and adverbial phrases?

The beauty of parkour is that you just improvise with the environment around you.

Before you watch

1 Work in pairs. Which sports (a–f) do people sometimes play or do in the street? Which sports do people mainly do in the street? Think of other examples of each type.

a soccer ....
b volleyball ....
c skateboarding ....
d basketball ....
e roller blading ....
f climbing ....

....

2 Look at the photo and answer the questions.

1 What does the sport of parkour, or free running, involve?

....
....

2 Who do you think it appeals to and why?

....
....

While you watch

3 Watch the video and check your answers from Exercise 2.

4 Watch the first part of the video (to 01:45) and choose the correct option.

1 Parkour is an example of a performance art that is found in *modern cities / poor urbanized areas.*
2 Parkour originated in *London / Paris.*
3 Parkour is something you can do without *any equipment / any formal training.*
4 The young men in the video took up parkour *because they were bored / to keep in shape.*
5 Abed says without parkour he *would feel out of shape / wouldn't know what to do.*

5 Watch the second part of the video (01:46 to end) and complete the sentences using one word in each space.

1 Abed's mother feels .... about her son's involvement in parkour.
2 Common injuries include .... and broken arms and legs.
3 In order to avoid injury, practitioners have to learn how to ....
4 Mohammad feels that initially people were .... the sport.
5 It's possible that this .... sport will one day bring these young men wider recognition.

6 Work in pairs. Complete the summary using the correct verbs. Then watch the video again to check.

Since its creation in France, parkour has ¹ .... around the world and recently has ² .... on in Palestine. It's a creative sport, where participants ³ .... moves to negotiate obstacles in their environment. For the underprivileged youth of Gaza, it's a great way to ⁴ .... themselves and ⁵ .... in shape at the same time.

Parkour is a risky sport because you can easily hurt yourself if you ⁶ .... awkwardly. But maybe one day these men might be asked to ⁷ .... on a bigger public stage.

After you watch

7 Roleplay **planning a sports campaign**

Work in pairs.

Imagine you want to promote sport as a way for people in your city to get in shape and stay healthy. You think the best way to do this is with street sports. Look at these questions and then plan a campaign.

- What is the target age group or groups?
- What kind of sport would most appeal to them?
- Where could they play or do this sport?
- Are training, equipment, and funds needed?
- Are there health and safety implications?
- How could you encourage people to join in?

Present your plan to another pair. Ask each other questions about the practicalities of each plan.

8 Work in groups and discuss the questions.

1 Do you think sports like parkour should be regulated? Why?
2 What are the advantages (and disadvantages) of "street sports"?
3 What sport would you nominate to be included in the next Olympic Games and why?

---

apathy (n) /ˈæpəθi/ a lack of interest; feeling unconcerned and unmotivated

awkward (adj) /ˈɔkwərd/ uncomfortable, clumsy

improvise (v) /ˈɪmprəˌvaɪz/ compose or perform something without any preparation

poverty line (n) /ˈpʊvərti ˌlaɪn/ the minimum level of income needed to live

stunt man (n) /stʌnt ˌmæn/ a person who simulates dangerous actions like falls and car chases in movies

underprivileged (adj) /ˌʌndərˈprɪvəlɪdʒd/ lacking social advantages; from a poor background

UNIT 6 REVIEW

Grammar

1 Complete the first part of the blog by putting the verbs (1–6) in the correct form: infinitive, *to* + infinitive, *-ing* form, or preposition + *-ing* form.

Back pain is a common health problem which affects 80 percent of us at some time in our lives. It prevents people ¹ _____ (work), causes people ² _____ (become) depressed, and affects general well-being.
You could be forgiven ³ _____ (think) that lower back pain is a curse of our modern lifestyle. Many in the West blame our sedentary habits. But back pain is something that people around the world seem ⁴ _____ (suffer) from, whether they spend all day ⁵ _____ (sit) at a desk or ⁶ _____ (work) in the fields.
Scientists believe that back pain comes from our being bipedal: walking upright on two feet. So, unless you **go in for** regular posture training or have a resistant physique, you will suffer from back pain at some point. What to do about it? You can **look into** exercise classes that help to build core muscle strength, but they are mainly a preventive measure. Some countries have developed cures, like Madagascar, where Baobab tree bark is used. But mostly treatment consists of months of painkillers and manipulation before the practitioner can **turn around** the situation. It seems that for the time being, we will just have to **put up with** back pain.

2 Read the rest of the blog. Who in the world suffers from back pain? What can be done about it?

3 Look at the phrasal verbs in bold in the second half of the blog. Replace each noun object with a pronoun. Think carefully about the position of the pronoun.

I CAN	
use correct verb patterns (verb + *-ing* or infinitive)	
use different kinds of phrasal verbs	

Vocabulary

4 Complete the sentences with the correct preposition.

1 If I am feeling run ____ , I get some rest.
2 I fast one day a week. ____ the face of it, it doesn't sound like much, but I feel amazing.
3 If I feel I am about to come ____ with a cold, I start taking lots of vitamin C.
4 A lot of athletes in their mid-thirties take ____ yoga to prolong their careers.
5 Regular exercise keeps you ____ good shape.
6 It's difficult to set ____ time for exercise, but you just have to build it into your routine.

5 Work in pairs. Discuss the statements in Exercise 4. Which do you agree with?

I CAN	
talk about exercise and health	
use idioms and phrasal verbs	

Real life

6 Look at the proposal to install gyms in the workplace. Complete the text with these words.

admittedly	grant	head
out	particularly	through

Workplace gyms are not a ¹ _____ original idea, I'll ² _____ you, but I think they could be very popular with employees. I haven't thought ³ _____ all the details, but the basic idea is to get people exercising during the workday.
⁴ _____ , this isn't going to be a cheap option for companies. One possibility would be to offer companies a tax break on the investment they make. I'm just thinking off the top of my ⁵ _____ here. I haven't worked ⁶ _____ exactly the best way to help companies fund this.

7 Work in pairs. Think of a health and fitness program to help teenagers follow a healthier lifestyle. Present your proposal to another pair. Use phrases to anticipate arguments.

I CAN	
present and discuss a proposal	
anticipate arguments and concede a point	

Speaking

8 Work in groups. How are people in your country encouraged to stay in shape? Eat healthily? Discuss.

Unit 7 Stories from history

A young Mongolian woman competes in an archery contest. In Genghis Khan's time, his cavalrymen could fire six arrows a minute, facing forward or backward.
Photograph by James L. Stanfield

FEATURES

1 Look at the photo and the caption. Discuss the questions.

1 What do you know about Genghis Khan?
2 What do you think is people's opinion of him in his native Mongolia?
3 What is his reputation in other countries?

2 Work in pairs. Discuss with your partner what these expressions used in narrating history mean.

> there are two sides to every story
> it's always the same old story
> or so the story goes
> the evidence tells its own story
> he wanted to get the inside story

3 Who are the famous leaders in your country's history? What achievements are they remembered for? Discuss.

7a The father of history

Reading

1 Work in pairs. Look at the quotation. What is the serious point it makes about history writing?

Perhaps nobody has changed the course of history as much as the historians.

Franklin P. Jones, humorist (1908–1980)

2 Read about Herodotus's history of the Persian invasion of Greece and answer the questions.
1 Who was Herodotus?
2 What is characteristic of his history writing?
3 Why did Xerxes of Persia invade Greece?
4 What is Demaratus's message about the Greeks?
5 How will Xerxes act on this information?

3 Read the extract again. What can you say about the following?

1 how Greece was organized in this period
2 Xerxes's character
3 how Xerxes's subjects felt about him
4 the values that were important to the Spartans

4 What do you think of Herodotus's way of presenting historical facts? Is it effective? Is it accurate? Explain your reasons.

> ▶ **WORDBUILDING noun formation**
>
> Many nouns in English have the same form as the verb they are derived from. Others are formed with a suffix: *-ment, -ion, -ance*.
> *installment, invasion, resistance*

The father of history

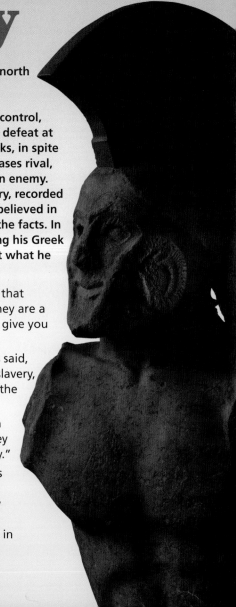

In 480 BC, the Persian king Xerxes I arrived in the north of Greece with an army of approximately 200,000 men, one of the largest armies ever amassed. In addition to hoping to bring Greece under Persian control, he was determined to get revenge for his father's defeat at the Battle of Marathon ten years earlier. The Greeks, in spite of being a number of independent, and in some cases rival, city-states at that time, united to face the common enemy. What followed is one of the great stories of history, recorded by Herodotus, "the father of history." Herodotus believed in the power of storytelling as much as in detailing the facts. In this passage from his *Histories*, Xerxes is consulting his Greek advisor, the exiled Spartan king Demaratus, about what he can expect from the Greek army.

"Demaratus, do you think the Greeks will make a stand against us? I imagine that even if they do, their resistance won't last long, on account of the fact that they are a divided people." After hesitating, Demaratus answered, "Do you want me to give you an honest answer or a pleasing one?"

Xerxes promised he would not punish him if he spoke honestly, so Demaratus said, "All Greeks are brave, but the Spartans especially so. They'll never submit to slavery, even if you secure the surrender of the other Greeks. If only a thousand take the field, they'll still meet you in battle."

Xerxes laughed at this. "You don't seriously think that a thousand men, or even fifty thousand, could stand against an army like mine? With a single master, they might fight harder. However, left to their own free choice, they'll act differently."

Demaratus replied, "You asked for the truth and I gave it. The Spartans are as good as any men, but when they fight together, they are the bravest of all. Because although they are free men, they are not in all respects free. The law is their master and they fear it more than your subjects fear you. Whatever the law commands, they do; and the command is always the same: never flee in battle, stand firm, and conquer or die."

Language focus linking words

5 Look at the sentences (1–6) and answer the questions (a and b).

1 **In addition to** hoping to bring Greece under Persian control, he was determined to get revenge.
2 The Greeks, **in spite of** being a number of independent city-states, united to face the enemy.
3 Their resistance won't last long, **on account of** the fact that they are a divided people.
4 **After** hesitating, Demaratus answered.
5 **However**, left to their own free choice, they'll act differently.
6 **Although** they are free men, they are not in all respects free.

a Which highlighted linking words introduce: a contrast, a reason, an additional point, time?
b Which conjunction(s) are followed by a noun or gerund? Which start a clause or a new sentence?

> ▶ **LINKING WORDS**
>
> ***and, after, although, because, but, since, when** (+ clause)*
> ***Although** it's history, it's also a great story.*
> *Since his army was so large, Xerxes felt confident of victory.*
>
> ***after, as well as, despite, in addition to, in spite of,***
> ***on account of** (+ gerund or noun)*
> *In addition to recording history, Herodotus told stories.*
>
> ***following, owing to** (+ noun)*
> *Following his father's defeat, Xerxes was set on revenge.*
>
> ***however, moreover, nevertheless** (+ new sentence)*
> *The Persian army was huge. Moreover, it was well equipped.*
>
> For more information and practice, see page 165.

6 Look at the language focus box and rewrite the sentences using the prompts so they have a similar meaning.

1 Herodotus is one of the world's most famous historians, but he only wrote one book.
  a Despite _____ .
  b Herodotus _____ . However, _____ .

2 Some people doubt that Herodotus's facts are reliable and have even called him "the father of lies."
  a In addition to _____ .
  b _____ . Moreover, _____ .

3 Historians are suspicious of Herodotus's *Histories* because many of his stories are based on what others told him.
  a _____ owing to _____ .
  b Since _____ .

4 When Herodotus had completed his *Histories*, he read them aloud at the Olympic Games.
  a After _____ .
  b Following _____ .

7 Complete the description of Xerxes's first battle with the Greeks using these linking words.

and	since	however	in addition to
when	owing to	following	in spite of

Xerxes was determined to reach and conquer the southern cities of Greece quickly. [1] _____ , his army first had to travel through the pass at Thermopylae, which is extremely narrow, [2] _____ the closeness of the mountains on one side and the sea on the other. [3] _____ the Greeks heard of the Persian route, they put 7,000 men under King Leonidas of Sparta [4] _____ sent them to protect the pass. It was a battle the Greeks did not expect to win, [5] _____ the Persian army was so much larger. [6] _____ this, they still managed to hold the Persians off for seven days until a local man, Ephialtes, betrayed the Greeks by showing the Persians a path behind the Greek lines. Leonidas, [7] _____ keeping 300 Spartans with him, persuaded 700 other Greeks to fight to the end. They did not last long, but [8] _____ this episode, Xerxes reassessed his opinion of the Greeks, in particular, the Spartans.

Vocabulary and speaking
stories from history

8 Match the words in bold (1–6) with the definitions in the box.

achievement	bad reputation	criminal
explorer	personal loss	unlucky

1 a **pioneer** who made an amazing discovery
2 a **jinxed** leader
3 someone who achieved fame or **notoriety**
4 an **outlaw** who helped people
5 an amazing **feat** in battle
6 someone who made a great **sacrifice** to help others

9 Work in groups. Each think of a story from history using the ideas in Exercise 8. Make notes and tell the story to the group. Then ask each other questions.

7b Microhistory

Listening

1 Working in groups, think about your favorite toy(s) from your childhood and discuss the questions.

1 What was your favorite toy?
2 Was the toy only available when you were a child, or can you still buy it now?
3 Did your parents pass down any toys or games to you from their childhood? What were they?

2 💿 **26** Listen to an interview about microhistory (see definition), then answer the questions.

> **microhistory:** the study of either the daily lives of individuals or communities, or of single events that helps us to understand life in the past. Microhistory asks questions like: Where did people meet socially? What did they eat? What were people's attitudes to children? How did they treat their elderly? What were their main festivals?

1 Which question in the definition did the interview help to answer?
2 What was the answer that they found?

3 💿 **26** Look at the questions. Listen again and choose the correct option to complete the sentences.

1 In the past, historians thought that childhood in the Middle Ages:
  a was an emotional time.
  b didn't really exist.
2 The interviewer isn't surprised that in the Middle Ages children worked because:
  a times were hard.
  b people did not live so long.
3 The objects were excavated:
  a from the river bed.
  b from an area next to the river.
4 When the archaeologist says they "struck gold" he means that they:
  a found valuable objects.
  b are likely to become rich.
5 The objects they found were:
  a mostly small replicas of everyday objects.
  b mostly military toys.
6 The birdcage and stool tell us something new about:
  a what children were interested in.
  b what people had in their houses.

4 What example(s) were given of toys that still exist today? Can you think of other toys that have stood the test of time?

Idioms luck

5 Work in pairs. Look at this phrase from the interview and match it to the correct definition (a–d). Then do the same with the other phrases (1–5). Two phrases have the same definition.

"… you could say we **struck gold**!"

1 miss the boat
2 blow your chance
3 get your break
4 not go your way
5 hit the jackpot

a have great luck
b achieve success through a lucky opportunity
c have bad luck
d lose an opportunity

6 Work in groups. Complete one of these sentences using examples from your own experience. Then tell the group what happened to you.

1 I felt nothing was going my way when…
2 I really hit the jackpot when I…
3 I blew my chance to… when I…
4 I got my break to… when…

Language focus subordinate clauses

7 Work in pairs. Look at the sentences from the interview (1–3) and the subordinate clauses in bold. Answer the questions (a–d).

1 **Compared to children today**, I imagine children then didn't have much of a childhood.
2 **As far as historians are concerned**, that is the accepted view of it.
3 **Considering people had much shorter lives**, you can understand why children were made to work.

a Can the sentences stand alone when the subordinate clause is removed?
b Can the subordinate clause stand alone without the main clause?
c Is the subject of the subordinate clause the same as the subject of the main clause?
d How does each subordinate clause give a more complete meaning to the sentence?

> ### ▶ SUBORDINATE CLAUSES
>
> *considering (that), assuming (that), in case* + subject + verb
> *Considering their age, children worked too hard.*
> *They protected the objects in case they got damaged.*
>
> *compared to, regardless of* (+ noun or gerund)
> *It's an important object, regardless of its financial value.*
>
> *as far as... is concerned, thinking about it*
> *Thinking about it, we should give them to the museum.*
>
> For more information and practice, see page 166.

8 Match the two parts of the sentences.

1 **Insofar as** the objects have great historical value,
2 **Assuming that** these *are* all medieval toys,
3 **Regardless of** what they tell us about children at the time,
4 **In case** any listeners want to see these items,

a the collection will be going on tour around the country.
b some of these objects are things we didn't know existed in medieval households.
c you could say we struck gold!
d they paint a different picture of childhood in the Middle Ages.

9 Pronunciation intonation in subordinate clauses

a 🔊 **27** Listen to the sentences in Exercise 8. Does the intonation rise or fall at the end of each subordinate clause?

b Work in pairs. Practice saying the sentences.

10 Complete the passage by choosing an appropriate subordinating conjunction.

> as far as... are concerned   contrary to
> given that   insofar as   in spite of
> in view of the fact that   supposing that

Philippe Ariès's book *Centuries of Childhood* was revolutionary [1] _____ it told history from the point of view of the ordinary person, not the ruling classes. But [2] _____ ordinary people were generally illiterate, it was difficult for Ariès to gather documentary evidence about their lives. [3] _____ some historians _____ , Ariès's research methods are unconventional and unreliable. But, [4] _____ this criticism, his work created a whole new interest in social history.

Ariès's main thesis is that in the Middle Ages there was no concept of childhood. [5] _____ there was no mandatory education, children were free to be trained for work around the age of seven. [6] _____ he is right, it tells us that, [7] _____ modern ideas about child development, it is actually society that chooses when a child becomes an adult.

Writing and speaking

11 Work in pairs. Think about your, your parents', and your grandparents' childhood. Discuss the questions with your partner.

• How much freedom were you given to do what you wanted?
• How much time did your parents spend playing with you?
• How much work were you expected to do (for example, around the house)?
• When did adulthood begin?

12 Write three or four sentences about how you think attitudes to childhood have changed over three generations.

7c Diamond shipwreck

Reading

1 Look at the map showing shipping routes in the 16th century from Portugal to the East. Discuss:

1 Why did ships make these voyages?
2 What dangers did sailors face on voyages like this?

2 Read the article about the voyage of one of these ships. Discuss the following questions with your partner.

1 What was the purpose of the voyage?
2 What happened four months into the journey?
3 What was ironic about the way the voyage ended?

3 Circle the word that does NOT fit in each sentence.

1 Among the objects on the *Bom Jesus* were… and… .
   a spices   b weapons   c treasure
2 The ships themselves were… vessels.
   a advanced   b well-built   c much traveled
3 Details of what happened are difficult to establish because of a lack of… evidence.
   a first-hand   b documentary   c new
4 This part of the Namibian coast is very… .
   a bleak   b hot   c unpopulated
5 The striking thing about the diamonds in this area is how… they are.
   a big   b accessible   c numerous
6 The voyage of the *Bom Jesus* ended in disaster because it was unable to resist the strong… .
   a tides   b currents   c winds

4 Find words in the article with the following meanings.

1 a great journey (para 2)
2 very strong and robust (para 3)
3 not very clear (para 4)
4 unfriendly (para 5)
5 a small suggestion or hint (para 8)

Critical thinking fact or conjecture

5 History is a mixture of known facts and conjecture (things which you guess might be true). Are the sentences fact (F) or conjecture (C)? Find evidence in the article to support your answer.

1 The wreck found on the Namibian coast was a 16th-century Portuguese trading ship.
2 The ship was in good condition when it set off.
3 The ship was in contact with the authorities in Portugal.
4 The ship was blown off course in a storm.
5 The ship sank after hitting some rocks.
6 The sailors managed to get ashore but died there.

6 Compare your answers in Exercise 5 with your partner's. How believable are the sentences that you have marked conjecture? Why is this?

Word focus *bear*

7 What is the meaning of *bear* in these phrases?

a …**bearing** the coat of arms (para 1)
b …**bearing** 300 sailors (para 3)

8 Work in pairs. Look at the other expressions with **bear** and discuss their meanings.

1 The sea wall **bore the brunt** of the storm, so that the boats suffered only minor damage.
2 The face on the coin **bears** little **resemblance** to the King himself.
3 He was never promoted and he **bore a grudge** against his employers for years.
4 The hole in the boat **bears witness** to the force of the storm.
5 Months of digging **bore fruit** when they uncovered the ship's mast.
6 **Bear in mind** that the ships of the day were made entirely of wood.

Speaking

9 Work in groups. You are each going to read two historical facts. After reading, ask each other to guess what the irony of each situation was.

Student A: Read the facts on page 154.

Student B: Read the facts on page 155.

Student C: Read the facts on page 156.

This improbable story would have been lost forever if it had not been for a geologist working on the coast of Namibia who came across a copper ingot. The ingot was the type traded for spices in the East Indies in the 16th century. Archaeologists would later find a staggering 22 tons of these ingots beneath the sand, as well as cannons, swords, ivory, muskets, chain mail, and exquisite gold coins bearing the coat of arms of King João III of Portugal. From this, archaeologists and historians have pieced together a remarkable story.

One fresh spring day in Lisbon in 1533, the great ships of the India fleet sailed grandly down the Tagus River and out into the Atlantic, flags flying. These ships were the pride of Portugal, the space shuttles of their day, off on a fifteen-month odyssey to bring back a fortune in pepper and spices from distant continents. Goa, Cochin, Mombasa, and Zanzibar, once remote places, were now familiar ports of call, thanks to Portuguese ingenuity and skill.

The ships that sailed that day were sturdy and capable; two of them were brand new and owned by the king himself. One was the *Bom Jesus*, captained by one Dom Francisco de Noronha and bearing 300 sailors, soldiers, merchants, priests, nobles, and slaves. She had on board a fortune in gold and ivory to trade at a famous spice port on the coast of India.

But four months or so after its grand departure from Lisbon, the fleet was struck and scattered by a huge storm. Details are sketchy. A report of the voyage by Captain Dom João Pereira, the fleet's commander, has been lost. All that remains is acknowledgement from a clerk in Lisbon that the report was received, and a mention that the *Bom Jesus* disappeared in wild weather somewhere off the Cape of Good Hope. It is easy to imagine what happened next: the ship was caught in powerful winds and currents and

driven helplessly northwards for hundreds of miles. Somewhere near the Namib Desert, it struck rocks about 500 feet from shore. The shuddering blow broke off the stern, spilling tons of copper ingots into the sea and sinking the *Bom Jesus*.

And the sailors? "In a storm, getting ashore would have been just about impossible," says one archaeologist. "On the other hand, the storm might have blown itself out and the ship drifted ashore on one of those quiet, foggy days we also get around here." And then what? This is one of the most inhospitable places on Earth, an uninhabited wasteland of sand and scrub. It was winter. The sailors were cold, wet, and exhausted. There was no hope of rescue, for nobody knew they were alive. No ship was likely to pass, since they were far off the trade routes. As for getting back to Portugal... they might as well have been shipwrecked on Mars.

Yet this place held an extraordinary secret. It was a desert so rich in high-quality diamonds that in the 1900s, the explorer Ernst Reuning made a bet with a companion about how long it would take to fill a tin cup with them. It took all of ten minutes.

For long ages, millions of diamonds had been washed down to the shore from deposits in the mountains far inland. Only the hardest gems, some weighing hundreds of carats, survived the journey. They spilled into the Atlantic at the river's mouth and were borne up the coast by the same cold current that would one day sweep the *Bom Jesus* to her end.

Whatever happened to the sailors of the *Bom Jesus*, none returned home. They died somewhere near this mysterious coast, with no inkling of the irony that beneath their feet were more than 100 million carats of diamonds. They had set off on a great journey in search of riches and died on a shore of unimaginable wealth.

---

ingot (n) /ˈɪŋɡət/ a bar of a precious metal such as gold or copper
musket (n) /ˈmʌskɪt/ an old-fashioned rifle
stern (n) /stɜːrn/ the rear end of a ship

Diamond
Shipwreck

7d I blame the weather

Real life asking for confirmation and clarification

1 Work in pairs. Discuss the questions.

1 What was the last lecture or talk you attended?
2 Why did you go and what did you learn?

2 Quickly read the abstract of a history lecture. Then cover the text and answer the questions.

1 What will the lecture be about?
2 What general question will it try to address?

LET'S TALK ABOUT THE WEATHER

2:00 p.m. Forth Lecture Hall

Abstract: Weather affects events. Think how your plans can be changed by snow or even just a little rain. Extend this to a larger scale, and you can imagine how more dramatic changes in the climate might have helped to shape human history. For example, how did a drought in Africa contribute to the decline of the Roman Empire? How did a cold spell in Europe lead to persecutions in the 17th century?

This lecture examines the connection between climate changes and specific events in world history and asks whether we pay too little attention to the environment in our studies of the past.

3 🔊 **28** Listen, then put the number of the questioner next to the topic they ask about.

a the meaning of the term "Little Ice Age" *3* ☐
b the connection between cold weather and punishment *4* ☐
c the connection between the weather and the rat population *1* ☐
d the connection between the weather and the fall of the Roman Empire *2* ☐

4 Speaking skill prefacing a question and seeking clarification

🔊 **28** Work in pairs. Look at the box. Listen again and check (✓) the phrases the questioners use to preface each question. What is the purpose of these phrases?

▶ PREFACING A QUESTION AND SEEKING CLARIFICATION

Prefacing a question
If I understood correctly, you said that…
I'd just like to make sure I understood what you said about…
I'd like to pick up on one thing you said about…
The logical conclusion of your argument is that…
You mentioned…
Maybe I missed something, but…

Seeking clarification
Am I right in thinking that [1] _____ ?
Can you expand a little more on that?
[2] _____ . Is that what you're saying?
Can you explain what you meant by [3] _____ ?
How do [4] _____ fit in with _____ ?

5 🔊 **28** Complete the questions used to seek clarification in the box (1–4).

6 Pronunciation intonation in questions

a 🔊 **29** Work in pairs. Listen again. Does the intonation rise or fall in each question? What rule do they follow about *wh-* and *yes/no* questions?

1 Am I right in thinking that the drought in Africa caused an increase in the number of rats?
2 Is that what you're saying?
3 Can you explain what you meant by that?
4 How do punishments fit in with the Little Ice Age?

b Practice reading the questions in Exercise 6a.

7 Work in pairs. You are each going to give a short talk about a historical event which was affected by weather. Look at the notes and prepare your talk. Then ask and answer questions. Remember to preface each question with a comment.

Student A: Turn to page 155.

Student B: Turn to page 156.

7e Krakatoa

Writing describing a past event

1 Look at the photo and caption. What kind of island is this? Do you know any others like it?

2 Work in pairs. Read the short historical account about Krakatoa and answer the questions. Then discuss your answers with your partner.

　1　What historical point does the writer make?
　2　What evidence does she give to support this?

In 1883, the volcano on the island of Krakatoa erupted with such force that the explosion could be heard 100 miles away and ash rose as high as 4 miles into the atmosphere. Until then, few people had ever heard of Krakatoa. It was just a small island in the straits between Java and Sumatra.

The major eruption took place on Monday, August 27, causing the deaths of tens of thousands of people on neighboring islands, and destroying two-thirds of Krakatoa itself. But the lasting climatic effects were just as dramatic. In the preceding months, the volcano had already been active, discharging so much ash into the sky that it blocked out the sun for miles around. However, the ash that entered the upper atmosphere after the main eruption was blown right around the globe on the trade winds. The following year, climatologists recorded a 2.2°F drop in global temperatures, which did not return to normal levels until some years later.

Unusual global weather patterns seem to have continued in the years following the eruption of Krakatoa. Nebraska, in the US, suffered an extraordinary winter in 1888, when temperatures dropped 18 degrees in three minutes and up to 50 inches of snow fell in 36 hours, unheard of in those days, when 24 inches was the average for a whole year. Proving a direct connection between these events and the eruption is, of course, impossible, but the evidence is quite compelling.

Krakatoa erupting, Indonesia

3 Writing skill sequencing events

a Work in pairs. How does the writer sequence the different events surrounding the eruption of Krakatoa? Put these events in the order they appear in the text.

　a　events following the eruption of 1883
　b　the events leading up to the eruption of 1883
　c　the eruption itself

b Read the account again and find time phrases about the past which correspond to each of the present time phrases (a–d).

Present	Past
a　up to now	1 ....
b　in recent months	2 ....
c　next year	3 ....
d　nowadays	4 ....

c Complete the sentences with the correct time phrases. Use the words given.

Viewed from the present	Viewed from a point in the past
some days ago	They had met [1] .... (earlier)
tomorrow	There were further eruptions [2] .... (following)
at the moment	No one was living on Krakatoa [3] .... (time)
yesterday	Loud noises were heard [4] .... (previous)
from now on	Krakatoa became famous [5] .... (then)

4 Write about an event that happened near you. Use the ideas below to help you. Describe the events leading up to the main event, the main event, and the aftermath. Write 200–250 words.

- an extreme weather event
- the visit of an important person
- a sporting event or festival
- a special music event or festival

5 Exchange accounts with your partner. Use these questions to check your accounts.

- Is the sequence of events clear?
- Are the facts presented objectively?
- Are arguments supported by clear evidence?
- Have the correct time phrases been used?

秦始皇像

Bringing a piece of heritage home

Before you watch

1 Work in pairs. Discuss your favorite type of museum. Which of these categories does it fall into? What do you like to see there?

art	design	ethnographical	general
war	science	transportation	natural history

2 Look at the picture. Describe what it shows and where you would find it.

While you watch

3 Watch the video. Who is collecting objects like the one in the picture and why?

4 Watch the first part of the video (to 01:05) and choose the correct option to complete the table.

1	Period of objects in exhibition: *Qing dynasty / Ming dynasty*
2	Owner of objects: *Chinese state / private collector*
3	Where items were bought: *foreign auctions / foreign antique shops*
4	Location of exhibition: *a train station / a shopping mall*
5	Value of collection: *$25 million / $100 million*

5 Watch the second part of the video (01:06 to end) and answer the questions.

1 Who is competing for these objects?

2 What is happening to their price?

3 Where has this phenomenon been seen before?

4 What kind of items did people buy as the phenomenon evolved?

5 What are the two reasons people buy?

---

auction (n) /ˈɔkʃən/ a sale where items are sold to people who offer the highest amount
embroidered (adj) /emˈbrɔɪdərd/ decorated with patterns or images sewn onto it
finery (n) /ˈfaɪnəri/ expensive and beautiful objects
hoard (n) /hɔrd/ a big collection of valuable items
lot (n) /lɑt/ an item for sale at an auction
repatriate (v) /riˈpeɪtriˌeɪt/ return objects or people to their home country
smash (v) /smæʃ/ break completely
stately (adj) /ˈsteɪtli/ dignified, grand

---

6 Complete the summary using one word in each space. Then watch the video again to check.

A growing number of private Chinese [1] _____ would like to [2] _____ objects that have ended up overseas. So they buy up pieces at [3] _____ all over the world and bring them back to China. Often it is one wealthy Chinese person [4] _____ against another to buy the piece and so prices have [5] _____ . But there is also a market for more [6] _____ pieces which people buy as an [7] _____ or to help preserve their country's [8] _____ .

After you watch

7 Roleplay **a meeting to negotiate a solution**

Work in groups of four.

As part of its exhibits, a British museum has some treasure that was found onboard a Portuguese 16th-century trading ship that had sunk at sea off the coast of South Africa (weapons, coins, and art objects). The treasure was discovered by a British explorer in the 19th century and brought back to Britain. When the explorer died, his family gave the treasure to the museum. Portugal says this treasure is an important part of its cultural heritage and would like it returned. You are going to act out a meeting to try to negotiate what to do with the treasure.

Possible areas for negotiation:

- selling the pieces back
- lending the pieces now and again
- sharing the pieces

Students A and B: Imagine you represent the museum. You think the treasure should stay in a world-famous museum. Read the information and the possible areas for negotiation and prepare your argument.

Students C and D: Imagine you represent the interests of Portugal. You would like the treasure returned. Read the information and the possible areas for negotiation and prepare your argument.

Act out the meeting to negotiate what to do with the treasure and try to come to a solution.

8 Work in groups. Think of three important objects in your country (like monuments or artifacts in a museum) that best reflect your country's heritage. Describe them to your group and explain why you think they are significant.

UNIT 7 REVIEW

Grammar

1 Read the text and answer the questions.

1   What were these people's contributions to the field of geography?
    a George Everest   c George Custer
    b Homer   d James Whistler

2   How is each of them remembered?

2 Choose the correct option to complete each subordinate clause.

Few geographers die famous. Take the geographer and surveyor George Everest. Considering ¹ *he had / having* the world's highest mountain named after him, you'd think we would associate Mount Everest with him. However, compared to ² *there are climbers / climbers* Hillary and Tenzing, who first conquered the mountain, Everest himself is relatively unknown.
Some geographers are remembered for other achievements. For example, although the Greek poet Homer ³ *is / being* sometimes referred to as "the father of geography," he is best remembered for writing the *Iliad* and the *Odyssey*. George Custer, in addition to ⁴ *he served / serving* as a cavalry commander in the US wars against the Plains Indians, where he suffered defeat at the Battle of the Little Bighorn, also served in the Corps of Topographical Engineers. Thanks to his skills, the army was able to map enemy positions during the Civil War. As far as his employers ⁵ *were / being* concerned, they would probably have preferred it if he had stuck to drawing maps!

My favorite unsung geographer, however, is James Whistler, the American artist best known for the painting "Whistler's Mother." Since ⁶ *he was / being* a talented draftsman, Whistler was employed by the US Coast Survey Engraving Division to make maps. He would often get bored by the work and start adding his own artistic flourishes to serious government documents, not to mention ⁷ *he doodled / doodling* on the office walls. Following ⁸ *there was one / one* such incident, when he added seagulls to a map of Anacapa, he was strongly disciplined.

I CAN	
use linking words to connect ideas	
make sentences with subordinate clauses	

Vocabulary

3 Complete the sentences about historical events using these words.

evidence	feat	ill-fated
old	outlaw	sacrifices

1   Robin Hood was a(n) _____ who stole from the rich and gave to the poor.
2   Napoleon's invasion of Russia was a(n) _____ expedition which ended in defeat.
3   The archaeological _____ suggests there was a town here.
4   Alexander the Great's conquest of Persia was an amazing _____ for such a young man.
5   Mother Theresa of Calcutta made great personal _____ to help the poor and sick.
6   It's always the same _____ story. Once people gain power, they forget about the people who helped to put them there.

4 Work in pairs. Use phrases from Exercise 3 to describe four historical events (like the sinking of the *Titanic* or the first landing on the Moon).

I CAN	
describe events from history	
talk about luck and chance	

Real life

5 Complete the comments made by different members of the audience at a lecture.

1   If I understood _____ , you said that the Portuguese ship was part of a fleet of ships.
2   I'd like to _____ up on something you said.
3   Maybe I _____ something, but I don't see why no one went to look for survivors.
4   Am I right _____ thinking that no one found any of the wreckage?
5   Can you _____ a little more on what the ship was carrying?
6   How do the weapons found on the ship _____ in with the fact that it was a peaceful mission?

6 Work in groups. Tell each other the name of a game that you know well. Then ask each other questions to check what you know about it already and to find out more information.

I CAN	
use phrases to preface a question	
ask for confirmation and clarification	

Speaking

7 Work in pairs. Describe an important recent event in your country's history.

Unit 8 Digital media

Van Gogh's self-portrait at the Musée d'Orsay
Photograph by Raul Touzon

FEATURES

1 Look at the photo. What are these people doing and why? Would you do the same? Why?

2 Work in pairs. Discuss the questions.

1 How do digital media change the way we experience life?
2 How do audiences use digital media at concerts and conferences these days?
3 Does the use of digital media enhance our experiences or spoil them?
4 Some research suggests people remember events more vividly when they do not use digital media. Does that surprise you? What is more important, the memory or the picture?

3 Categorize the activities according to how you use them (a–c). Then discuss your answers.

a things that you do yourself
b things you benefit from others' doing
c things you never do

chat online	tweet	post comments on forums
upload photos	write a blog	use social networking sites
review products	download music	

8a Sinkholes

Reading

1 Work in pairs. Do you read blogs? Which ones? Discuss with your partner.

2 Look at the features of blogs (a–e). Discuss which features encourage you to read blogs and which don't. Explain your reasons.

Blogs offer:
a   an insider's view on a subject
b   a personal account
c   a writer's passion for a subject
d   a genuine, even if sometimes biased opinion
e   the chance of dialogue with the writer

3 Look at the photo below. Write questions that you would like answered about the photo. Then read the blog and see if it answered your questions.

4 Read the blog again and choose the best option to complete the sentences.

1   The blogger went to Guatemala himself to *see the hole / understand what had happened*.
2   The hole looked *man-made / natural*.
3   He suggests that Guatemala City rests on *insecure foundations / saturated earth*.
4   The official explanation is that *the sewer system was faulty / an unexpected weather event caused it*.
5   This sinkhole in Guatemala City is *unlike any other / not the first of its kind*.

Sinkholes

I've spent ten years photographing sinkholes and heard all sorts of explanations—some plausible, some just wild—about why they occur. So when I saw these dramatic pictures on the news of a new sinkhole in Guatemala City, I headed down there to look for myself rather than take anyone else's word for it.

It's a scary sight. The hole, which is 60 feet (18 m) wide and is estimated to be over 300 feet (100 m) deep, looks like someone has used an enormous drill. It's not the first time this has happened here. In 2007, a similar sinkhole appeared in Guatemala City and was reported to have swallowed about a dozen homes.

Most sinkholes are caused by a build-up of water in the soil over a natural cavity in limestone rock. The weight of the saturated soil causes the roof of the cavity to collapse with everything above it. But in this case, there's no limestone bedrock. In fact, there's no solid rock at all. The city is built on rather loose volcanic debris. What is believed to have happened is that water leaked from the sewer system and hollowed out the ground under the foundations of buildings. At a certain point, the ground just collapsed in this extraordinary pipe shape.

So strictly speaking, this isn't a real sinkhole. It's a different phenomenon that no one has named yet. Whatever you call it, the effect is both amazing and frightening. One local official said that it had happened after a freak tropical storm overloaded the water system and that it is not expected to happen again. Local residents seemed less sure. One said to me, "My family and I are getting out of here as soon as we can!"

Other sinkholes like this are known to exist and I'd be very interested to hear from any readers if you've seen anything similar.

cavity (n) /ˈkævɪti/ a hollow space in a natural structure
limestone (n) /ˈlaɪmˌstoʊn/ a type of porous rock

5 Look again at the features of blogs in Exercise 2. Which features do this blog offer the reader? Underline the parts of the blog that show you this.

> ▶ **WORDBUILDING compound nouns**
>
> Compound nouns are a combination of a noun + noun. They are often used for objects and materials.
> *bedrock, guidebook, limestone*

Language focus passive reporting verbs

6 Look at these two sentences (A and B) which use passive reporting verbs. Answer the questions (1–4).

Type A: **It is known that** most sinkholes **are caused** by a build-up of water.

Type B: The hole **is estimated to be** over 300 feet deep.

1 What grammatical form follows the reporting verb in each sentence?
2 Do we know who the agent of each of the passive reporting verbs is?
3 Why is a passive, not an active verb used?
4 Why do news reports use this type of verb?

7 Find four more type B sentences with passive reporting verbs in the article. What are the times of the events they refer to: present, past, or future?

> ▶ **PASSIVE REPORTING VERBS**
>
> **Present**
> A: *It is known that sinkholes occur in limestone rock.*
> B: *Sinkholes are known to occur in limestone rock.*
>
> A: *It is believed that the hole is growing larger.*
> B: *The hole is believed to be growing larger.*
>
> **Past**
> A: *It is said that the sinkholes appeared recently.*
> B: *The sinkholes are said to have appeared recently.*
>
> A: *It was reported that the sewers were leaking.*
> B: *The sewers were reported to be leaking.*
>
> A: *It wasn't thought that anyone had been injured.*
> B: *No one was thought to have been injured.*
>
> **Future**
> A: *It is expected that repair work will begin soon.*
> B: *Repair work is expected to begin soon.*
>
> For more information and practice, see page 166.

8 Look at the language focus box. Rewrite the sentences with passive reporting verbs you found in Exercise 7 into type A sentences.

Example:
1 The hole **is estimated to be** 300 feet deep.
   It is estimated that the hole is 300 feet deep.

9 Rewrite the sentences about sinkholes in Yucatán using passive reporting verbs.

1 People say that the cenotes in Yucatán are the most beautiful sinkholes in the world.
   The cenotes in Yucatán _____ .
2 Historians think they were important to the Mayan people.
   They _____ .
3 We already knew that the Mayans built important settlements near the cenotes.
   The Mayans _____ .
4 The Mayans believed that the cenotes led to the next world after death.
   It _____ .
5 Tourist agencies report that these water holes are increasingly popular with tourists.
   These water holes _____ .
6 In the future, agencies expect that the more popular ones will be closed to the public.
   In the future, the more popular ones

   _____ .

Speaking and writing

10 Work in pairs. Imagine you are describing one of the items below to someone who has never seen it. Tell your partner about your experience visiting it.

• a place of historical interest (like a building or an archaeological site)
• a place of geographical interest (like a mountain or a national park)
• a cultural event (like a festival or a ceremony)

11 Write your description in the form of a short (150 words) blog. Use passive reporting verbs. Look at the features of blog writing in Exercise 2.

8b Creating a buzz

Speaking and listening

1 Work in groups. Complete and then discuss this short questionnaire about brands and advertising.

1 Which brands of clothes, food, and household products are you especially loyal to?
2 What keeps you loyal to these brands?
3 What kind of advertising are you most likely to pay attention to: TV, magazine, online, other?
4 Has any new company or product attracted your interest recently?
5 How did they do this?

2 Look at the photo and answer the questions.

1 What are they selling?
2 What benefits are they offering the buyer?
3 How are they advertising them?

3 🎵 **30** Listen to an interview and answer the questions. According to Sarah Palmer:

1 What must your customers become if you are to be a successful marketer?
2 How often do companies manage to achieve "a straight sell"?
3 What should companies encourage customers to do on the social networking site?
4 How can marketers of ordinary products engage their customers?

4 🎵 **30** Listen again and mark the sentences true (T) or false (F).

1 It's not enough to be focused on the customer.
2 People aren't really interested in reading facts about the company.
3 National Geographic uses competitions to involve visitors.
4 National Geographic does not try to sell you anything directly.
5 Even with an everyday product, there are ways the seller can involve the customer.
6 The tea company has a website that educates the visitor.

Idioms business buzzwords

5 Work in pairs. A *buzzword* is a word or an expression that is trendy at the moment. There are many examples in business. Look at the words in bold and discuss what they mean.

1 We hear about companies being **customer-focused** all the time these days.
2 You want them to **buy into** your story.
3 We've been looking at examples of **best practices** in social media marketing.

6 Match the business buzzwords (1–9) with the correct definition (a–i).

1 **At the end of the day**, it's your choice whether to participate or not.
2 How much are we talking about? Give me a **ballpark figure**.
3 It's a great idea, but what's your **game plan**?
4 Keep me **in the loop**. I want to be informed.
5 How hard can it be? It**'s not rocket science**.
6 Great. I'm glad that we**'re on the same page**.
7 The disappointing sales were a big **reality check**.
8 We're looking for really fresh ideas, so try to **think outside the box**.
9 It's **a win-win situation**.

a advantageous to both sides
b be imaginative
c moment to face the true facts
d rough estimate
e simple
f strategy
g ultimately
h understand each other
i up-to-date with events

Language focus expressions with *no*

7 Match the two parts of the sentences. Then check the audioscript on page 179.

1 There's no point…
2 These days, a company has no hope…
3 There's no doubt…
4 Is there no mention…
5 They have no alternative…
6 No matter…

a of doing that unless they use social media.
b what you're selling, if you can involve people, you'll find an audience.
c of selling at all?
d being focused on your customers if they're not focused on you.
e but to present the product in an ordinary way.
f that a straight sell can work occasionally.

▶ **EXPRESSIONS WITH *NO***

no + noun + *-ing*
There's no point (in) waiting.
We had no difficulty (in) persuading them.

no + noun + *of* + *-ing*
There's no way of telling.
I had no intention of going there in person.

no + noun + *that*
There's no question that it's a popular brand.

no… except/but to + infinitive
We had no choice but to do what they said.
We had no alternative except to invite them.

no matter + relative pronoun
No matter where you go, you find the same thing.

For more information and practice, see page 167.

---

8 Look at the language focus box. Then rewrite the sentences using the words given.

1 It's a well-constructed website. (question)
There's _____ .
2 I found it very easy to navigate my way around the site. (difficulty)
I had _____ .
3 Also, whichever page I visited, there was always something interesting to look at. (matter)
Also, _____ .
4 I liked the fact that I didn't have to buy anything. (suggestion)
I liked the fact that there was _____ .
5 I was surprised that it didn't talk about shipping costs. (mention)
I was surprised that there was _____ .
6 You are forced to accept their shipping rates. (choice)
You have _____ .
7 I think that the retailer must make the buying process transparent. (matter)
I think that _____ .
8 I didn't intend to buy anything. (intention)
I had _____ .

9 Work in pairs. What commercial website have you visited recently? Why did you visit it? Was it a good or a bad experience? Complete these sentences and discuss them with your partner.

1 I had no problems…
2 There's no question that…
3 No matter…

Speaking

10 Work in groups. Look at the company profile below. Think of three suitable interactive elements for their social networking site that will attract and engage new customers. Use ideas that you discussed in Exercises 1 and 2 on page 96. Compare your ideas with other groups in the class.

Mosushi is a mobile vendor of Japanese food. Based in a large city, it has five small vans that sell Japanese meals and snacks, teas, and fruit juices from street locations. The company would like to get more of a following on social networks so that it can expand its business.

8c A hacker's life

Reading

1 Work in pairs. How do you (or could you) keep your Internet use private and your personal details secure? Think of four ways, using the words to help you. Compare your ideas with another pair and discuss which are most useful.

back up	download	identity	password
theft	transaction	Wi-Fi	

2 Look at the two definitions of "hacker." Which fits your idea of a hacker? Now read the article on page 99. What is the author's view?

---

hacker (n) /ˈhækər/

1 a nonprofessional but skillful computer programmer
2 a person who uses computers to gain unauthorized access to data

---

3 Read the article again and answer the questions. Compare your answers with your partner's.

1 What do DefCon hackers do to help improve Internet security?
2 What are most hackers not?
3 What do hackers look at besides online security?
4 What do they do with the information they find?
5 What does the writer like about the people at DefCon?
6 What is *Capture the Flag*?
7 What does the writer say about the majority of people who use the Internet?
8 What really motivates the hackers at DefCon?

4 Has your opinion of hackers changed after reading this article? How? Discuss with your partner.

Critical thinking identifying personal opinions

5 Work in pairs. Underline the adjectives and adverbs in the article that the writer uses to express his personal opinion.

Example:
But then comes the <u>worrying</u> realization that…

6 What would you say, in summary, were the writer's personal opinions about the following?

1 the mixture of people he met at DefCon
2 the security of personal data on the Internet
3 how we should feel about hackers

Word focus *break*

7 Work in pairs. Find three expressions with *break* (in paragraphs 1, 3, and 5) and discuss with your partner what each expression means.

8 Match the expressions with *break* (1–5) with the correct definitions (a–e).

1 The manager called everyone together to **break the news** about the company closing.
2 During the first lesson, the teacher got us to play a couple of games to **break the ice**.
3 They are hoping that their new social networking site will really **break the mold**.
4 You really should buy a new pair of shoes. It won't **break the bank**.
5 We didn't make a profit but I think we at least **broke even**.

a be very different
b help people relax
c make neither a profit nor a loss
d tell (someone) something important
e use up all one's money

9 Write a sentence using one of the expressions with *break*. Read it to your partner, omitting the phrase, and ask them to guess what the missing phrase is.

Speaking

10 Work in pairs. Some important data is missing from an office computer. You are going to act out a meeting between a small business owner and an Internet security consultant.

Student A: Turn to page 154. Look at the notes and prepare your answers.

Student B: Turn to page 155. Look at the notes. Then prepare to ask questions and give advice.

A hacker's life

Hackers compete in *Capture the Flag*.

Have you ever locked yourself out of your house and had to try to break in? First you get a sense of accomplishment in succeeding. But then comes the worrying realization that if *you* can break into your own place as an amateur, a professional could do it five times faster. So you look for the weak point in your security and fix it. Well, that's more or less how the DefCon hackers conference works.

Every year, hackers meet in Las Vegas to test their knowledge and capabilities. Mention the word "hacker" and many of us picture a seventeen-year-old geek sitting in a bedroom, illegally hacking into the US Pentagon's defense secrets. But that is actually a gross misrepresentation of what most hackers do.

The activities that take place at DefCon have an enormous impact on our daily lives. Here, computer addicts who can't break the habit or resist the challenge of finding security gaps scrutinize all kinds of systems, from the Internet to mobile communications to household door locks. And then they try to hack them. In doing so, they do us all a great service by passing on their findings to industry, which can then plug the security holes.

A graphic example of this is when I attended a presentation on electronic door locks. Ironically, one of the most secure locks they demonstrated was a 4,000-year-old Egyptian tumbler lock. But when it came to more modern devices, the presenters revealed significant weaknesses in several brands of electro-mechanical locks. A bio-lock that uses a fingerprint scan for entry was defeated, easily, using a paper clip. (Unfortunately, although all the manufacturers of the insecure locks were alerted, not all responded.)

DefCon is a vast mix of cultures as well as a culture in itself. People in dark clothes and ripped jeans talk to people in golf shirts and khakis. Social status here is based on knowledge and accomplishment, not clothing labels or cars. It's kind of refreshing. There are government agents here, as well as video game enthusiasts. Not that people ask each other where they work; that would break hacker etiquette.

To attract the brightest hackers, DefCon runs a competition called *Capture the Flag*, which pits elite hackers against each other in a cybergame of network attack and defense that goes on 24 hours a day. In a large, dimly lit conference hall, small groups of hackers try either to protect or to break into the system. There are huge video projections on the walls, and pizza boxes and coffee cups are strewn everywhere. The room is mesmerizing.

In another room, another contest is taking place. Here participants have five minutes to free themselves from handcuffs, escape from a cell, get past a guard, retrieve their passport from a locked filing cabinet, leave through another locked door, and make their escape to freedom.

If you're someone who dismisses the DefCon attendees as a bunch of geeks and social misfits, then you probably have the same password for 90 percent of your online existence. Which means you are doomed. Because even if you think you're being clever by using your grandmother's birth date backwards as a password, you're no match for these people. There is no greater ignorance to be found online than that of an average Internet user. I'm happy to admit that I'm one of them. I'm also aware that there are other people out there, big business among them, who are trying to get more and more access to our personal data. Sadly, we have few tools to protect ourselves. But there is a group of people who are passionate about online freedom and have the means to help us protect our privacy. Many of them can be found at DefCon.

---

do someone a service (v) /ˌdu ˈsʌmwʌn ə ˈsɜrvɪs/ help someone
etiquette (n) /ˈetɪkɪt/ code of polite behavior
handcuffs (n) /ˈhændˌkʌfs/ a pair of metal rings placed on the wrists to restrain someone
khakis (n) /ˈkækiz/ light-colored casual pants
scrutinize /ˈskrut(ə)nˌaɪz / examine something closely

8d A podcast

Vaadhoo Island in the Maldives

Real life making a podcast

1 Work in pairs. Discuss the questions.

1 How do you prefer to access news stories and reports?
   a print
   b Internet
   c video
   d audio

2 What kind of news stories and reports interest you particularly? Explain why.

arts and culture	business	politics
science and environment	sports	travel

2 🔊 31 Look at the photo and describe what you see. What kind of news report is this going to be? Listen and check your answer.

3 🔊 31 Listen again and answer the questions.

1 What did scientists already know about the cause of these blue ocean lights?
2 What more do they know now?

4 Speaking skill **hedging language**

🔊 31 When we aren't absolutely certain of the facts, we commonly use "hedging" language. Listen again and match the hedging expressions the speakers use with the facts (1–6).

1 … one of the most spectacular sights in nature.
2 … spend most of their lives in deep ocean waters.
3 … being able to light yourself up is useful.
4 … just lighting your way as you move around.
5 … electrical signals in the phytoplankton cause a chemical reaction.
6 … the electrical signal is generated by motion in the water.

▶ **HEDGING LANGUAGE**

It seems / appears that…
… tend(s) to…
… which suggests that…
It's reasonable to assume that…
We can probably conclude that…
There are estimated / thought to be…
Arguably…
Probably / Possibly / Most likely / Perhaps…

5 Pronunciation word stress

a 🔊 32 Listen again to the opening sentence of the interview. Underline where the stress falls in the words in bold. Where does the stress generally fall in (a) two-syllable words and (b) in words of three or more syllables?

"**Today** we're going to look at some new **evidence** about what is **arguably** one of the most **spectacular** sights in **nature**: the **phenomenon** of waves glowing at night and **mirroring** the stars with lots of **tiny**, blue lights."

b Work in pairs. Where does the stress fall in the words in bold in this sentence? Practice reading it correctly.

"It's **reasonable** to **assume** that the **electrical signal** is **generated** by **motion** in the **water**."

c What do you notice about these two-syllable verbs with stress on the second syllable: *propose, confirm, describe, explain, include*?

6 Work in two groups of three. You are going to make a news podcast about a new discovery.

Group A: Turn to page 154. Read the information.

Group B: Turn to page 155. Read the information.

- Discuss what you are going to say and prepare the news story. Remember to use hedging language.
- Practice reading the story aloud.
- Deliver your podcast to the other group.

8e The invisible man

Writing an online news report

1 Look at the photo. What is the man doing? Why? Read the news report and check your answer.

2 After it was first published, this news story "went viral," appearing on lots of websites all over the Internet. Why did it have such wide appeal?

3 Work in pairs. Read the advice to news writers. Then read the report again and find the answer to *Who? What? Where? When? Why?* and *How?*

> A news report includes the answers to the five *W*s and the *H*: *Who is it about? What did they do? Where and when did this happen? Why did they do it?* and *How did they do it?* The reader must be able to find the answers to these questions easily and quickly, before the report gives other details and information.

4 Writing skill cautious language

a News reports (and academic reports) use cautious language when the information given cannot be verified 100%. Find an example of each of the following types of cautious language in the report.

1 the verbs *seem* or *appear*
2 passive reporting verbs
3 adverbs of degree or frequency
4 adverbs that speculate about a fact

b Rewrite these sentences using the words given to express more caution about each of the facts.

1 His pictures carry a strong social message. (generally)
2 He became internationally famous when a New York art dealer bought some of his works. (apparently)
3 His work makes people think more about their surroundings. (might)
4 He wants to draw our attention to what we cannot see in a picture. (seems)
5 Bolin used friends at first to help him paint his pictures. (said)

5 Write a short news report about something that happened in your town or school recently. Make sure your report answers the five Ws and the H. Write around 150 words.

THE
INVISIBLE MAN

In his latest work, created in the summer of 2011 at his Beijing studio, Chinese artist Liu Bolin blends into a background of a supermarket soft drink display. When his assistants finished painting him in, he seemed to have disappeared. Entitled *Plasticizer*, the piece is supposed to express Bolin's shock at the discovery of plasticizer in food products. Plasticizers are additives generally used to make non-food products less rigid.

Such pictures have made Bolin internationally famous, which is ironic because they started out as a statement about how unwanted he felt by society. Bolin loves the challenge of blending into any surroundings: a building site, a telephone booth, a national monument. No trick photography or photoshopping is used and careful planning is needed for each image. First he tells the photographer how he would like the picture to look. Then his assistants paint him in, a process that can take up to ten hours while Bolin stands completely still, presumably in some discomfort.

His pictures appear to have struck a chord with many people because more recently, Bolin has branched out and created camouflage photos in New York, Paris, Venice, Rome, and London.

6 Exchange news reports with your partner. Does the news report:

- answer the six basic questions?
- use cautious language appropriately?

Talking dictionaries

The Tuvan people have a very rich lexicon.

Before you watch

1 Work in pairs and discuss the questions.

1 Can you think of three languages that are spoken in more than one country? Which is the most widespread?

2 Is your language spoken in another country? If so, where?

3 Is another language, such as English, replacing your language or other languages in your country?

2 How can we save lesser spoken languages from being dominated or replaced by "world" languages? Is it important to do this? Why?

While you watch

3 Watch the video and compare your answers from Exercise 2 with what the speaker says.

4 Watch the first part of the video (to 01:02) and answer the questions.

1 How many of the world's languages are endangered?

2 Why are these languages dying out?

3 What are the "savvy" communities doing to preserve their languages?

5 Watch the second part of the video (01:03 to 02:29) and then complete the summary of the Talking Dictionaries project using one word per space.

The aim of Talking Dictionaries is to give endangered languages a first-ever [1] _____ on the [2] _____ .
An example is Siletz Dee-ni from Oregon, US, which has only one [3] _____ speaker .
This speaker has recorded [4] _____ of words, which have been made into a talking dictionary. When you see the rich vocabulary of the language, it helps you appreciate the cultural [5] _____ .
The dictionary can then be used as a tool to [6] _____ the language.

6 Watch the third part of the video (02:30 to end) and answer the questions.

1 What did the Papua New Guinea villagers ask the Enduring Voices team?

2 What message did seeing the Matukar Panau talking dictionary on the Internet send to people?

3 What is special about the Tuvan talking dictionary?

4 To whom do the Talking Dictionaries team want to spread the message of the importance of linguistic diversity?

7 Which words do you remember from the two talking dictionaries that you saw? What did they tell you about those particular cultures? Watch the video again to check.

1 Siletz Dee-ni (Oregon, US)

2 Matukar Panau (Papua New Guinea)

After you watch

8 Roleplay creating a talking dictionary

Work in groups of three or four. Make your own small talking dictionary as follows:

- List five or six words or short phrases which are typical of your language and culture (for social life, food, geography, weather).
- Write an English translation for each.

Read your phrases and their translations to your group. Then ask each other questions about why you chose these particular phrases.

9 Work in groups. Do you think that the Internet helps promote cultural diversity or does it make cultures more similar and homogenous? Discuss. Give examples to support your arguments.

---

collaboration (n) /kə,læbəˈreɪʃən/ working together on something
devalue (v) /diˈvælju/ make something less valuable than it is
indigenous (adj) /ɪnˈdɪdʒɪnəs/ native to a particular country or location
migratory (adj) /ˈmaɪgrə,tɔri/ moving from one place to live in another
pertaining (to) (v) /pərˈteɪnɪŋ/ describing; related to
platform (n) /ˈplætfɔrm/ a computer software framework in which you can run other programs
revitalize (v) /riˈvaɪtˈəl,aɪz/ put the life back into something
savvy (adj) /ˈsævi/ knowledgeable
worthwhile (adj) /ˈwɜrθˈwaɪl/ having value

UNIT 8 REVIEW

Grammar

1 Read the blog about the Mariana Trench and make passive reporting verbs from the words in italics.

2 Read the blog again and answer the questions.

   1   Where and what is the Mariana Trench?
   2   What was Cameron's aim in visiting it?

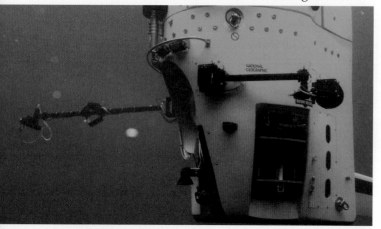

¹*It / say / be* one of the greatest achievements in exploration since we put a man on the Moon. James Cameron recently made the headlines by diving almost seven miles (11 k) in a one-person submersible to what ²*think / be* the deepest part of the ocean, the Mariana Trench. This great chasm, 120 times larger than the Grand Canyon, is where the Earth's Pacific plate slides under the Philippines plate.

Better known as the director of the movies *Titanic* and *Avatar*, Cameron is one of just three people to reach Earth's deepest point, and the only one to stay long enough to look around. Although ³*it / already / know* how ⁴*the Mariana Trench / be / form*, Cameron hoped to discover more about its biology.

In 1960, Swiss engineer Jacques Piccard and US Navy Captain Don Walsh ⁵*report / spend* 20 minutes in the Mariana depths, but they saw nothing because their submarine disturbed too much mud on the ocean floor. Cameron's submersible was equipped with stereo digital cameras to take 3D shots, and a large bank of LED lights. ⁶*It / hope / that / his movie / shed* new light on life in one of the most extreme environments on our planet.

3 Complete the statements which use phrases with *no*. Write one word in each space.
   1   No matter _____ you rank it in the history of exploration, there's no doubt _____ James Cameron's achievement is a remarkable one.
   2   Cameron had no way _____ telling what he would find, but he had no intention _____ letting that deter him from diving.
   3   He had no difficulty _____ getting funding for the project, but with so many people backing him, he had no choice _____ to dive.

4 Work in pairs. Think of a place that someone discovered or explored for the first time. Make a sentence describing what people thought about this place using a passive reporting verb.

I CAN	
report what has been said (passive reporting verbs)	☐
use phrases with *no*	☐

Vocabulary

5 Choose the best option to complete the sentences.

   1   I *position / post* a lot of comments on car forums.
   2   He *puts on / writes* a weekly blog about movies.
   3   People think social media marketing is complicated but it's not *space / rocket* science!
   4   By thinking outside the *box, / frame,* they came up with a really innovative website.
   5   Their *match / game* plan is to sell a lot of ads.
   6   The customer is happy and the company is happy. It's a *win-win / gain-gain* situation.

6 Work in pairs. What's your favorite website? Is it interactive? Why do you like it?

I CAN	
talk about digital media	☐
understand business buzzwords	☐

Real life

7 Rewrite the statements to make them less certain.

   1   James Cameron has an obsession with exploring the deep seas. (seems)
   2   The most difficult thing was going down alone in the submersible. (arguably)
   3   He tweeted: "Hitting bottom never felt so good." (reported)
   4   People who usually undertake such missions are scientists, not film directors. (tend)
   5   In the future, these missions will be manned rather than unmanned. (likely)
   6   The Mariana Trench is 7 miles deep. (estimated)

8 Work in pairs. Make a short podcast about James Cameron's exploration of the deep sea. Then present your podcast to another pair.

I CAN	
make a news report	☐
use hedging language	☐

Speaking

9 Work in pairs. Describe to your partner how you make use of digital media (a) in your work and (b) in your social life. How would your life be different without it?

Unit 9 The music in us

A young boy watches street performers.
Photograph by Greg Dale

FEATURES

1 Look at the photo and answer the questions.

1 What is a *street performer*?
2 Is it common to see them in your country? Where?
3 What kind of music do they play?

2 Put the words in the right category (a–e).

ballad	dance	eclectic	folk	instrumental
melodic	solo artist	soothing	sophisticated	

a genres of music   d describing music
b musicians   e describing taste
c compositions

3 Work in groups. Discuss these questions.

1 How important is music to you? What kind of music do
you listen to? Where and when?
2 Do you prefer live music or recorded music? Why?

9a World music

Reading

1 Work in groups and answer the questions.

1 How important is music in your culture?
2 Is there one style of music that dominates?
3 How different are musical tastes across generations?
4 Do you listen to music from other countries and cultures? If so, who or what?

2 Read the interview with a musician and say which of these statements best sums up his view of music and culture.

a Music isn't really very different across cultures.
b Cultural differences in music are fascinating.
c Fortunately, music is becoming more standardized across the world.

3 Match the types of music (1–4) with the point they are supposed to illustrate (a–d).

1 American teenagers and sitar music
2 international pop music
3 Mexican-Irish songs
4 80s rock

a There's a wealth of diverse musical styles out there.
b Each generation believes it owns the music of its time.
c There is music out there with universal appeal.
d Music doesn't always have universal appeal.

4 Work in pairs. Has Western pop music influenced traditional music in your country? Is this a good thing or not? Discuss with your partner.

WORLD MUSIC

INTERVIEW OF THE WEEK

He's been traveling for just under two years, so we thought it was time we caught up with musician Justin Cape.

WM: Justin, you've spent a lot of time studying other musical styles and traditions. Are you trying to make music that has a more universal appeal?

JC: That's not my goal really. Global commercial forces have already homogenized music styles quite a lot. I noticed that on my travels. I just get excited about exploring different types of music.

WM: But you have sophisticated tastes. For many people, different styles of music aren't always very accessible, are they?

JC: No, they can seem alien, but I don't think that's so surprising; it's just habit, like the food you eat. Not many American teenagers listen to Indian sitar music, just as not many nomads in the Sahara eat hamburgers and fries. But I think often, if you give it a chance, it can be incredibly rewarding.

WM: And what are you listening to at the moment?

JC: A group from Mali called Tinariwen. They play a very upbeat mix of Middle Eastern and African music. I'm also a big fan of Ry Cooder, another musical nomad. He really mines the world's music styles. He started out exploring different kinds of American music: blues, gospel, R&B. Then he worked with musicians in Cuba and Mali. And he's just produced a CD of Mexican-Irish songs, which are fantastic!

WM: Is what people sing about different from culture to culture?

JC: Not really. Any differences are as much generational as cultural. Each new generation feels that "their" music is speaking just to them; that it's addressing things that have never been experienced before. In Western music, we speak about music in generational terms: 60s soul, 80s rock, and so on. But to answer your question, I think even if music is very different from place to place, its themes are pretty universal.

Language focus the adverb *just*

5 *Just* has a lot of meanings and is used often in spoken English. Match the sentences (1–6) with the correct meaning of *just* (a–f).

1 He's been traveling for **just** under two years.
2 It's **just** habit, like the food you eat.
3 Not many American teenagers listen to Indian sitar music, **just** as not many nomads in the Sahara eat hamburgers and fries.
4 I **just** get excited about exploring music.
5 And he's **just** produced a CD of Mexican-Irish songs, which are fantastic!
6 Each new generation feels that "their" music is speaking **just** to them.

a very recently   e a little
b simply   f no particular
c only   meaning
d exactly

> ▶ **THE ADVERB *JUST***
>
> ***just* + main verb**
> *They've just finished a tour of Asia.*
> *I'm just waiting for the song to finish downloading.*
>
> ***just* + preposition**
> *She's just under 80 years old, but you wouldn't know it.*
> *He has just about finished recording the album.*
>
> ***just* + noun**
> *He doesn't have a sore throat. It's just the way he sings!*
>
> ***just* + adjective**
> *It's just sad that she doesn't play live more often.*
>
> ***just* + conjunction**
> *The concert was just as you said it would be.*
> Notes
> 1 *just* is placed before the word it emphasizes
> 2 *just about = almost*
>
> For more information and practice, see page 168.

6 Work in pairs. Look at the language focus box and notice the position of *just* in each sentence. Then put *just* in the sentences below. There is sometimes more than one possible position. What is the meaning of *just* in each case?

1 If you took the time to listen to Ry Cooder, you'd definitely like him.
2 I've heard his new single on the radio.
3 It's over ten years since they last performed.
4 Hearing her sing gives me goosebumps.
5 The concert is in an old theater behind the bank on Main Street.
6 Thank you for the CD; it's what I wanted.
7 I can't understand why you like his music!
8 I'm as interested in the lyrics as the music.

7 Pronunciation word stress: *just*

a 🔊 **33** Listen to how *just* is pronounced. In what situations would you hear each phrase?

1 Just a minute.
2 Phew! Just in time.
3 I'm sorry, I just don't get it.
4 Thanks, I just had one.
5 Thanks, I'm just looking.
6 Hi, did you just call?
7 We're just friends.
8 I just wondered.

b Work in pairs. Make short conversations using these phrases and practice pronouncing them with the appropriate stress.

Speaking and vocabulary themes of songs

8 Work in groups. The list below contains the hundred most used words in English Language pop song titles in the last hundred years (without *the, to, I, you, my, don't*). First check you know what the words mean. Then follow this procedure.

1 Each think of three of your favorite pop song titles in English and two in your own language.
2 Check if the song titles contain one or more of these words.
3 Discuss what the most common themes are in the songs that you thought of.

> ain't alone angel arms around away
> baby bad beautiful believe blue boy
> change Christmas comes crazy cry
> dance days dear dream ever everybody
> everything eyes fall feel fire fool forever
> girl gone gonna goodbye happy heart
> heaven hey hold kiss la lady leave life
> light lonely love lover mama man mind
> mine miss moon moonlight morning mister
> music night nobody oh people play
> please rain red remember river rock roll
> rose sing smile somebody something song
> soul star stay stop street summer sun
> sweet sweetheart talk tears theme things
> think tonight town true walk wanna
> wish woman wonderful world young

9b Healing music

Listening

1 Work in pairs. Answer the questions.

1 How do different types of music affect your mood?
2 When do you listen to music to affect your mood? While driving?

2 Which of the following therapeutic properties do you think music has? Explain your reasons.

a relieving stress
b relieving pain
c acting as an anesthetic
d helping sleep
e helping with learning disabilities
f preventing heart disease
g helping with speech difficulties
h combating memory loss

3 🎵 **34** Listen to a talk by a neuroscientist about music therapy. Which therapeutic properties in Exercise 2 does she mention?

4 🎵 **34** Complete the notes. Then listen and check your answers.

1 Area of the brain activated by music:
_____
2 The body releases endorphins to _____ and produce _____
3 Same parts of the brain are used to process _____ and _____ .
4 Music could help people with _____ and other _____
5 Dr. Schlaug treated people who _____ .
6 The results of Schlaug's music therapy were really _____ .
7 Music therapy for memory loss is important because _____

> ▶ **WORDBUILDING negative prefixes**
>
> We can use a number of different negative prefixes in English as well as the common *un-* and *in-* prefixes: *a-, dis-, dys-, non-.*
> *asymmetrical, dyslexia, non-toxic*

Idioms music

5 Look at this idiom used by the speaker. What do you think it means?

"This news should be **music to our ears**."

6 Match these music idioms (1–7) with their meaning.

accept responsibility	give a contrary opinion
know what's going on	make a fuss
seem very relevant to	shout about one's achievements
take things as they come	

1 You**'ve changed your tune**. You said you didn't like rock music.
2 What she said about working long hours really **struck a chord with** the audience because they were mostly nurses.
3 It's a mistake to go to a job interview with a particular strategy. Just **play it by ear**.
4 Don't worry about John negotiating the deal for us. He **knows the score**.
5 I don't mean to **blow my own horn**, but I think my performance was the best.
6 Sooner or later someone will find out that I cheated and I'll have to **face the music**.
7 In the end he did help me clean up, but he **made a big song and dance about it**.

7 Work in pairs. Describe examples of the following.

1 someone who likes to blow their own horn
2 a time when you made a big mistake and had to face the music
3 something you read recently that really struck a chord with you
4 a situation in which it is best to play it by ear

Language focus expressing purpose

8 Work in pairs. Look at the sentences from the talk which express purpose (1–5) and answer the questions (a–d).

1 Endorphins are released at times of stress **to** help us deal with pain.
2 Hospitals now use music **for** pain relief after an operation.
3 Perhaps you are someone who has to strain **so as to** hear what people are saying.
4 I'm not saying you should take up the violin **so that** you can hear people better at parties.
5 I'm not saying you should take up the violin **in order to** be a better linguist.

a Which sentences use *to* + infinitive to express purpose?
b What modal verb follows *so that*? Can any other modal verb follow it?
c What part of speech must follow *for* when expressing purpose?
d Are *so as to* and *in order to* more or less formal than the simple *to* + infinitive?

> ▶ **EXPRESSING PURPOSE**
>
> **Infinitive of purpose**
> *I gave up playing the piano (in order) to concentrate on my classes.*
> *I turned down the music so as not to disturb the neighbors.*
>
> **for**
> *He listens to classical music for relaxation.*
> *He plays in a band not for money but for fun.*
>
> **avoid**
> *We kept the music low to avoid annoying the neighbors.*
>
> **so that / in order that**
> *The song sample is there so that you can hear it before you buy it.*
> *He wrote the lyrics down so that he wouldn't forget them.*
>
> For more information and practice, see page 168.

9 Look at the language focus box. Then use the prompts to rewrite the sentences so that they have the same meaning.

1 He took up the guitar because he wanted to join his brother's band.
  a He took up the guitar so that _____ .
  b He took up the guitar in order to _____ .

2 I play the trumpet because it helps me relax.
  a I play the trumpet to _____ .
  b I play the trumpet for _____ .
3 They sing familiar songs so that they don't confuse the patients.
  a They sing familiar songs so as _____ .
  b They sing familiar songs to avoid _____ .

10 Rewrite the phrases in italics using the words given.

> When asked to pronounce new sounds in another language, we often prefer to pronounce sounds that we are already familiar with [1] *because we don't want to sound silly* (avoid). It seems that we have to lose our inhibitions [2] *if we want to pronounce another set of sounds properly* (order). But there are various things you can do [3] *if you want to improve* (to) your English pronunciation.
>
> First, try to think of the sounds of a language as music. Second, try to exaggerate the sounds of the target language a little [4] *because then you get* (as) close to the reality of native pronunciation. Finally, practice singing songs in the target language [5] *because it helps you to lose* (so that) your inhibitions. It's amazing how much better someone can imitate pronunciation in a song than the ordinary spoken word.

Speaking

11 Work in groups. You are music consultants that advise companies and organizations on how to use music to achieve a particular effect or mood.

Group A: Think of a plan for using music in schools.

Group B: Think of a plan for using music in an airport.

Then present your ideas to the other group.

Reading

1 Work in pairs. Discuss what you know about these four famous pop artists (a–d).

- dead or alive
- nationality
- type of music played
- names of songs
- other things they are known for

a Michael Jackson c Bob Marley
b John Lennon   d Elvis Presley

2 Read the review. Would the writer agree, partly agree, or disagree with these headlines about Bob Marley?

1 THE MAN WHO BROUGHT **REGGAE** TO THE WORLD

2 MILLIONS IN THIRD WORLD LOOK TO MARLEY AS A HERO

3 SOCIAL DISADVANTAGES INSPIRE MARLEY SONGS

4 MARLEY WAS AN ABSENT FATHER

5 NEW FILM REVEALS MUCH ABOUT REGGAE STAR'S LIFE

6 SINGER WHO SPREAD MESSAGE OF HARMONY

3 In pairs, discuss what makes Bob Marley stand out as a pop artist.

4 Find words in the review with the following meanings.

1 small sections or parts of a film (para 2)
2 a disadvantaged and troubled area of a city (para 3)
3 a person who doesn't fit in to a group (para 3)
4 common, even dominant (para 5)
5 different sides or parties in a dispute (para 6)
6 in a state of great happiness (para 7)

Critical thinking identifying text types

5 In pairs, discuss which type of review (a–c) best describes the one you have just read. Give reasons.

a a short description of a book, movie, or event with practical information for readers or viewers on how to read or see it
b an appraisal of a book, movie, or event with the reviewer's recommendation to the reader or viewer
c a description of the book, movie, or event and an analysis which adds the reviewer's own knowledge on the subject

6 In what situations is each type of review in Exercise 5 most useful? Discuss with your partner.

Word focus *hit*

7 What does the word *hit* mean in this sentence?

"His first **hit** came when he was only eighteen years old."

8 Match the words in bold with their definition of *hit* (a–f).

1 With music, it's **hit or miss**: not every song sells.
2 They **took** a big **hit** when the stock market crashed.
3 The video game that you bought was **a real hit** with Jack; he hasn't stopped playing it.
4 I think you **hit a nerve** when you told Benny that he needed to study harder. Did you see his expression?
5 I think I'd better **hit the road** or I'll be home late.
6 The joke he told didn't **hit the right note** with the audience. They didn't laugh much.

a be appropriate   d mention a sensitive point
b a big success   e not consistently successful
c leave   f suffer a financial loss

Speaking

9 Work in groups. You are going to organize a charity concert to raise money for children in poverty. Decide on the following:

- the name and venue
- what age group you want to attract
- which artists you will invite to perform
- how it will raise money
- how you will link the event to the theme of children in poverty

ONE LOVE

What makes Bob Marley such an important figure in popular music? Globally, perhaps only Elvis, the Beatles, and Michael Jackson are bigger names. Marley was not the first person to introduce reggae to a wider audience outside the West Indies, but he was, and remains, the only global reggae superstar. Yet, unlike the artists just mentioned, in many developing countries, Marley is celebrated as some kind of redeeming figure, a symbol of hope. To understand why this is, one needs to know more about the man and his background.

Kevin Macdonald's recent documentary, *Marley*, while not providing all the answers, contains a lot of previously unseen footage. Through interviews, performances, and recording sessions, the film provides an insight into the mind and motivation of a musician whose life was cut tragically short; Marley died of cancer in 1981 at 36.

Born in a poor ghetto of Kingston, Jamaica, Marley had a passion for music and began recording at a young age, his first hit coming when he was only eighteen. His difficult environment instilled in him a keen sense of social justice, which he expressed in his music. His mixed ethnic background taught him what it felt like to be an outsider. His father was a white Jamaican who worked as a British marine officer; his mother was a black Jamaican who had married at eighteen.

His father was rarely present and died when Bob was only ten. Did this absence have any bearing on Marley's behavior towards his own eleven children? In the movie, his daughter Cedella talks about her difficulty getting her father to notice her. But neither she, nor any one else in the family, has a bad word to say about him. There is no sense that he did not have time for them; simply that he was prioritizing. Marley's calling was first and foremost to music and its power to effect change.

Shortly after his marriage to Rita Anderson in 1966, Marley became a Rastafarian, a faith that champions the right of Africans taken into slavery in the West Indies to return one day to Africa. So while themes of social injustice and hardship in the shanty towns of Kingston characterize early songs like *Trenchtown Rock* and *I Shot the Sheriff*, it is the theme of a displaced people that is prevalent in later songs like *Exodus* and *Redemption Song*. But whether the songs deal with injustice or dislocation, almost all contain sentiments of unity and love.

Marley maintained that, "People want to listen to a message. This could be passed through me or anybody. I am not a leader, but a messenger." But this is too modest. He experienced genuine hardship and even put his life on the line for justice. In 1976, he took great risks organizing a free concert in his home town of Kingston. It was intended to unite the warring political factions in Jamaica, but while preparing for it, he was the victim of an assassination attempt that left him wounded.

That his songs come from the heart and appeal to others who face hardship is certainly one key to Marley's enduring status as a songwriter. But what stays with you after watching this film is the magic of his performances. The music still sounds fresh, and Marley himself is lost in it, living each note as he spins and jumps ecstatically around the stage.

At two and a half hours, this documentary still leaves many unanswered questions about the man who became Jamaica's first superstar. But isn't that the nature of great people who die young? They leave us wanting more. Kevin Macdonald's *Marley* is in select theaters starting May 3.

Real life your favorite music

1 Work in pairs. Read the description. Do you have a similar program in your country? Discuss it with your partner.

Desert Island Discs is a radio show that has been running on BBC Radio since 1942. Each week a guest is "invited" to be a castaway on a desert island. He or she is allowed to "bring" eight pieces of music, a book, and one luxury item. During the show, the guests talk about their life and the reasons for their choices of music.

2 🎵 **35** Listen to a "castaway" talking about himself and answer the questions.

1 What is this man's job?
2 In what way has he been successful?
3 What kind of music is the first piece he chooses and why does he choose it?

3 Speaking skill responding to difficult questions

🎵 **35** Often when we respond to questions, we need to give ourselves a little time to think. Look at the phrases in the box. Then listen again and answer the questions.

a What questions does the interviewer ask?
b Which phrases does Frank Steel use in his answers?

▶ **RESPONDING TO DIFFICULT QUESTIONS**

That's a good / an interesting question.
I've never really thought about it.
It's not (It isn't) something I've thought a lot about.
I don't really look at it like that.
I honestly don't know.
I couldn't really tell you.
That's hard to say.
Frankly, I've got no idea.

---

4 Pronunciation intonation to express uncertainty

a 🎵 **36** We often use a "wavering" intonation—rising and falling in the same phrase or sentence—to express uncertainty. Listen to the phrases in the box and practice saying them.

b 🎵 **37** Say these phrases with a "wavering" intonation. Then listen and check.

1 perhaps	3 I'm not sure
2 maybe	4 I can't say

5 Work in pairs. You are going to act out a *Desert Island Discs* interview. Follow these steps.

- Write down some details about yourself so that the interviewer has some information to work with. Include your job and education, interests, and personal achievements.
- Exchange notes with your partner and each prepare questions to ask the other.
- Think of two pieces of music you would take and why. Also think of one luxury item.
- Act out the interview, then change roles.

6 Did you find out anything interesting or new about your partner? Tell the class.

9e Fado

Writing a description

1 In pairs, describe to each other a traditional form of music in your country: its style, themes, history, and popular appeal now.

2 Read the description of *fado*, and answer the questions.

   1 How would you describe it?
   2 With whom is it popular?

3 Look at the elements of a description and find an example of each one in the text.

   1 It uses powerful adjectives.
   2 It describes feelings.
   3 It tries to convey an atmosphere.
   4 It uses similes.
   5 The author speaks to his audience as one of them.

4 Writing skill parallel structures

a Look at the sentences from the description. Notice how the words that follow the phrases in bold balance. For example, in 1, *either* and *or* are followed by a pronoun + verb. What parallel structures are used in the other sentences (2–4)?

   1 ... **either** you'll love it **or** you'll hate it.
   2 **Like** the blues, fado tells…, **but unlike** the blues, it focuses…
   3 ... of being away from **either** a loved one **or** your home, **or** something you can never regain.
   4 Mariza has broadened fado's appeal **by** fusing it with other musical traditions and **by** touring the world with her music.

b Rewrite these sentences using parallel structures.

   1 Mariza is young, talented, and she has lots of energy.
     Mariza is young, talented, and energetic.
   2 She sings both traditional songs and she sings more modern songs.
   3 You can either reserve in advance or it's possible to pay at the door.
   4 You can spend hours wandering around the old town, visiting cafés, and you can listen to live music.
   5 The music fuses traditional Spanish folk music and there are elements of North African music.

THE *FADO* OF LISBON by Jay Rowsell

People say about fado that either you'll love it or you'll hate it. One thing is certain: you can't ignore it. It has been compared to the blues because the songs are sad, but with fado the intensity of the emotion is greater, piercing the listener's body like a knife. Like the blues, fado tells of pain and hardship, but unlike the blues, it focuses on the pain of separation: of being away from either a loved one or your home, or something you can never regain. Perhaps that is not surprising when you consider that Portugal is a country with a long tradition of sailors and voyagers.

When I first saw a *fadista* perform in a dimly lit café one sultry evening in Lisbon twenty years ago, I was ignorant both of the fado music tradition and of the Portuguese language. But that didn't matter, because the sheer drama of the music told its own story. In those days, fado was a style of music known only in Portugal and a few of its former colonies: Brazil, Angola, and Mozambique. Now, with the help of stars like Mariza, it has an international following. Mariza has broadened fado's appeal by fusing it with other musical traditions, like Spanish flamenco and Brazilian jazz, and by touring the world with her music. But to hear traditional fado, you should go where its roots are: the Alfama district of Lisbon. You may hate it, but I suspect you will love it.

5 Write a 200-word description of a traditional type of music or dance. Include:

- information about the history of this tradition
- a description of how it is performed, what its appeal is, and the feelings it arouses
- where you can still find it being performed

6 Exchange descriptions. Did your descriptions:

- give a sense of the atmosphere?
- include strong descriptive language?
- speak to the reader personally?
- use parallel structures correctly?
- make you want to explore this kind of music?

It's the story of a rags to riches tale in Jamaica.

Before you watch

1 Work in pairs. Read the quotations (a–f) by the singer Bob Marley. Then discuss with your partner what adjectives could describe his attitude to life.

a Just because you are happy does not mean that the day is perfect but that you have looked beyond its imperfections.

b The truth is, everyone is going to hurt you. You just got to find the ones worth suffering for.

c Some people feel the rain. Others just get wet.

d Love the life you live. Live the life you love.

e The day you stop racing is the day you win the race.

f Better to die fighting for freedom than be a prisoner all the days of your life.

2 Work in pairs. If you were going to interview the director of a documentary about a famous musician's life, what questions would you ask? Write three key questions. Then compare your questions with another pair.

1 ....

2 ....

3 ....

While you watch

3 Watch the interview with Kevin Macdonald, the director of *Marley*, and compare your questions from Exercise 2 with the ones the interviewer asks.

4 Watch the first part of the video (to 00:54) and answer the questions.

1 What aspect of Marley's life did Kevin Macdonald feel had not been covered yet?

....

2 How does he describe the way people react when they hear Marley's music these days?

....

3 What does he hope the film will achieve?

....

5 Watch the second part of the video (00:55 to 01:51). Underline the words Kevin Macdonald uses when he describes Bob Marley's life story.

touching	fascinating
rags to riches	family troubles
personal suffering	crime
political activity	extraordinary
intense	racial issues
amazing	tough
violence	gangsters

6 Watch the third part of the video (01:52 to end) and complete the sentences about Bob Marley.

1 The first thing people like about him is that he is ....

2 More significantly he is very ....

3 He tries to offer people in hardship some ....

4 Because he's lived through tough times himself, you ....

5 He's the most listened-to artist in the world because his message is ....

6 The things he sings about are things we can all ....

After you watch

7 Roleplay an interview with the director

Work in pairs.

Student A: You are a movie director who has made a documentary about the life of a famous person. Think about the reasons you chose this person and what story you wanted to tell.

Student B: You are a reporter. You are going to interview a movie director about a recent documentary he or she has made about the life of a famous person. Prepare questions.

Act out the interview, then change roles and act out the interview again. Student B should choose a different famous person.

8 Work in groups and discuss these questions.

1 What situations can you think of where music brings people together?

2 What examples can you think of in your own culture?

afresh (adv) /ə'freʃ/ from the start again, as if for the first time
numerically (adv) /nu'merikli/ in terms of numbers
privilege (n) /'prɪvəlɪdʒ/ an honor
rags (n) /rægz/ old, poor clothes
sincere (adj) /sɪn'sɪər/ meaning what you say
solace (n) /'sɑlɪs/ comfort
tribulations (n) /ˌtrɪbjə'leɪʃənz/ difficulties, hardship

UNIT 9 REVIEW

Grammar

1 Read the article about the 1971 Concert for Bangladesh. What was its purpose? In what three ways was it successful?

2 Rewrite the sentences (1–4) in the first two paragraphs of the article using these words.

1 so as to	3 for
2 to	4 so that

The Concert for Bangladesh in 1971 was the first large benefit concert of its kind, staged [1] *in order to help victims of a disaster*. It was organized by Beatle George Harrison and Indian musician Ravi Shankar and attracted an audience of 40,000 people.

The show's aim was to raise money [2] *for the relief* of the refugee crisis following the cyclone that hit the country in 1970 and the Bangladesh Liberation War. The concert itself raised over $250,000, not counting the profits from the live album. The money went to UNICEF [3] *so that they could distribute it* to where it was needed most. Other famous music artists of the day, such as Bob Dylan, Billy Preston, and Eric Clapton, also performed [4] *to ensure as wide an audience as possible for the music*.

But the aim of the concert wasn't only to raise money. The organizers wanted people to be more aware of Bangladesh's problems. In this sense, according to Shankar, "It was fantastic." It also turned out to be the start of a new movement in benefit concerts. Under fifteen years later, Live Aid, a response to the Ethiopian famine, attracted a global TV audience of almost two billion.

3 Work in pairs. Insert the word *just* in the most appropriate place in each sentence in the last paragraph. In the first sentence you need to replace a word with *just*.

I CAN	
express purpose in different ways	
use *just* with different meanings	

Vocabulary

4 Match the words about music (1–8) with the correct definition (a–g).

1	eclectic taste	5	instrumental
2	strike a chord	6	face the music
3	a street performer	7	a ballad
4	play it by ear	8	soothing

a accept responsibility
b liking different kinds of music
c take things as they come
d having a calming effect
e one who plays music for money on the street
f seem relevant to
g a sentimental or romantic song
h (music) without singing

5 Work in pairs. Describe a song or a genre of music that you like and explain why you like it.

I CAN	
talk about music	
use music idioms	

Real life

6 Complete the dialogue.

A: How often do you actively listen to music?
B: I couldn't really [1] _____ you. Well, if you count turning on the radio, then maybe three or four times a day.
A: Do you use music when doing certain things, like driving or working at your computer?
B: I've never really [2] _____ about it, but, yes, I do. I often listen to music when I'm working.
A: And does it help you work, make you more productive?
B: That's a(n) [3] _____ question. I suspect that it's really more of a distraction.
A: How do you think you would feel without music in your life?
B: That's hard to [4] _____ . It would be less fun, I imagine. No, I [5] _____ don't know.

7 Work in pairs. Act out a similar conversation by asking each other the questions in Exercise 6.

I CAN	
talk about (my favorite) music and why I like it	
give myself time to think when responding to difficult questions	

Speaking

8 Work in pairs. Describe a piece of music that you have heard being played a lot on the radio or TV recently. Explain why you like it or dislike it.

Unit 10 Social living

Cinco de Mayo, a festival
celebrating the Mexican American
community, in Denver, US
Photograph by John McEvoy

FEATURES

1 Work in pairs. Look at the photo and caption. What festivals
or public holidays in your country celebrate a spirit of
community? How do they do this? Discuss with your partner.

2 Match the adjectives (a–d) with these words used to talk about
communities (1–4).

1 groups	a rich
2 migrants	b extended
3 family	c first-generation
4 heritage	d ethnic

3 Look at the questions and discuss with your partner.

1 Is there a strong sense of community where you live? What
kind of social gatherings take place, like street parties,
meals with friends, dances?
2 Do you think it's confusing to have two cultures, or is it a
positive thing? Why?

10a Good citizens

Rob Kevan volunteering in Snowdonia National Park

Listening

1 Work in pairs. Choose the correct option to complete each collocation.

1 _play_ **a part** in society
   a act   b play   c make
2 _do_ **one's part** for the community
   a make   b do   c take
3 _lend_ someone **a helping hand**
   a lend   b bring   c do
4 _take_ **responsibility** for your environment
   a hold   b keep   c take
5 _show_ **concern** for others who are less fortunate
   a take   b make   c show
6 _have_ **a say** in decisions that affect you
   a make   b take   c have

2 Look at the photo. In what way is Rob a good citizen? Which phrase(s) from Exercise 1 could be used to describe what Rob is doing?

3 🔊 **38** Listen and answer the questions.

1 What aspect of citizenship are schools focusing on?
2 What does the sociologist think young people should be encouraged to think about?
3 Do opinions of the duties of a good citizen vary from country to country?
4 What is an example of one of our basic duties to each other?

4 🔊 **38** Look at the phrases in bold used by the sociologist. Then listen again and write down what he is referring to or the example given in each case.

1 … **a hot topic** at the moment… _citizenship education_ _teaching children about laws/ institutions_
2 … I know **the intentions are good**…
3 … there were **some duties on a more human level**… _help people understand reasoning_
4 There were also **some unexpected findings**. _opinions of duties_ _Switzerland_

5 Work in groups. Think of three more public-spirited actions that people perform in their communities.

> ▶ **WORDBUILDING compound adjectives**
>
> Compound adjectives, which are a combination of an adjective + past participle, are sometimes connected by a hyphen.
> _clear-cut, open-minded, public-spirited_

Language focus tag questions

6 💿 **39** Listen to the questions below (1–6). Which one(s):

a ask(s) an open question?
b check(s) what you understand to be the case?
c isn't/aren't really asking a question but just offering agreement?

1 Surely any training is better than none, isn't it?
2 And what is the point?
3 And you think that kind of duty is closer to the spirit of good citizenship, do you?
4 And how did people rate these duties?
5 I imagine there wasn't that much difference in the way different nationalities responded, was there?
6 That is surprising, isn't it?

7 💿 **39** Listen again to the questions in Exercise 6 and answer the questions.

1 Does each question rise or fall at the end?
2 How would the meaning change in questions 1, 5, and 6 if the intonation were reversed?
3 What effect does the word "surely" have on the meaning in question 1?

> ▶ **TAG QUESTIONS**
>
> **Tag questions: checking (rising intonation)**
> *You haven't seen my glasses anywhere, have you?*
> *He works for the council now, doesn't he?*
> *You think that's right, do you?*
>
> **Tag questions: agreement (falling intonation)**
> *People just want an easy life, don't they?*
> *It isn't fair, is it?*
>
> **surely: opinions**
> *Surely that would be a better solution?*
>
> For more information and practice, see page 169.

8 Look at the language focus box. Then rewrite the statements in italics in these conversations as an appropriate tag question or *surely* question. There is sometimes more than one possibility.

1 A: *You follow the news a lot.*
   B: Yes, I do.
   A: *So you think it's important to keep up with political events.*
   B: Yes, very important.
2 A: *People aren't generally very public-spirited here.*
   B: No, I they aren't.
3 A: *It's up to each individual how much they participate in public life.*
   B: Not really. If they all kept to themselves, there would be no community.
   A: *Yes, but there will always be some people who want to get involved.*
   B: *So you think it can just be left to others.*

4 A: *It isn't pleasant to live in run-down surroundings.*
   B: No, but what can you do?
   A: *But you care what the city looks like.*
   B: Of course. I just don't have time to do anything about it.

9 Work in pairs. Discuss the tags for these questions. Then check your answers with your teacher.

1 I'm disturbing you, _____? (negative tag)
2 Nothing bad happened, _____? (affirmative tag)
3 You're ready to go, _____? (negative tag)
4 I know you, _____? (negative tag)

10 Pronunciation tag questions

a Work in pairs. Decide which sentences probably have a rising intonation at the end and which a falling intonation. Explain why.

1 You couldn't give me a hand, could you?
2 He would say that, wouldn't he?
3 You think I'm overreacting, do you?
4 Surely the answer is four, isn't it?
5 She didn't give a great performance, did she?
6 Let's go, shall we?
7 Nobody noticed I wasn't there, did they?

b 💿 **40** Listen and check your answers. Then practice saying the questions with your partner.

Speaking

11 Work in groups. Look at the statements from an international citizenship survey and rank them in order of importance. Then ask each other questions about your answers.

> *Surely people shouldn't have to vote in elections if they don't want to?*

It is the duty of a citizen:

1 always to vote in elections.
2 always to obey laws and regulations.
3 to be active in social associations.
4 to try to understand the reasoning of people with other opinions.
5 to choose products for ethical or environmental reasons, even if they cost more.
6 to help people at home and abroad who are worse off than yourself.

10b The civilized insect

Reading

1 Work in pairs. What do you know about ants? Think about habitat, diet, society, predators, etc. Discuss with your partner.

2 Look at these funny quotes from the animated movie *Antz*. What do they tell you about ants?

"When you're the middle child in a family of five million, you don't get any attention.

I wasn't cut out to be a worker. My whole life, I've never been able to lift more than ten times my body weight."

3 Read the article. What is the main reason ants are so successful?

4 Look at the text again. Are these statements true (T) or false (F)?

1 Ants aren't found in very cold places.
2 Ants' bodies vary in shape and size according to their function.
3 In some ways, ants can be said to think before they act.
4 They use strength in numbers to overcome enemies.
5 Individually, ants are more intelligent than people give them credit for.

The civilized insect

Ants number approximately ten thousand trillion worldwide. Each individual ant hardly weighs anything, but put together they weigh roughly the same as all of mankind. They also live nearly everywhere, except on icy mountain peaks and around the poles. No one knows precisely how many species there are, but it is estimated at over 20,000. For animals their size, ants have been incredibly successful, largely owing to their highly sophisticated social behavior.

In colonies that range in size from a few hundred to tens of millions, they organize their lives with a clear division of labor: a queen or queens whose job it is to reproduce; some fertile males who die shortly after mating with the queen; and sterile females who make up the main population of workers and soldiers, toiling away in a determined fashion. In some species, the bodies of these sterile females are adapted to different jobs: building and expanding the nest, foraging for food, defending against predators, and so on.

How they achieve this level of organization is even more amazing. Where we use sound and sight to communicate, ants depend primarily on pheromones, chemicals emitted by individuals and smelled or tasted by nestmates. A given species produces just ten to twenty signals, which, unlike human language, are entirely instinctive messages. A pheromone trail left by a foraging ant will lead others straight to where the food is. When an individual ant comes under attack or is dying, it sends out an alarm pheromone to alert the colony to mobilize as a defense unit.

In fact, when it comes to the art of war, ants are unsurpassed. They are completely fearless and will readily take on prey much larger than themselves, attacking in deadly swarms and overwhelming their target. Such is their dedication to the common good of the colony that workers

will also sacrifice their lives to help defeat an enemy.

Behaving in this altruistic and dedicated manner, these little creatures have flourished on Earth for more than 140 million years, long outlasting dinosaurs. Because they think as one, they have a collective intelligence greater than the sum of its individual parts, something you could hardly say of most species.

---

altruistic (a) /ˌæltruˈɪstɪk/ unselfish
colony (n) /ˈkɑləni / a group of animals or insects that live together
forage (v) /ˈfɔrɪdʒ/ search for food
sterile (adj) /ˈstɛrəl/ not capable of reproducing

Language focus adverbs

5 Answer the questions about the adverbs and adjectives in the article.

1 What kind of word does *precisely* complement? (para 1)
2 What kind of word does *incredibly* complement? (para 1)
3 How would you say *hardly weighs anything* using the word "almost"? (para 1)
4 In paragraph 3, is *straight* an adjective or an adverb in this context?
5 Why does the author say *in a determined fashion* rather than adding *-ly* to the adjective? (para 2)

> **ADVERBS**
>
> **Adverb + verb**
> *Ants react **quickly** when they are in danger.*
>
> **Adverb + adjective**
> *Ants' nests are **carefully** constructed.*
>
> **Adverbs with the same form as the adjective**
> *When threatened, ants mobilize **fast**.*
> *Ants work **hard** to improve the colony.*
>
> **Adverbs meaning *almost ... not***
> *There is **barely** any place on Earth that ants do not inhabit.*
>
> **Adverbs not formed with the *-ly* suffix**
> *They carry out their work **in a lively way**.*
> *They live **in an organized manner**.*
>
> For more information and practice, see page 170.

6 Look at the language focus box. Find one more example of each type of adverb form in paragraphs 4 and 5 of the article.

7 Transform the adjectives given into adverbs or adverbial phrases and put them into the correct place in each clause or sentence.

1 Ants are sophisticated creatures. (social)
2 Ants are cooperative, but they don't act towards each other. (friendly)
3 An ant can lift up to twenty times its body weight, whereas most people can lift their own. (bare)
4 You could say an ant's brain was big (hard), but in fact it has the biggest brain-to-body-size ratio of any insect.
5 A worker ant doesn't live (about 50 days) but a queen can live for decades. (long)
6 Some ants, when they attack other ant colonies, emit false pheromone signals to confuse the enemy. (clever)
7 Not all ants like to work. (hard)
8 The slave-maker ant steals eggs and makes the hatched ants work for it. (new)

Idioms animal verbs

8 Work in pairs. There are many verbs, used mainly in spoken English, that are derived from the names of animals. Each reflects a characteristic of that animal, for example, *to horse around* = to play or fool around. Look at the "animal verbs" and say what you think each means and the animal characteristic it reflects.

1 Stop **bugging** me—I need to finish this paper!
2 Take that shortcut; it **snakes through** downtown and will bring us to the highway.
3 You **wolfed** that **down**. Didn't you eat lunch?
4 He always tries to **duck out of** doing hard work.
5 The press have **hounded** him day and night ever since he broke the world 100 meter record.
6 He's just **parroting** what the teacher said. Hasn't he got his own views on the subject?

9 What animal verbs do you use in your own language? Do they translate into English?

Speaking

10 Work in pairs. Look at the photos.

Student A: Turn to page 154 and read the facts.

Student B: Turn to page 156 and read the facts.

Then take turns asking and answering the questions.

a How and why do starlings flock together?
b Why do bees make honey and why are they so important to human beings?

10c Living free?

Reading

1 What is meant by the term *hunter-gatherer*? How is their life different from farmers?

2 Work in pairs. Look at the map. What does it tell you? Why do you think this is?

3 Read the article and say which statement best summarizes what the author thinks about the Hadza way of life.

  a It's a good life but not practical for us nowadays.
  b It guarantees both health and harmony in society.
  c It's sustainable and we ought to imitate it.

4 Read the article again quickly and mark the things the Hazda have (✓) and don't have (✗). Then compare answers with your partner.

- working animals
- enemies
- sufficient food
- basic tools
- a lot of free time
- a government
- their own strict routines
- a difficult environment

5 Work in pairs. Explain what these phrases mean.

  1 Agriculture's rise, however, came with a price. (para 2)
  2 they've left hardly a footprint on the land (para 3)
  3 this honor confers no particular power (para 4)
  4 the Hadza are such gentle stewards of the land (para 5)
  5 the Hadza have lost exclusive possession of much of their homeland (para 5)
  6 Their entire life is one insanely committed camping trip. (para 6)

Critical thinking reading between the lines

6 Sometimes in articles, an author's views are not explicitly stated, but have to be inferred by reading between the lines. Answer these questions by reading between the lines.

  1 Do you think the author admires the Hadza, or not especially?
  2 Do you think the author has particular views on the question of how land should be used?

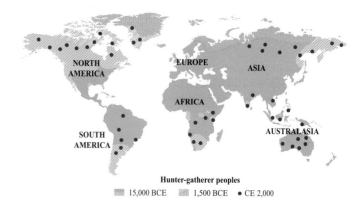

Hunter-gatherer peoples
▨ 15,000 BCE ▨ 1,500 BCE • CE 2,000

7 Work in groups. Compare your answers from Exercise 6 and refer to parts of the text that support your view. Did you agree or not?

Word focus *free*

8 Look at this phrase from the article. What does it tell you about the Hadza?

"There are many things to envy about the Hadza, including what **free spirits** they appear to be."

9 Work in pairs. Look at these other expressions using *free* and discuss what each one means.

  1 **Feel free** to make yourself a cup of tea or coffee.
  2 I wonder what he'll want in return for his help. **There's no such thing as a free lunch**.
  3 When the chairman lost control, the debate became **a free-for-all**.
  4 They were very particular about the text, but they gave us **free rein** on the design.
  5 Even though he was guilty, he **got off scot-free**.

10 Choose two of the following and talk about them from your own experience.

- a discussion that became a free-for-all
- a time you were given free rein to do something
- someone who is a free spirit

Speaking

11 Work in groups. You are going to take part in a discussion about the future of the Hadza lands. Look at your role and act out the discussion.

Student A: Turn to page 154.

Student B: Turn to page 155.

Student C: Turn to page 156.

The Hadza hunter-gatherers of Tanzania live a life that has not changed much in over 10,000 years. They have no crops, no livestock, no permanent shelters. In spite of long exposure to agricultural groups around them, who have domesticated both plants and animals, the Hadza have maintained their foraging lifestyle.

The story of the spread of agriculture is the story of growing population density. Villages formed, then cities, then nations. And in a relatively brief period, the hunter-gatherer lifestyle was extinguished in all but a few places. Agriculture's rise, however, came with a price. It introduced infectious disease epidemics, social stratification, intermittent famines, and large-scale war. Professor Jared Diamond of UCLA has called the adoption of agriculture "the worst mistake in human history"—one from which we have never recovered.

Looking at the Hadza, you can see why he came to this conclusion. They do not engage in warfare. They do not live densely enough to be threatened by an infectious outbreak. They have no known history of famine. The Hadza diet is more stable and varied than that of most of the world's citizens. They live almost entirely free of possessions. The things they own—a cooking pot, a water container, an ax—can be wrapped in a blanket and carried over a shoulder. They enjoy an extraordinary amount of leisure time, "working"—actively pursuing food—only four to six hours a day. And over all these thousands of years, they've left hardly a footprint on the land.

Hadza women gather berries and baobab fruit and dig edible tubers. Men collect honey and hunt. They will eat almost anything they can kill, from birds to wildebeest. The Hadza recognize no official leaders. Camps are traditionally named after a senior male, but this honor confers no particular power. No Hadza adult has authority over any other. None has more wealth; rather, they all have no wealth. There are few social obligations—no birthdays, no holidays, no anniversaries. People sleep whenever they want. Some stay up at night and doze during the heat of the day.

The chief reason the Hadza have been able to maintain their lifestyle so long is that their homeland is not an inviting place. The soil is briny; fresh water is scarce; the bugs can be intolerable. For tens of thousands of years, it seems, no one else wanted to live here. Recently, however, escalating population pressures have brought a flood of people into Hadza lands. The fact that the Hadza are such gentle stewards of the land has, in a way, hurt them; the region has generally been viewed by outsiders as unused, a place sorely in need of development. The Hadza, who by nature are not a combative people, have almost always moved away rather than fight. But now there is nowhere to retreat. Over the past century, the Hadza have lost exclusive possession of much of their homeland.

Living
free?

There are many things to envy about the Hadza, including what free spirits they appear to be. Free from schedules, jobs, bosses, bills, traffic, taxes, laws, social duties, and money. Free to grab food and run shirtless through nature. But who of us could live like them? Their entire life is one insanely committed camping trip. It's incredibly risky. Medical help is far away. One bad fall from a tree, one bite from a black mamba snake, and you're dead. Nearly half of all children do not make it to age fifteen. They have to cope with extreme heat and swarming tsetse flies. The fact is that it's too late for us to go back to a Hadza lifestyle. Of greater concern is that soon it may be impossible for them to remain in one.

confer (v) /kənˈfɜr/ give something (to somebody)
doze (v) /doʊz/ sleep lightly
social stratification (n) /ˈsoʊʃəl ˌstrætəfɪˈkeɪʃən/ different levels or classes in society
thorn (n) /θɔrn/ sharp point on a plant stem

10d An interesting subject

Real life making conversation

1 Work in pairs. Which of the following points are characteristics of a good listener? Discuss.

a maintains eye contact
b shows appreciation
c tries to predict what the other person is going to say
d waits before giving their views
e asks questions
f relates what they hear to their own experience

2 Are you a good listener? Which of the points in Exercise 1 are you good or bad at doing?

3 🔊 **41** You are going to hear a conversation about an assignment. Quickly read the task. Then listen and answer the questions.

1 Why does the first speaker initiate the conversation?
2 What topic has the second student chosen for his essay?
3 Is the first speaker interested to know more? Why?

> Throughout history, people have tried to establish ideal or "utopian" societies for others to follow. Research one of them and write an essay describing its principles and why you think it was an effective or ineffective model.

George Pullman

4 Speaking skill showing interest

🔊 **41** The speakers use phrases to show interest and keep the conversation going. Listen again and complete the phrases.

1 B: I've been researching a model society set up in the 1880s in Chicago by George Pullman…
   A: _____? _____ interesting.
2 B: … he based his society on capitalist principles, thinking that capitalism was the best way for a society to fulfill its material and spiritual needs.
   A: _____ .
   B: Yes, _____?
3 B: He owned all the buildings and rented them to the workers.
   A: _____ .
   B: No, _____?
4 A: So _____ it probably failed in the end then.
   B: _____ —these things often do.

> ▶ **SHOWING INTEREST**
>
> **Showing interest**
>
> | | |
> |---|---|
> | I got a "B" on my essay. | → Really? |
> | I'm going to Spain next month. | → Are you? |
> | Wonderful concert! | → Yeah, wasn't it? |
> | The weather doesn't look very good. | → No, it doesn't, does it? |
> | He left his job. | → Did he really? |
> | I'll give you a call some time. | → Please do. |
>
> **Responding naturally**
>
> | | |
> |---|---|
> | What are you doing here? | → Waiting. |
> | Are you going to the conference? | → I hope / think / suppose so. |
> | Will the store still be open? | → I don't think so. / I'm afraid not. / I doubt it. |
> | I'm coming down with a cold. | → Me too. |
> | I can't wait for summer. | → Me neither. |

5 Imagine you are researching an essay on a particular topic. Choose a subject that you know. With your partner, act out two conversations like the one you heard in Exercise 3.

I'm writing a paper on the Maya.

Oh, really?

Yes. Did you know they were incredibly advanced astronomers?

I think so… they had a very precise calendar, didn't they?

10e A good start in life

Writing a discursive essay

1 Choose the four items (a–h) that you think most help people to achieve professional success.

   a   wealthy parents
   b   a strong work ethic
   c   good social connections
   d   supportive friends or community
   e   ambitious parents
   f   a good education
   g   a high social status
   h   something else?

2 Work in groups. Discuss your answers. Does social background (upbringing, education, parents' jobs) play a big part in determining a child's prospects in life?

3 Read the essay. What is the main argument? Do you agree? Why?

4 **Writing skill critical thinking in writing**

Look at the four steps we use when writing a discursive essay (1–4). Which of the ideas from the essay (a–c) is the hypothesis, the thesis, and part of the analysis?

   1   think first about what the probable answer / your position is (your hypothesis)
   2   develop this into your main argument (your thesis)
   3   find evidence to support your argument (the analysis)
   4   repeat your main argument in the conclusion

   a   Children's prospects are clearly connected to their own opinion of what they can achieve.
   b   Those from high-income families hoped to become lawyers or doctors.
   c   Social background is important for success because it shapes your expectations in life.

Is social background an IMPORTANT FACTOR *in success?*

It is generally thought that to have a good chance of succeeding in life you need to have certain social advantages: wealthy parents, a high social status, and a privileged education. But I would argue that provided children are given the basic necessities of life—being fed and clothed properly, and being loved and cared for—then their prospects are determined only by their own opinion of what they can achieve. And that can be changed.

In a recent study, children in the city of Baltimore, US, were interviewed about their prospects. Their ambitions reflected their own experience. Those from high-income families hoped to become lawyers or doctors, because those were typical professions of their parents' friends. Those from poorer backgrounds wanted to be professional athletes or musicians, because those were the people who had succeeded in their communities. However, they expected to be electricians or hairdressers. At school, the more privileged children performed better, because they knew that if they got good grades, their prospects of becoming a lawyer or doctor were good. The children from poorer backgrounds had no such incentive and performed much worse. However, when their school offered cash prizes on condition that their grades improved, the improvement was immediate.

This shows that children's prospects are clearly connected to their expectations. While they have low ambitions, they will see no benefit in working hard at school and, as a result, they will not succeed. Some people always start life worse off than others, but where they end up is a question of what they believe is possible.

5 Write an essay of 250–300 words on the topic *How does social background affect a child's prospects in life?* Use the ideas that you discussed in Exercise 2.

6 Exchange essays with your partner. Use these questions to check your essays.

- Is the main argument clear?
- Does the essay outline the main argument at the beginning and end of the essay? Is it clear?
- Does the analysis support the main argument?
- Do you find the arguments logical and convincing?

Initiation with ants
Video

A grueling initiation is about to begin.

Before you watch

1 Work in pairs. Look at the definition of *initiation*. Can you think of an example of ceremonies for these occasions (a–d)?

> **initiation (n)** /ɪˌnɪʃiˈeɪʃən/ a ceremony or task that gives a person formal admission or acceptance into a club, organization, community, or family

a being born
b passing from childhood into adulthood
c marriage
d another occasion

2 You are going to watch a video about an initiation ceremony. What part do you think ants will play?

While you watch

3 Watch the video and check your answer from Exercise 2.

4 Watch the first part of the video (to 00:50) and complete the table about the initiation ritual.

1	The signal for the start of the initiation:
2	Length of ritual:
3	Age of participants:
4	Animal used in ritual:
5	Purpose of ritual:
6	Number of times participant must perform it:

5 Watch the second part of the video (00:51 to end) and answer the questions.

1 How powerful is the sting of these ants?

2 How is it possible to place the ants in the gloves without being stung?

3 Why don't the ants escape from the gloves?

4 What is the purpose of the dance?

5 What happens after the gloves are removed?

6 How does the new initiate react to his ordeal?

6 What does the chief say about the wider purpose of this ritual? Do you agree with him? Why?

7 Complete the summary based on the video, then check it.

The Sateré-Mawé tribe of the Amazon ¹_____ an extreme ritual for ²_____ that acts as ³_____ into manhood. Bullet ants ⁴_____ gloves, which ⁵_____ by the initiates ⁶_____ ten minutes while ⁷_____. These ants ⁸_____ sting of a bee and the initiates ⁹_____ gloves ¹⁰_____ twenty times. After the gloves are taken off, ¹¹_____ 24 hours. The chief of the tribe says that ¹²_____.

After you watch

8 Roleplay an interview about a ceremony

Work in pairs.

Student A: You are going to talk about a ceremony in your country. Choose a ceremony from the list or your own idea and prepare to talk about it.

- a naming ceremony for a child
- a rite of passage into adulthood
- a graduation ceremony
- a wedding ceremony

Student B: Imagine you are a foreign journalist. You are going to interview a local person about a local ceremony. Look at these points and prepare your questions.

- what the purpose of the ceremony is
- who participates
- what form the ceremony takes
- the origins and significance of the ceremony
- what it means to locals and what they like about it

Act out the interview, then change roles and act out the interview again. Student B should choose a new ceremony.

9 What's the most difficult thing you have had to do in front of a group of your peers?

---

carnivore (n) /ˈkɑrnɪˌvɔr/ meat eater
excruciating (adj) /ɪkˈskruʃiˌeɪtɪŋ/ very painful
medicine man (n) /ˈmedɪsɪn ˌmæn/ the person in a tribe who is supposed to be able to heal illnesses
mitt (n) /mɪt/ a glove without finger compartments
neurotoxic (adj) /ˌnʊroʊˈtɑksɪk/ poisonous to the nerves
stab (n) /stæb/ a wound made by a pointed object
stupor (n) /ˈstupər/ a state of near unconsciousness
swarm (n) /swɔrm/ a large group of insects, like bees
unfazed (adj) /ʌnˈfeɪzd/ not troubled or bothered
writhe (v) /raɪð/ move about in pain or trying to get free

UNIT 10 REVIEW

Grammar

1 Complete the interview by:

   a transforming the adjectives given (1–6) into their correct adverbial form.

   b rewriting the questions (a–d) as tag questions.

2 Read the interview again and answer the questions.

   1 What was the key to saving the coral reef in this area?

   2 Why is the proposed new development a danger to the marine park?

I = Interviewer, J = Javier Hernandez

I: Cabo Pulmo National Marine Park is a great example of how citizens can act [1] _____ (concerted) to effect change. We interviewed local environmentalist Javier Hernandez to find out more. Javier, [a] *was your main purpose to protect the reef*?

J: Yes, that's right. We were concerned because the reef was deteriorating [2] _____ (fast) and we needed help to save it.

I: And [b] *did you get the help of the government*?

J: Yes. By campaigning and lobbying [3] _____ (hard), we were able to get fishing banned in this area. After all the intensive fishing of the last 25 years, there were [4] _____ (hard) any fish left. The fish were part of a fragile ecosystem that supports the coral.

I: And [c] *has that changed*?

J: Absolutely. The project has been [5] _____ (incredible) successful. Stocks of fish have risen by 450 percent.

I: So [d] *can you relax now that you have won this particular battle*?

J: No! There's now a proposal to build an enormous tourist complex right next to the marine park, with a new marina, countless hotels, and stores. We're negotiating with the developers. The negotiations are being conducted [6] _____ (friendly), but if they fail, we are worried about the negative impact on the marine park.

Vocabulary

3 Complete the collocations.

   1 We are a very close-k_____ community.

   2 My father is a second-g_____ immigrant.

   3 I don't see a lot of my e_____ family: uncles, aunts, cousins, and so on.

   4 I try to do my p_____ for the community by helping to coach the local youth football team.

   5 My neighbors are always willing to lend a helping h_____ when someone needs it.

   6 Big festivals are part of our cultural h_____ .

4 Work in pairs. Discuss which of the statements in Exercise 3 are true about you. Explain your answers.

Real life

5 Match the statements (1–6) with the correct short response (a–f).

   1 I waited an hour to get a bus home last night.

   2 Are they going to close the street to traffic?

   3 I think the new community center is great!

   4 The team was amazing!

   5 I'll let you know if I need any more details.

   6 We're going to Madagascar this summer.

a Please do.	d Yes, they were, weren't they?
b I think so.	
c Are you? How exciting!	e Did you really?
	f Me too.

6 Work in pairs. Tell each other your news: what has happened to you recently, what your plans are, what you think about a recent event. Show interest and ask questions to get more information.

Speaking

7 Work in pairs. Discuss what aspects of social living you like best and which aspects you think are the most important for a healthy society.

Unit 11 Reason and emotion

Tree branch swing, India
Photograph by Jhulan Mahanta

FEATURES

1 Work in pairs. Look at the photo and describe the boy's feelings. Do you think that some emotions are universal? Which ones? Why?

2 Look at the adjectives for describing emotions. Put two adjectives under each heading. Which word in each pair has the stronger meaning?

annoyed	astonished	content	despondent	ecstatic
livid	miserable	petrified	scared	taken aback

Anger	Fear	Surprise	Happiness	Sadness
_____	_____	_____	_____	_____
_____	_____	_____	_____	_____

3 Choose two of the adjectives from Exercise 2 and talk about the last time or a memorable time when you felt this emotion.

I was really annoyed when I turned up for a concert the other week and they told me it had been canceled. They offered me a refund, but they should have contacted me ahead of time!

11a Emotional intelligence

Listening

1 Look at the definition of *emotional intelligence*. How emotionally intelligent do you think you are? Do you know anyone who is particularly emotionally intelligent?

> **emotional intelligence (EI)** the ability to recognize, judge, and control one's own and others' emotions

2 🔊 **42** Listen to an interview with a psychologist and answer the questions.

   a What service does she offer?
   b Why do people need it?

3 🔊 **42** Read the sentences. Then listen again and choose the correct option to complete them.

   1 EIQ's training helps people to tell positive from negative *influences / emotions*.
   2 More and more people around the world suffer from being *confused / nervous and worried*.
   3 Hikikomori are young Japanese who avoid *other people / their parents*.
   4 EIQ can help people overcome their fear of public *speaking / places*.
   5 Micro-expressions appear on the face only for a few *seconds / parts of a second*.
   6 Micro-expressions often show people's *darker / hidden* feelings.
   7 The presenter's micro-expression revealed his *surprise / irritation*.
   8 The doctor wanted to feel *more detached from / closer to* his patients.

4 Do you think Naomi is right that life has become more difficult to deal with emotionally? Why?

Idioms feelings

5 The idiom *on edge* was used in the interview to describe people who feel tense and nervous. Match the idioms with the feelings they describe.

> **Idioms**
> a little down   all over the place   on edge
> hot under the collar   speechless   upbeat

> **Feelings**
> angry   confused and disorganized
> optimistic   sad   tense and nervous
> very surprised

6 Work in pairs. Look at these sentences. Check your answers from Exercise 5.

   1 Sorry, I think I sent you the wrong document. And I've left my memory stick at home. I'm **all over the place** today.
   2 Don't worry about Paolo. He's just **a little down** after failing the test.
   3 Carla's very **on edge** today. Is she worried about something?
   4 I'm **upbeat** about our prospects of winning.
   5 He got **hot under the collar** when the dinner guests arrived an hour late.
   6 Frankly, I was **speechless** when she said she didn't think it would work. It was her idea in the first place!

Language focus unreal past

7 Look at the sentences (1–6) where the speaker uses a past form to talk about hypothetical situations in the present or future. Match them with the descriptions (a–d).

1 Do you wish that you **felt** more in control of things?
2 Perhaps it's time you **looked** into "emotional intelligence training."
3 Suppose you **were** someone who felt very on edge when speaking in public.
4 I'd rather your listeners **took** one of our courses.
5 What if I **were to tell** you that you'd already made one of these?
6 If only I **was** better at building rapport.

a   a wish
b   a picture of an unreal situation
c   a preference for what someone would like to happen
d   a sentence that says what should be done now

▶ **UNREAL PAST**

would rather / would just as soon
I'd rather you found someone else to give the talk.
I'd just as soon people decided for themselves.

I wish / if only
I wish / If only life was less stressful.
I wish / If only he would relax a bit more.

what if / supposing / suppose
What if we were to offer you a free trial?
Supposing he reacted badly. What would you do?

it's (high) time
It's (high) time that we got a new computer.

For more information and practice, see page 171.

---

8 Look at the language focus box. Then rewrite the sentences below using the words given.

1 I think he might be persuaded by more money.
   (Supposing / we / offer)
2 He really needs to organize his life better.
   (It's time / he)
3 Driving an hour to work each day is stressful.
   (I wish / have to)
4 I never have time to take a real vacation.
   (If only / I / be / able)
5 Can you let me see the letter before you send it?
   (I'd rather / you / show)
6 People do everything in such a hurry.
   (I wish / people / slow down)
7 He might refuse. What would you do then?
   (What if / he / say)
8 Do you have any good advice for me?
   (What / you / do / if)

9 Complete the conversation with one word in each space.

A: What if someone [1]_____ to offer you emotional intelligence training? What [2]_____ you say?
B: I think I [3]_____ be a little taken aback. I'd [4]_____ other people didn't tell me how I should feel or respond emotionally.
A: Don't you wish that you [5]_____ understand your own emotions better?
B: Maybe, but that doesn't mean I [6]_____ go and get training for it. [7]_____ the person didn't have any real qualifications? I'd just as [8]_____ trust my own instincts.

Speaking

10 Work in groups. Discuss the list of things that irritate people about modern life. Think of two more things each and explain why they irritate you. Agree on the three that are most irritating.

1   being stuck in traffic
2   waiting for things to download on the computer
3   receiving unsolicited calls at home from sales and marketing companies
4   people who talk loudly on their cell phones in public places
5   people cutting in front of you in line
6   parents who embarrass you thinking they are cool
7   delays on a flight, train, or bus
8   waiting for someone who is always late

I hate listening to other people's phone calls!
I would rather be stuck in traffic!

11b Thinking Fast and Slow

Reading

1 Work in pairs and discuss each situation. Would you follow your instinct or intuition? Or would you take your time thinking about it?

1. deciding whether to rent the first apartment you have looked at
2. expressing something in English that you are not sure of
3. giving money to someone collecting for a charity on the street
4. deciding what to wear to a party
5. giving your opinion in a debate

2 Read the article about rational and irrational thinking and say which statement (a–c) best summarizes Kahneman's theories.

a. We can often be irrational in our thinking.
b. We are essentially rational in our thinking.
c. We are completely unpredictable in our thinking.

3 Match the questions in the article (1–3) with what they tell us about the way we think (a–c).

a. that we carry a lot of preconceptions about the world with us
b. that we are not logical when it comes to taking risks
c. that we can be influenced in our thinking by irrelevant information

Thinking
FAST & SLOW

Psychologist Daniel Kahneman's work on how rational minds sometimes think irrationally won him the Nobel Prize in Economics because it is key to understanding people's behavior. Kahneman researched our irrational traits by asking intriguing questions. Here are three examples from his book *Thinking Fast and Slow*. Answer each one without thinking too hard. Should you get them wrong, don't worry: most of us do.

1. Roughly how many United Nations states are African?

2. Linda is a single 31-year-old, bright, and concerned with issues of social justice. Which statement is more probable: a) Linda works in a bank, or b) Linda works in a bank and is active in the feminist movement?

3 a. You can either have $500 for certain, or a 50 percent chance of winning $1,000. Which would you choose?

3 b. You can either lose $500 for certain, or have a 50 percent chance of losing $1,000. Which would you choose?

The answer to the first question is 53, but that's not important. What is psychologically interesting is that had someone already mentioned that the temperature today was 82° Fahrenheit, your answer would have been a higher number than if you had been told it was 28° Centigrade. The answer to the second question is that neither is more probable. However, an overwhelming number of people answer b. Were the same question presented as a logical formula, few would make this mistake. But we are influenced by the plausible details, preferring the human story to the hard logic. Logically, you should choose the same option in both 3a and 3b, but it seems that most of us take fewer risks when there's a chance of winning something. However, offered a chance to get out of a losing situation, most of us will take the gamble.

What Kahneman is trying to demonstrate is that our intuition can be unreliable and irrational. He describes our brain as having two systems: System One, where we form intuitive responses, and System Two, where more conscious, deliberate thought occurs. The problem is that on many occasions, System One is always trying to help, often with imperfect information. And the result can be imperfect, such as when making financial decisions. Some even say that had it not been for this irrational thinking, the banking crisis of 2008 might not have occurred.

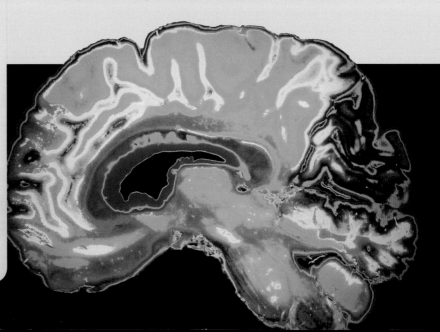

4 Find adjectives in the article with the following meanings.

1 interesting (para 1)
2 very large (para 2)
3 believable (para 2)
4 slow and careful (para 3)
5 incomplete, unsatisfactory (para 3)

5 Have you made any financial decisions that weren't based on rational calculation? What were they? Did they work out for you?

> ▶ **WORDBUILDING heteronyms**
>
> There are some words in English ending in *-ate* that have the same form as an adjective and as a verb. We use pronunciation to distinguish between them.
> *deliberate*: verb /dəˌlɪbərɪt/; adjective /dɪˌlɪbrət/

6 Pronunciation heteronyms

🔊 **43** Listen to the pairs of sentences. What is the difference in the pronunciation of the final syllable of each word in bold?

1 a Was that a **deliberate** mistake?
   b Don't **deliberate** for too long.
2 a We need to **separate** the groups.
   b That's a **separate** issue.
3 a He's very **articulate**.
   b He couldn't **articulate** what he meant.
4 a Let's not **duplicate** the work.
   b I have a **duplicate** copy.

Language focus inversion in conditionals

7 Look at these sentences from the article. Can you express exactly the same idea, beginning each sentence with *if*?

1 Should you get them wrong, don't worry.
2 Had someone already mentioned that the temperature today was 82° Fahrenheit, your answer would have been a higher number.
3 Were the same question presented as a logical formula, few would make this mistake.
4 Some even say that had it not been for this irrational thinking, the banking crisis of 2008 might not have occurred.

> ▶ **INVERSION IN CONDITIONALS**
>
> *should*
> *Should you need to contact me, I'll be at the Jianguo hotel.*
>
> **second conditional**
> *Were the price lower, I wouldn't hesitate to buy it.*
> *Were it not for me, you wouldn't be living here.*
>
> **third and mixed conditional**
> *Had I known earlier, I would have informed you.*
> *Had he not written the book, no one would know about this.*
>
> Notes
> 1 We use inversion in slightly more formal speech or writing.
> 2 The use of *for* + noun or *for* + *the fact that* is quite common in second and third conditional inversions.
> 3 We use the *were to* form only to talk about future possibilities, not unreal present situations.
>
> For more information and practice, see page 171.

8 Look at the language focus box. Then rewrite these conditional sentences using inversion.

1 If someone asks who told you, don't give them my name.
2 If I had thought about it for longer, I would have gotten the answer right.
3 They wouldn't be in this situation now if they had taken my advice.
4 If we took the risk, I am sure that we wouldn't regret it.
5 Would the world be a better place if everyone thought more carefully before acting?
6 If something is unclear, you can always call and ask.

9 Work in pairs. Write five sentences about yourself using inversion. Use the sentence stems below or make up your own. Then compare sentences with your partner.

1 Were it not for my parents…
2 I wouldn't be living here…
3 Had it not been for the bad weather…
4 I wouldn't have reached such a high level of English…
5 Had it not been for the fact that I…
6 I would have become a…

Speaking

10 Work in pairs. Look at these other Kahneman puzzles, taking no more than 30 seconds to answer each one. What point is Kahneman trying to make about the way we think in each case? Can you think of other situations where it isn't helpful to be an intuitive thinker?

1 A bat and a ball cost $1.10. The bat costs one dollar more than the ball. How much does the bat cost?
2 Imagine that you bought a ticket to see a play for $30. As you enter the theater, you discover that you have lost the ticket. The theater keeps no record of ticket purchasers. Would you pay $30 for another ticket to see the play?

11c Us. And them.

Reading

1 Look at the photos of the robots and answer the questions.

1 Which is real? Which are science fiction?
2 What do you think robots are able to do? What things can't they do?

2 Read the article and choose the correct option (a–c). At their current stage of development, robots can:

a only carry out industrial tasks.
b replace people in some simple jobs.
c already think and feel emotion.

3 Work in pairs. Write notes about what each robot can and can't do.

Yume   HERB   Vanderbilt prototype

4 Find words in the text with the following meanings.

1 make a sudden movement (para 1)
2 go to sleep briefly (para 2)
3 a great flow, a waterfall (para 4)
4 propelling or throwing an object at speed (para 6)
5 people without exerience in something (para 7)
6 copying (para 9)

Critical thinking understanding style

5 The author uses various techniques to keep this scientific subject light and prevent it becoming too serious. Match the phrases from the article (1–6) with the technique used (a–c).

1 ... a role that admittedly is not the most demanding. (para 2)
2 ... like a person who has lost interest... (para 2)
3 ... HERB isn't going to win any prizes for beauty (para 5)
4 ... a necessity if he is to help an elderly widow to the bathroom without catapulting her through the door. (para 6)
5 Picking up a drink is not a very difficult task for most of us. (para 7)
6 ... he takes the safest course of action and simply stands there, honking at everybody. (para 8)

a an amusing image
b an understatement
c a comparison with human appearance or behavior

6 Work in pairs. Compare your answers from Exercise 5 with your partner's. Did these techniques improve the article for you or not? Explain your reasons.

Word focus *move*

7 Work in pairs. Look at this expression with *move* from the text and discuss what it means. Then complete the other expressions with *move* using the words given.

"HERB is **on the move** but he still has his limitations."

mountains	a muscle
to tears	up in the world

1 Her story of having to look after her sick brother **moved everyone** _____ .
2 That's your Ferrari? You**'re moving** _____ .
3 Don't **move** _____ ! There's a bee on your collar. I'm going to brush it off.
4 Jack was called away on an emergency and will be out for a week. We're going to have to **move** _____ to make the deadline without him.

Speaking

8 Work in pairs. Which of the following occupations do you think robots should *not* be allowed to participate in and why?

a police work   c childcare
b healthcare   d public transportation

9 Ethical issues are always raised by technological progress. What rules should govern the use of these technologies?

- applications on phones that allow you to know where the user is
- genetic modification of foods
- open access to books and music on the Internet

US. & AND THEM.

Someone types a command into a laptop, and Actroid-DER jerks upright. She raises her arms and the corners of her mouth lift to form a smile. She blinks, then turns her face toward me. "Are you surprised that I'm a robot?" she asks. "I look just like a human, don't I?"

Her comment has the effect of drawing my attention to the many ways that she does not. Developed in Japan by the Kokoro Company, the Actroid-DER android can be rented to serve as a kind of receptionist at corporate events, a role that admittedly is not the most demanding. But in spite of the $250,000 spent on her development, Yume, as she is known, moves jerkily, and her inelastic features give her lovely face a crazed look. She also appears to nod off between remarks, like a person who has lost interest in a conversation.

Actroid androids are part of a new generation of robots, designed to function not as industrial machines but as agents capable of taking on roles in our homes, schools, and offices: cooking, folding the laundry, even babysitting our children. "In five or ten years, robots will routinely be functioning in human environments," says Reid Simmons, a professor at Carnegie Mellon University.

Such a prospect leads to a cascade of questions. How much everyday human function do we want in our machines? What should they look like? Do we want androids like Yume in our kitchens or are they just creepy? Will these robots change the way we relate to each other?

In another building not far away, HERB sits motionless, lost in thought. Short for *Home Exploring Robotic Butler*, HERB is being developed by Carnegie Mellon as a prototype service bot to care for the elderly and disabled. With Segway wheels for legs and computers for a body, HERB isn't going to win any prizes for beauty. But unlike Yume, HERB does have something like a mental life.

Traditional robots can be programmed to carry out very precise actions, but only within a very structured environment, like a factory production line. HERB is being programmed to "think" for himself: to negotiate human spaces and move around without bumping into people who are themselves in motion. HERB's perception system consists of a video camera and a laser navigation device which control his mechanical arm. The arm is pressure-sensitive: a necessity if he is to help an elderly widow to the bathroom without catapulting her through the door.

HERB can pick up a juice box, hold it upright, and place it down again gently. He can tell its shape and how easily it can break. To the uninitiated, these accomplishments might seem unimpressive. Picking up a drink is not a very difficult task for most of us. It's also a simple act for an industrial robot programmed for that specific action. But the difference between a social robot like HERB and a conventional factory bot is that HERB knows the object is a juice box, and not a teacup or a glass of milk. This understanding involves a great deal of mathematics and computer science, but it boils down to taking in information and processing it intelligently in the context of what he already knows about his world.

So HERB is on the move, but he still has his limitations. At the moment, he just has a digital bicycle horn that he honks to let people know he's getting near them; if a room is crowded, he takes the safest course of action and simply stands there, honking at everybody.

Other robots are now probing the world of human emotions. One prototype developed at Vanderbilt University plays a simple ball game with children. The robot monitors a child's emotions by measuring minute changes in heartbeat, sweating, and gaze. When it senses boredom or irritation, it changes the game until signals indicate the child is having fun again. There is no linguistic interaction, but it is a first step toward replicating a key aspect of humanity: recognizing others' feelings, and adjusting your behavior accordingly. But of course, as Yume admits, "I'm not human! I'll never be exactly like you."

android (n) /ˈændrɔɪd/ a robot with a human form
bot (n) /bɑt/ abbreviation for robot
prototype (n) /ˈprooʊtəˌtaɪp/ a first version of a machine

Unit 11 **Reason and emotion** 135

11d A sensitive subject

Real life recognizing feelings

1 Work in pairs. Read this part of a guide about communicating with people. Think of a situation when you didn't follow this advice. What happened? Discuss with your partner.

There are many opportunities for misunderstandings to arise in communication with others, whether in work relationships or simply between friends. And there is also a lot of advice about how to avoid them. But there is one simple tool in all types of communication that we should all bear in mind: if you feel something is wrong, ask. So if something strikes you as funny or strange or rude, or you think you have upset or offended the other person, just ask… sensitively, of course. Otherwise you will be left wondering what someone meant by a gesture or expression, or whether they were offended by, or misunderstood, something you said.

2 🔊 **44** Listen and answer the questions.

1   What is the relationship between each pair of speakers?
2   What is the subject of each conversation?

3 🔊 **44** Listen again. In each conversation there was a point of misunderstanding between the speakers. What was it?

a   Conversation 1: ....
b   Conversation 2: ....
c   Conversation 3: ....

4   Speaking skill recognizing others' feelings

🔊 **44** Look at the box. Then listen to the conversations again. Which expressions were used in the following situations?

1   Fernando asked Phil if everything was OK.
2   Alicia recognized Becky's feelings.
3   Becky corrected the impression she gave.
4   Megumi asked Paul about his feelings.
5   Paul corrected the impression he gave.

> ▶ **RECOGNIZING OTHERS' FEELINGS**
>
> You look a little puzzled / surprised / upset.
> You seem concerned / worried.
>
> I'm sorry, I didn't mean to offend you.
> Did I say something to upset you?
> Did I say something funny?
> Sorry, I don't understand what's so funny / what the joke is.
>
> Sorry, perhaps that sounded a little abrupt.
> I'm sorry, that came out wrong.
> Please don't think I'm rude / ungrateful / nosy, but…

5   Pronunciation adjectives ending in -ed

a 🔊 **45** Work in pairs. How are these adjectives pronounced? Listen and check.

alarmed	concerned	distressed	embarrassed
insulted	offended	shocked	surprised
worried			

b What are the rules about the pronunciation of adjectives ending in *-ed*? Think of three other adjectives describing feelings that end in *-ed*. How are they pronounced?

c Practice saying the words in Exercise 5a again with the correct pronunciation.

6 Work in pairs. Improvise a conversation based on one of the situations below. Use phrases from the box in Exercise 4.

• a misunderstanding between colleagues about who was supposed to do a certain job
• a friend finding something funny that was not intended to be a joke
• a discussion between colleagues about some work that was not done correctly

11e Don't get me wrong

Writing an email message

1 Work in pairs. Discuss the questions.

1 It's said that up to 40 percent of all emails are misinterpreted in some way. Why do you think this happens?
2 When was the last time you had an email misunderstanding? What happened?

2 Read the paragraphs and compare the answers you discussed in Exercise 1.

It's very easy to be misunderstood in an email. That's because people treat email like a face-to-face conversation, where exchanges can be very short and to the point. But of course they are *not* the same. In face-to-face conversation, we communicate our feelings with gestures, expressions, and tone of voice, as well as words.

In email writing, both the writer and reader imagine the tone. So if the reader is feeling particularly sensitive, he or she might take offense at something that the writer intended to be a joke. Or if the writer tries to express urgency about something that needs doing, the reader might interpret this as impatience, frustration, or anger, when really it's nothing of the kind.

3 Match each email that caused a misunderstanding (A–F) with how the reader interpreted it (1–6).

1 You have ignored my wishes.
2 You are asking for my advice on something I am not included in.
3 You think I can't spell.
4 You think I'm always slow to get things done.
5 You think my ideas are worthless.
6 You think I am ignoring you.

A I got your report. I honestly didn't expect to see it until the end of the month.

B Thanks for letting me know about the party next Saturday. I thought you were going to do it on one of the days I said I could come, but never mind.

C I read your suggestions and I think we will stick to the original plan.

D Five of us have been offered the chance to visit the new Williams factory next week. There are two other people whom I want to invite, not to include you: Vikram and Malik. What do you think?

E Thanks for the email. I don't know about the "optinos" because I don't know what that means! But if you want my opinion, I think the Berkeley chairs are the best option.

F I emailed you two days ago. Please reply today or we'll miss the deadline.

4 Writing skill avoiding misunderstandings

Use the phrases for avoiding misunderstanding (1–8) to rewrite the emails and make them clearer. In some cases you can use more than one phrase, but in D you only need to correct the grammar.

1 Don't take this the wrong way.
2 No offense intended.
3 I don't want to pressure you.
4 I'm joking, of course.
5 It took me somewhat by surprise.
6 Many thanks for getting back to me so quickly.
7 I do appreciate all your work on this.
8 I am not offended in any way.

5 A colleague at work has told you that your department is going to be closed down. Write an email to your boss to find out: why the decision was made, if he had anything to do with it, and what is going to happen to the employees in your department.

6 Exchange emails with your partner. Check if:

- the email is clear in its purpose.
- it contains any mistakes (grammar or spelling).
- its tone is clear and cannot be misinterpreted.

11f Self-teaching robots

Video

This robot solves problems like we do.

Before you watch

1 Work in pairs. Look at the list (a–d) of "intelligent" machines and programs that make decisions for themselves. Which are useful and which annoying?

a a parking sensor on a car
b a warning system in a car that tells you when you are not wearing a seatbelt
c an automatic spelling check on a computer or phone
d speech recognition systems in a car or computer

2 How do you think a robot could "learn" new things? Discuss with your partner.

While you watch

3 Watch the video and answer the questions.

1 How does the robot teach itself?

2 What are the creators' ambitions for this type of robot?

4 Watch the first part of the video again (to 01:21) and complete the notes.

> **Name of robot:**
> The Real World [1] _____ (RWGPS)
> **Creator:**
> Tokyo [2] _____
> [3] _____ of project:
> Dr. Osamu Hasegawa
> **Aim of project:**
> to [4] _____ robots and the real world
> **Task given to robot:**
> serving [5] _____
> **Information NOT given to robot:**
> prior knowledge of [6] _____
> **How the robot solves the problem:**
> analyzes [7] _____ and applies filters

5 Watch the second part of the video (01:22 to end) and mark the sentences true (T) or false (F).

1 The robot was programmed to pick up a cup.
2 The robot uses information from the Internet to make an "intelligent" decision.

3 The robot uses Google to research specific items, much like we do.
4 Learning moral values is not a realistic ambition for this robot.

After you watch

6 **Roleplay presenting an idea for a household robot**

Work in pairs.

Imagine you have been asked to present an idea for a robot which can do some household chores. Look at the list of chores (a–h) and decide which one would be most useful. Design the concept for a robot to do this chore. Consider how sophisticated the robot would have to be and how it would work (in simple terms). It could be either an android-type robot or a simpler, more industrial-type robot. Try to anticipate potential problems.

a ironing
b vacuum cleaning
c sorting and taking out the trash
d making the beds
e watering the plants
f walking the dog
g dusting/cleaning surfaces
h cooking

Present your ideas to another pair and answer their questions.

7 Work in groups and discuss these questions.

1 Did watching the video and listening to your classmates' ideas change your opinion about the possibilities for robots to help humans? Why?
2 What other chores or tasks in your daily life would you like robots to help you with? How realistic do you think it is that this will be a possibility in the future?

> **core** (n) /kɔr/ the heart or center of something
> **educated guess** (n) /ˈedʒʊ,keɪtɪd ˈges/ a speculation based on a reasonable amount of knowledge or information
> **invaluable** (adj) /ɪnˈvæljuəbəl/ very valuable
> **irrelevant** (adj) /ɪˈreləvənt/ unimportant; not related to the subject in question
> **moral values** (n) /ˈmɔrəl ˈvæljuz/ a set of beliefs about what is right and wrong
> **scour** (v) /skaʊər/ search a place very thoroughly

UNIT 11 REVIEW

Grammar

1 Complete the article by putting the verbs in the correct form. Note that the last two are examples of inversion in a conditional sentence.

2 Answer the questions about the article.

    1 What is the problem with this type of test?
    2 Is this the participants' fault? Why?

3 Work in pairs. Answer the statements (1–6) in the article. Discuss what you think each answer tells you about a person's emotional intelligence.

Look at these statements from a test of emotional intelligence and choose one of the following answers: *certainly true*, *probably true*, *probably untrue*, or *certainly untrue*.

1 I'd rather not _____ (give) my opinion if it risks offending someone.
2 I'd rather others _____ (tell) me the truth even if it is sometimes painful.
3 I wish I _____ (can) control some of my bad habits, but I can't.
4 If I _____ (have) to list my main strengths, I'd have no trouble thinking of them.
5 Unless _____ (someone / praise) my work, I am not happy with it.
6 _____ (I / be asked) to do something unethical, I would refuse.

Did you answer the questions honestly? Probably not entirely.
7 _____ (you / be instructed) to be as honest as possible before you started, you might have been more truthful, but only a little. Why is this? The problem with measuring emotional intelligence is that it relies heavily on the subjects' knowing their own feelings and being truthful in their responses. Many of us would be inclined to give untruthful responses about our weaknesses because we all have a natural tendency to play down our faults.

Vocabulary

4 Choose the correct option.

    1 I'm not panicking. I just feel a bit *on edge / upbeat*.
    2 I wasn't just angry. I was absolutely *hot under the collar / livid*.
    3 To say I was surprised is an understatement. I was completely *ecstatic / speechless*.
    4 Don't worry. He's not miserable; he's just feeling *astonished / a little down* at the moment.
    6 I am absolutely *petrified / scared* of spiders.

5 Work in pairs. Think about your first day in a new job or at a new university. Describe what happened and what your feelings were.

Real life

6 Work in pairs. Read the situations and complete the phrases that recognize other people's feelings.

    1 *The other person is looking anxious.*
        _____ concerned. Is everything OK?
    2 *You are aware that what you said was quite direct.*
        I'm sorry, maybe that _____ .
    3 *You want to decline an offer politely.*
        Please don't _____ , but I think I can manage.
    4 *The other person looks a little hurt by what you said.*
        I'm sorry, I hope _____ .
    5 *You said something that you didn't intend to say.*
        I'm sorry, that came _____ .

7 Work in pairs. Improvise a short conversation where there's been a misunderstanding. Your friend borrowed your laptop but hasn't returned it so you speak to her about it, or some other situation.

Speaking

8 Work in pairs. Are you a more rational person or do you like to trust your feelings? Discuss with your partner and give an example of this.

Unit 12 Landscapes

A landscape in Tuscany, Italy
Photograph by Gianluca Colla

FEATURES

1 Working in pairs, look at the photo. How would you describe the landscape? What kind of landscapes do you like (natural, agricultural, urban)? Why?

2 Write in the adjectives that are used to describe these features of landscapes. More than one answer may be possible.

bleak	cloudless	idyllic	lush	monotonous	nighttime
open	rich	rolling	rustic	snow-capped	sparse

a _____ environment   a _____ skyline

_____ vegetation   _____ hills

a _____, flat landscape   _____ meadows

a _____ sky   _____ farmland

_____-_____ mountains   _____ plains

a pretty _____ scene   _____, gentle countryside

3 Work in groups. Think of examples of the following in your country and tell the rest of the group.

- a landscape that you associate with your childhood
- dramatic changes of scenery
- blots on the landscape

12a Under the big sky

Reading

1 Look at these two quotations about the American West. What do you think the West represents for Americans? What do *you* associate with the West?

> Washington is not a place to live in. Go West, young man, go West and grow up with the country.
>
> *Horace Greeley, editor*

> So I pulled the sun screen down and… and kept on moving west. For West is where we all plan to go some day.
>
> *Robert Penn Warren, poet*

2 Work in pairs. Look at the photo and think of three adjectives or adjective + noun collocations you would use to describe this landscape. Discuss with your partner.

3 Read the article and answer the questions.

1 Where has Allard worked and what kind of photos does he take?
2 What does he feel about the American West?

Under the big sky

In a career spanning fifty-odd years, American portrait and landscape photographer William Albert Allard has shown us people and places as he sees them. Much of his work, well over forty photographic assignments in fact, has been for *National Geographic*. One of his colleagues said, "Before Bill arrived, the stuff in the magazine was travel-postcard photography." He claimed that Allard was instrumental in bringing a more intimate and personal style to photojournalism in the magazine. The assignments have taken him to dozens of countries all over the world, but Allard's heart remained in the West, as he explained in an article.

"It was a summer day in 1969. There had been no rain for weeks. A seventeen-year-old boy from Stanford, Montana, said you can tell it's really dry when a single rider can kick up a dust trail. We stopped with our horses at a stream. The water was cool and tasted of the earth. 'Do you ever feel like leaving your community here?' I asked.

"'No,' the boy said. 'It must be kind of rough on the outside, all alone, trying to make a living. Don't you think?' 'Yes,' I told him. 'It can be all of that.'

"Since that innocent exchange, I've spent much of my life traveling the world. I've seen a lot of wonderful places. But the American West never left me. It kept drawing me back.

"Raised further east in Minneapolis, I didn't get my first look at the West until around 1965. I can still remember one early morning in Wyoming, the first light on high mountain meadows, the wisps of clouds within my reach. That look demanded another look, and another, until I found myself seeking any excuse, some idea for a story that would lead me back from the East, where I had moved, to that grand expanse.

"If we're lucky, we all find some place special to us. Even though it may change with time, if we love it deeply enough, there is a part of it within us to the end. That's how I feel about the West."

4 Look at the statements. Then find and underline phrases in the article which support these statements.

1 Allard brings his own individual perspective to his photography. (para 1)
2 *National Geographic* photos used to be unexceptional. (para 1)
3 Riding horses is part of Montana's culture. (para 2)
4 The West had a magnetic pull on Allard. (para 4)
5 Land and sky seem close together in the West. (para 5)

Language focus approximation

5 Compare the pairs of sentences. What effect do the words in bold have on the meaning?

1 a In a career spanning fifty years.
  b In a career spanning fifty-**odd** years.
2 a Before Bill arrived, the photos in the magazine were travel-postcard photography.
  b Before Bill arrived, the **stuff** in the magazine was travel-postcard photography.
3 a It must be rough on the outside.
  b It must be **kind of** rough on the outside.
4 a I found myself seeking an idea for a story.
  b I found myself seeking **some** idea for a story.

6 Find examples of the following in the text.

1 two more approximate numbers (paragraph 1)
2 an approximate date (paragraph 3)
3 one more use of *some* (in paragraph 6) to mean an unspecified thing

---

▶ APPROXIMATION

Numbers
fifty-odd years; fifteen or so people
forty magazine articles, give or take
some / around / about / roughly six houses
dozens of letters; in the next day or two
(well) under / over a hundred messages

Adjectives
it's kind of* difficult
a grayish color

some
We all have some place which is special.
Can you give me some idea when you will arrive?

Vague words
One moment, please. I'll just get my things.
There's some strange stuff* in my coffee.

* more colloquial
Note: The suffix *-ish* is usually added to words describing physical features (like size, color, or time).

For more information and practice, see page 172.

---

7 Look at the language focus box. Read the text below and replace the underlined words with expressions of approximation.

[1] Five years ago, I took a trip to Madagascar to photograph the landscape. An amateur photographer I had met at [2] a party told me it had the most wonderful scenery. Normally, I spend [3] two months researching a place before I go there. But in this case, I had only a [4] short amount of time before I had to be back. So, I packed my [5] belongings and left the next day. During the course of the assignment, I took [6] 2,000 pictures. The photographer that recommended Madagascar said the landscape was [7] varied. That was a huge understatement. There's desert, marshes, rainforest, sandy beaches, and rocky coves; and all of this is home to [8] more than 200,000 different species of plants and animals.

8 Work in pairs. Use expressions of approximation to describe the following.

• how near you live to the sea (about)
• the number of months/years you've been living here (odd)
• the color of some aspect of the landscape around you (hills, trees, buildings) (*-ish*)
• the number of high-rise buildings in your town or city (over)
• the kind of leisure activities people can do in this area (stuff)

Speaking

9 Work in pairs. Describe to your partner a place that is special to you, including these items.

• where it is and its main features
• what the land is used for
• your favorite season (or time of day) there
• what you do there
• why it is special to you

12b Nature close up

"Narrow road to a far province." *Haiku*

Listening

1 The 17th-century Japanese poet Basho is famous for his haikus about nature. Look at the haiku and say what the form of a haiku is: how many lines, how many syllables per line, and how many syllables in total.

2 🔊 **46** Listen and answer the questions.

subject of our nature.

1 What attracted the biographer to Basho?
2 Why did Basho make his long journey across Japan? *Get away from it all - get closer*
Was quite a celebrity
3 Why does she think haikus are good at describing nature? *→ polished - beauty of* *nature*

3 🔊 **46** Work in pairs. What did the biographer say about each of the things below? Discuss with your partner. Then listen again and check. *simplicity of nature in a few words.*

1 a particular flower *- brilliant color*
2 the spray from a waterfall *- light catches spray of water*
3 a floating leaf *- floating the... reflection*
4 a frog *making a splash*
5 an avenue of trees

> ▶ **WORDBUILDING suffix *-ity***
>
> We add *-ity* to some adjectives to form a noun describing a state.
> *intense → intensity*
> Note that there are some irregular formations.
> *celebrated → celebrity, simple → simplicity*

Idioms **adjective collocations**

4 Does the expression in bold below mean *extremely clear* or *moderately clear*?

"reflections in a **crystal clear** stream"

5 In all these other expressions except two, the first word does the intensifying. Underline the two expressions where the second word intensifies.

bone dry	rock hard
brand new	scared stiff
fast asleep	sopping wet
freezing cold	stone cold
lightning quick	wide open
pitch black	worried sick

An old silent pond…
A frog jumps into the pond,
splash! Silence again.

Basho

6 Work in pairs. Choose three of the phrases from Exercise 5 and put them into sentences that describe situations from your own experience. Then tell your partner.

> *Once on vacation, we got lost and had to find our way back in the pitch black. I was scared stiff.*

Language focus qualifiers

7 Look at the sentences (a–f) and the underlined qualifiers. Answer the questions.

1 What kind of word is being qualified?
2 What effect does the qualifier have on this word?

a Observing nature is <u>a bit of</u> a luxury.
b That's <u>quite</u> interesting, because one of his preoccupations was observing nature.
c But <u>fairly</u> late in life, he decided he needed to get away from it all.
d He was actually already <u>quite</u> a well-known poet in his lifetime.
e So he traveled a distance of <u>slightly</u> less than 1,200 miles.
f It <u>rather</u> upset him.

▶ QUALIFIERS

quite, pretty, really, kind of, and fairly
It's quite / fairly / pretty / kind of unusual to see a double rainbow.
It's quite a steep path.
It's a fairly / pretty easy climb.
I really enjoyed meeting her.

rather
It's a rather long way. OR *It's rather a long way.*
The book was rather good, I thought.

slightly, a little, a bit
I was slightly / a little / a bit disappointed to miss the sunset.
The other beach is slightly / a bit / a little further away.
I regret it slightly / a little / a bit.
Notes
1 *quite* comes before "a" when modifying adjective + noun
2 the meaning of these words can depend on the intonation

For more information and practice, see page 173.

---

8 Look at the language focus box. Then cross out the qualifier which does not fit in each sentence.

1 Basho was *rather / quite / fairly* a modest man.
2 Basho also suffered *a bit / quite / slightly* from health problems.
3 It's *a bit of / pretty / quite* difficult to imagine how he managed such a journey.
4 The route he took has now become *a bit of / pretty / quite* a famous trail in Japan.
5 A haiku is a *fairly / pretty / quite* short poem.
6 Sometimes, when translated, they are *really / a bit / slightly* shorter.
7 I *pretty / quite / rather* like reading his poetry.
8 It's *quite / rather / a little* easy to see why it's so popular.

9 Make sentences about your feelings about the following. Use qualifiers from the language focus box to express your feelings about:

- going for long walks.
- reading poetry.
- how easy it is to enjoy nature in your area.

Speaking and writing

10 Work in pairs. Think of two more examples of "nature close up," like the ones in the photos: small things that strike you as interesting or beautiful. Describe them to your partner and explain why you chose them.

> *I really like snow storms. Everyone stays in and even the busy city streets seem rather peaceful and clean.*

> *Yes, snow is pretty relaxing... until you have to shovel!*

11 Now put one of your ideas from Exercise 10 and try to put it into the form of a haiku. Follow the rules of a haiku from Exercise 1.

12c Room with a view

Reading

1 Work in pairs. Do you have pictures on your walls at home: paintings, posters, or photos? What are they of?

2 Look at the photo of a picture on a wall in a room. Then read the article about a camera obscura and note down the steps in the process used to make this picture. Compare notes with your partner.

3 Read the article again. Are the sentences true (T) or false (F), or is there not enough information (N)?

1 The picture produced by a camera obscura is always clear.
2 The effect produced by a camera obscura has been known to people for centuries.
3 The modern camera is based on the same principle as the camera obscura.
4 The technical explanation for this phenomenon is not very complicated.
5 Vermeer used a type of camera obscura to achieve effects in his paintings that other artists were not able to.
6 Morell was the first person to try to photograph the effects produced by a camera obscura.
7 Morell's first photograph of a camera obscura image was of a toy shop outside his house.
8 Morell wanted to create a new movement within art photography.

Critical thinking identifying aims

4 Which of these things could be done using information in the article? Give reasons.

1 make a camera obscura
2 make a shoebox camera
3 take a photo of an image in a camera obscura

5 Which of these were the author's reasons for describing the camera obscura?

a so readers could do it themselves
b so readers could appreciate both how it is done and the results
c so readers could appreciate only the results

Word focus *space* and *room*

6 Work in pairs. Look at the text from the article (a–b). Are the words *space* and *room* interchangeable? What about in the other sentences (1–3)?

a …when light enters a dark **space** through a tiny hole. (para 2)
b He chose a **room** in his own house in Quincy, a Boston suburb. (para 6)

1 Do you have any **room** in your bag for my laptop?
2 I'm sorry I took so long. I couldn't find a parking **space**.
3 I love the feeling of wide open **space** around me.

7 Look at the sentences and say (a) which word (*space* or *room*) completes the expressions, and (b) what each expression means. Sometimes both words are possible.

1 I really think you should **give her some** _____ . She's very upset after the argument with Wei.
2 Everyone knows that he's unreliable, but no one wants to say it. That's **the elephant in the** _____ .
3 After exams, we'll have some **breathing** _____ .
4 His English is much better, but there's still _____ **for improvement**.

Speaking

8 Work in pairs. Discuss how you think the photographic effect below was achieved. Check the answer on page 153.

9 Prepare a description of one of the techniques below used to produce a particular effect. Explain it to your partner.

- a cooking technique (like making perfect rice)
- a dancing technique (like moonwalking)
- a DIY technique (like hanging wallpaper)
- a technique in a particular sport (like tennis)

ROOM WITH A VIEW

It's 1988 and Cuban-born Abelardo Morell is in a classroom in Boston teaching an introductory photography course. He covers the classroom windows with black plastic, making the space as dark as possible, and cuts a dime-sized hole in the plastic. Almost instantly the back wall comes alive like a movie screen, its surface covered with an upside-down, fuzzy image of people and cars moving along the street outside, sky on floor, ground on ceiling, as if the laws of gravity have gone haywire.

Something strange and wonderful happens when light enters a dark space through a tiny hole. Aristotle described the phenomenon in the 4th century BC. Leonardo da Vinci sketched the process, and 19th-century seaside tourists lined up to see demonstrations of it.

Morell had turned his classroom into a camera obscura ("dark room" in Latin), perhaps the earliest known imaging device, and the ancestor of the photographic camera. Like an eye, a camera obscura receives images through a small opening. Light enters the hole at an angle, the rays reflected from tops of objects, like trees, traveling downwards, and those from the lower plane, say flowers, traveling upwards, all crossing inside the dark space and forming an inverted image. It seems like a miracle, but in fact it's basic physics. The brain automatically rights the eye's image; in a regular camera, a mirror flips the image. Here, it remains upside down.

A portable version of the camera obscura, a box with a small hole fitted with a lens, first became popular in the 17th century and was used by painters like Vermeer and Canaletto as a drawing aid. Some claim that Vermeer must have traced over the image to achieve such accurate perspective in his paintings. Scientists also used the camera obscura to observe solar eclipses, just as children do today with pinhole cameras made from shoe boxes. Then, in the early 1800s, innovators began inserting chemically treated paper or metal plates at the back of the boxy camera obscura

to capture the image, and the art of photography was born.

When Morell saw how fascinated his students were by the ghost-like images that appeared on the wall, he decided to try to photograph the effect. To his knowledge, it had never been done before. It took months to master the technique, to figure out the right size of hole to allow both brightness and sharpness and to determine the right exposure time.

He chose a room in his own house in Quincy, a Boston suburb. He set his camera on a tripod in his son's bedroom in front of the camera obscura image, opened the shutter, and left the room—for eight hours. The result was mesmerizing. The developed picture showed inverted trees and houses across the street hovering over the boy's toys like a

scene from a fairy tale. "I was giddy," Morell said. "It felt like the moment photography was invented." From that eureka moment, Morell has gone on to produce a series of original and enthralling photographs. His views range from New York City panoramas to warm Italian vistas.

Replacing film with a more light-sensitive digital sensor, he cut exposure times from hours to minutes, permitting him to capture clouds and shadows. He is most excited about his work with a floorless tent: a portable camera obscura that he takes to rooftops or parks or city streets to project images directly onto the ground. By melting the boundaries between landscape and dreamscape, Morell hopes that he will "refresh how people see the world."

dime (n) /daɪm/ a small American coin
eureka /yʊˈrikə/ a Greek expression meaning "I've found it!"
exposure (n) /ɪkˈspoʊʒər/ the time the light is allowed to enter the camera
flip (v) /flɪp/ turn over
giddy (adj) /ˈgɪdi/ greatly excited
lens (n) /lenz/ a piece of glass through which the image enters the camera
shutter (n) /ˈʃʌtər/ the part of a camera that opens and shuts to allow the image in

12d A stain on the urban landscape

Real life a debate

1 Read the text. Can you guess what word should go in each space?

> Although it's said the Great Wall of China is the only man-made thing you can see from space, in fact it is man-made pollution in our cities that is most visible on the landscape: ¹ _____ pollution in the day and ² _____ pollution at night.

2 In pairs, look at the facts below about the world's top six most congested cities. Guess which cities they are.

1 In 2008, this South American city had a record 160-mile (265 km) traffic jam.
2 In 2010, a 62-mile (100 km) traffic jam took ten days to clear in this Asian capital.
3 This is Europe's most congested city.
4 Europe's most romantic city also holds the record for the worst traffic jam ever: 18 million cars!
5 In this eastern European capital, 38 percent of the roads are always congested.
6 This city in Latin America records the world's highest "commuter pain" (stress, lost time, and poor health).

3 Think of two ways traffic congestion could be reduced in big cities. Then exchange ideas with another pair.

4 Speaking skill interrupting

a 🔊 **47** Listen to an extract from a local meeting about traffic congestion in a city and answer the questions.

1 What ideas to reduce traffic congestion are presented?
2 What are the two points of debate about the first idea?

b 🔊 **47** During the discussion, different speakers interrupted each other. Look at the box. Then listen again and underline the phrases that the speakers used to interrupt and prevent interruptions.

▶ INTERRUPTING

Interrupting
Excuse me, can I just interrupt you there?
Can I just say something in answer to that?
No, hang on a minute…
No, I'm sorry I have to stop you there…
Yes, but…

Preventing interruptions
Excuse me, can I just finish what I was saying?
Just a moment, please…
OK, you can make your point in a minute.

5 Pronunciation intonation in interruptions

a 🔊 **48** Being polite while interrupting is important. Listen to how some of the phrases in the box are pronounced with a firm but gentle tone.

b Work in pairs. Practice saying the phrases without sounding too hard or unfriendly.

6 Work in groups. Use the ideas you discussed in Exercise 3 for a meeting. Think about the main issues and possible objections or concerns. Play the roles of the chair and the participants at the meeting. Use the language in the box to help you interrupt each other.

12e A unique service

Writing a speculative letter

1 Work in pairs. Imagine you have just started a new business. What methods could you use to attract customers?

2 Look at this list of tips for approaching clients cold (without any previous contact). In pairs, discuss which you think are most important and why.

   a focus on a specific group or type of customers

   b decide which means of communication they will prefer

   c make sure the company is the right size (not too big or small in relation to what you offer)

   d be conscious of how much they will want to spend

   e be clear about your offer and what is different about it

   f offer some "bait": a discount or extra service

3 Read the letter. Does it follow the tips in Exercise 2? Underline the parts of the letter that correspond to each tip.

4 Writing skill **persuasive language**

a Find examples of the following persuasive techniques in the letter.

   1 making strong claims
   2 using clear, short sentences
   3 recognizing what the other person wants
   4 empathizing by describing experiences you have in common
   5 suggesting possible options or solutions

b Match the techniques (1–5) in Exercise 4a with these sentences.

   a Clearly, no one wants to be a victim of computer fraud.
   b And why not?
   c You could try the system out for a week before you commit to paying anything.
   d Our approach is unique. *1*
   e We know how frustrating it is to lose important data.

EXOSCAPE
Garden & landscape designs
exoscape.net

Dear Ms. Liu:

Please excuse my direct method of approach. We are currently writing to a number of medium-sized local businesses like yours to see if you would like to join the growing number of businesses benefiting from the unique service we offer.

Exoscape is a young team of landscape gardeners and exterior designers. We specialize in transforming the outer appearance of buildings and grounds. Clearly, you don't want to spend a lot of money on this. But it is amazing what effects can be achieved at a low cost with the addition of plants and well-placed lighting.

We all look at our surroundings from time to time and think they need freshening up. If you have recently, why not pick up the phone and give us a call? If you would like to know more about us first, please visit our website. It lists our services and tells you what our clients are saying about us.

We are currently offering an initial 30-minute consultation free of charge. You might want to take advantage of this offer before it expires at the end of the month.

I look forward to hearing from you.

Yours sincerely,

Jin Cho

5 A lot of companies send out documents (letters, marketing literature) with poor English, giving a bad impression to customers and business partners. You are a translator and copywriter who offers a service checking the English in documents. Write a speculative letter offering your services to local companies. Write between 150 and 200 words.

6 Exchange letters with your partner. Check the following:

   • Is the letter persuasive?
   • Is the service described clearly?
   • Does it make a special offer?

Nothing, just nothing. Not even one stick.

Before you watch

1 Work in pairs. What do you know about where oil is normally found and how it is extracted? Discuss with your partner. Use these words to help you.

> deposits   drill   oil rig   pump out   rock

2 Look at the photo and the title of the video and answer the questions.

1 Where do you think the oil is found here?

2 What impact does extracting the oil have on the landscape?

3 Why has this method of extracting oil become popular recently?

While you watch

3 Watch the video and check your answers above.

4 Watch the first part of the video (to 02:13) and answer the questions.

1 The woman says you can no longer see what?

2 What is this area normally home to?

3 What level of oil reserves does Canada have?

4 What was photographer Peter Essick's mission?

5 Watch the second part of the video (02:14 to 2:37). Complete the description of the mining process using one word in each space.

First the [1] _____ is cut down. Then the top [2] _____ is removed and the sand [3] _____ by enormous shovels. It's then carried by dump [4] _____ to a processing facility. Each truck can carry almost 440 tons of oil-rich sand. After processing, the synthetic crude is shipped via [5] _____ to refineries in the United States.

6 Watch the third part of the video (02:38 to end). Has Canada's oil boom had a positive (P), negative (N), or unknown (U) effect on the following?

a the cost of living in the area
b employment opportunities in the area
c local people's lives in general
d the soil
e the climate
f wildlife

After you watch

7 Roleplay an interview about the Canada oil sands

Work in pairs.

Student A: Imagine you are a reporter from a local newspaper. You are going to interview a spokesperson for an oil company that extracts oil from the Canada oil sands. Look at these points and prepare a list of questions.

- why this kind of oil exploitation is necessary
- what the company is doing to mitigate the impact of its activities

Student B: Imagine you are a spokesperson for an oil company that extracts oil from the Canada oil sands. A reporter from a local paper is going to interview you. Consider these points and prepare what you are going to say.

- the arguments defending what you are doing
- how you plan to protect the environment from lasting damage

Act out the interview, then change roles and act out the interview again.

8 Work in groups. Look at these other ways in which people exploit natural resources. Which are the most damaging to the environment? Which are the least damaging? Discuss what can be done to mitigate the effects of the damage in each case.

- growing trees for wood and paper
- large-scale fishing
- farming, especially for meat
- hydroelectric power
- coal mining

---

bitumen (n) /baɪˈtumən/ tar, a thick, black, oil-based substance
bog (n) /bɒg/ a marsh or wetland
boreal (adj) /ˈbɔriəl/ belonging to the Arctic climate zone
crude (adj) /krud/ not refined; in its unprocessed form
muskeg (n) /ˈmʌskeg/ an acidic type of soil
nesting spot (n) /ˈnestɪŋ ˌspɑt/ a place where birds can make their nests
peat (n) /pit/ soft, partly carbonized vegetable matter found in bogs and marshes
strip mining (n) /ˈstrɪp ˌmaɪnɪŋ/ getting at material near the surface by removing the topsoil
viscous (adj) /ˈvɪskəs/ thick, of a liquid
wilderness (n) /ˈwɪldərnɪs/ an area of wild, deserted land

UNIT 12 REVIEW

Grammar

1 Look at the photo. Where do you think this is? What is the man doing? Read the article and check your answer.

2 Use these words to qualify and approximate the expressions in italics (1–8) in the article. In some cases you may need to add other small words.

1 really	4 -ish	7 rather
2 some	5 bit	8 kind
3 or so	6 dozens	

Although it has a modern and cosmopolitan capital, Iceland is characterized by some of the most dramatic landscapes to be found anywhere on Earth. It is also [1] *a dynamic landscape*, a fact nowhere more in evidence than on the highly active volcanic Westman islands, [2] *six miles* south of the main island. In the last [3] *50 years*, they have seen enormous changes. One, Surtsey, only appeared in 1963 following a volcanic eruption, and another, Vestmannaeyjar, was evacuated in 1973 after a devastating eruption.

Visitors are attracted to these extraordinary islands by the puffin population. These [4] *small* black and white birds can be seen in their thousands perched on cliffs and steep grassy slopes. Lucky visitors can witness the ancient and traditional art of puffin catching or sky fishing. Using large nets on long poles, [5] *like* butterfly nets, hunters stalk the puffins perilously close to the cliff's edge, and when they take flight, they catch them in their nets. [6] *Puffins* can be caught in this way each day. It's dangerous work, but for the local hunters puffin meat is a staple food. I was [7] *taken aback* by the flavor at first, but the meat was [8] *tasty*.

3 Work in pairs. Describe a sight you can commonly see in the countryside in your country.

I CAN
use language of approximation
modify the meaning of words using qualifiers

Vocabulary

4 Complete the descriptions using these words.

bone	brand	lush	monotonous
rolling	rustic	skyline	wide

1 The countryside is very green and gentle in this area: _____ hills and _____ meadows, with a few _____-looking barns.
2 This is an area of _____ open plains with few buildings in sight. The summers are long and there is little rain, so the earth becomes _____ dry. Some find it a _____ landscape, but I love the feeling of space and the big sky.
3 It's a _____-new business district with tall, glass buildings and paved walkways. By day it's buzzing with people and the nighttime _____ is dramatic.

5 Work in pairs. Describe the landscape around your home, college, or workplace.

I CAN
describe features of a landscape
use adjective collocations

Real life

6 Rewrite these phrases for interrupting and preventing interruptions so that they are gentler.

1 I have to interrupt you there.
2 I have to answer that.
3 Stop there.
4 Let me finish.
5 Make your point in a minute.
6 One moment.

7 Work in pairs. Explain to each other what you think is most important when learning English. Try to interrupt when the other person is speaking and prevent interruptions when you are speaking.

I CAN
participate in a debate
interrupt politely and prevent interruptions

Speaking

8 Work in pairs. Turn to the photo of a landscape or scene from nature that you liked best in Unit 12. Explain why you like it.

UNIT 1c Exercise 11, page 14

Group A
1 **misgiving** (n) /mɪsˈgɪvɪŋ/ doubt or apprehension
2 **spurn** (v) /spɜrn/ reject
3 **zany** (adj) /ˈzeɪni/ eccentric, unconventional; a little crazy

Example:
If the word was "immortal," a correct definition would be: "Immortal means living forever, never dying. For example, 'the immortal words of Shakespeare' or 'Shakespeare has achieved immortal fame.'"
A false definition would be: "Immortal means behaving in a way which is not right. For example, 'Earning that much money when others earn very little is immortal.'"

UNIT 2c Exercise 11, page 26

Quiz

How would you feel in the following situations? Read the questions and answer A, B, or C. Then look at the key on page 154 to find out what your comfort zone is. Discuss the results.

A comfortable, even excited about the prospect
B a little uncomfortable, but willing to try
C uncomfortable and reluctant to do it

1 At a Karaoke club, a friend forces you to go on stage to sing Frank Sinatra's "My Way."
2 You are asked to give a 45-minute talk about your company to a group of 250 high school students next month.
3 A famous person you admire (writer, actor) is sitting near you on a train. You want to get an autograph.
4 A friend, who is a biking fanatic, has invited you on a biking vacation in the mountains.
5 A group of friends has organized an adventure weekend involving canoeing in white water rapids, rock climbing, and caving.
6 You are asked if you would mind being filmed at work by a TV crew making a fly-on-the-wall documentary about your company.
7 You are unexpectedly offered a promotion to a job with more pay but also much more responsibility and less security. (You will be judged by your results.)
8 Your next door neighbor's daughter practices the violin for two hours every evening and the sound is loud and horrible. You need to speak to them directly about it.

UNIT 3d Exercise 7, page 40

Student A

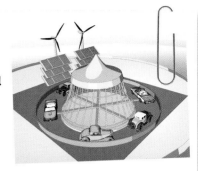

By Francesca Martelli: A children's carousel powered by wind and solar energy. It will have little carriages in the shape of antique cars made over the decades by the city's car manufacturer. Francesca hopes the project can be partially funded by the car manufacturer.

UNIT 4d Exercise 7, page 52

Student A
A typical coffee shop produces over two tons of waste coffee grounds each year. Your idea is to use them to grow mushrooms, which you can then sell to supermarkets. By using waste coffee grounds to grow mushrooms, you would be (a) recycling the waste and (b) reducing the cost of the compost you need to grow your mushrooms.

UNIT 5d Exercise 5, page 64

Student A: Passage 1
"When I told friends in London that I was going to travel around Europe and write a book about it, they said, 'Oh, you must speak a lot of languages.' 'Why, no,' I would reply with a certain pride, 'only English,' and they would look at me as if I were crazy. But that's the glory of foreign travel, as far as I'm concerned. I don't want to know what people are talking about. I can't think of anything that excites a greater sense of childlike wonder than to be in a country where you are ignorant of almost everything. Suddenly you're five years old again. You can't read anything, you have only the most rudimentary sense of how things work, you can't even reliably cross a street without endangering your life. Your whole existence becomes a series of interesting guesses."

Unit 12c Exercise 8, page 146

Light trails: This effect is achieved by leaving the camera shutter open. A longer exposure time will give you more light trails, and make them longer. However, if the shutter is open too long, the brightness of each trail will fade.

UNIT 1c Exercise 11, page 14

Group B
1 **howl** (v) /haʊl/ let out a long, pained cry like a dog or wolf
2 **jaded** (adj) /'dʒeɪdɪd/ bored; lacking enthusiasm
3 **reprieve** (n) /rɪ'priːv/ a temporary delay in a punishment

Example:
If the word was "immortal," a correct definition would be: "Immortal means living forever, never dying. For example, 'the immortal words of Shakespeare' or 'Shakespeare has achieved immortal fame.'"
A false definition would be: "Immortal means behaving in a way which is not right. For example, 'Earning that much money when others earn very little is immortal.'"

UNIT 2c Exercise 11, page 26

Answers to Quiz

Mostly As: You feel confident with new challenges and are happy to be in the spotlight. That's great, but be careful not to overextend yourself.

Mostly Bs: You are careful, but you want to expand your comfort zone by doing things that challenge you.

Mostly Cs: You are someone who likes to stay well within your comfort zone. That's OK, but remember that leaving it now and then can be empowering.

UNIT 4d Exercise 7, page 52

Student B
Your idea is to make it easier for people to scrap their old cars. Currently, when cars reach the end of their life, owners must pay a scrap metal dealer $100 to come and collect them from their homes. You would collect people's scrap cars for free. You would then (a) try to recycle as many parts as possible before (b) taking them to the scrap metal dealer to get money for the remaining metal or parts.

UNIT 7c Exercise 9, page 86

Student A
Read the facts. The underlined words give a clue.

1 Fact: Alfred Nobel was the man after whom the Nobel peace prize was named, but…
   Irony: he was also the inventor of dynamite.
2 Fact: Jim Fixx, the author of *The Complete Book of Running*, was the man who promoted jogging as a way to get healthy exercise. But at the age of 52, while out jogging…
   Irony: he had a heart attack and died.

UNIT 8c Exercise 10, page 98

Student A
You own a small travel agency which employs six people. Some data is missing but it is unclear whether someone hacked into the computer or an employee took the data or deleted it by accident. Think about:
- how many computers your office uses
- how you protect your information (passwords, virus protection)
- what you use the Internet for (what external sites you use and what transactions you do)
- how you keep all sensitive documents, digital or written

UNIT 8d Exercise 6, page 100

Group A: Why do stars twinkle?
The traditional answer is that the light from them is disturbed by movement of air in our own atmosphere. If that is true, why don't planets twinkle too? Now some scientists think that it must have something to do with the distance (planets are much nearer) and that there is something getting in the way. What that "something" is, no one knows.

UNIT 10b Exercise 10, page 121

Student A
Starlings flocking is one of the most amazing sights in nature. Some time around dusk, starlings come together and circle the sky in large groups for a few minutes. Murmurations of starlings happen everywhere, including cities; I've watched a murmuration in Framingham, right near the malls. It is thought that they do this to be less vulnerable to predators. Flying in close formation, they change direction every few seconds. No one is quite sure how they do this without crashing into each other. One study showed that each bird follows the movement of the seven nearest birds, and all have very quick reaction times. After circling in the air for some time, suddenly they all come down to ground together, as if being sucked to earth.

UNIT 10c Exercise 11, page 122

Student A
You are an ecologist. You want to help the Hadza preserve their way of life. To do this, you think that a large area of land needs to be strictly conserved, so that no development, including building and farming, can take place there. You would also like the Hadza to be left in peace and not become a tourist attraction for visitors on safari.

UNIT 3d Exercise 7, page 40

Student B

By Rana Suweilah: A giant LED screen mounted on a wall of black granite taken from the nearby mountains. In front of the wall will be a large paved area with seating, where people can skate or play games. The screen will show video footage of construction workers in the 1950s, building skyscrapers downtown.

UNIT 4d Exercise 7, page 52

Student C
It's annoying to come home after work and find that the mailman has been unable to deliver a package because no one was home. Your idea is to provide an evening redelivery service for packages. Currently, if no one is at home, the package is returned to the local post office, which people have to go to in person. Using your system, people would pay an annual fee for you to collect these packages and redeliver them at a more convenient time.

UNIT 6c Exercise 8, page 74

Student A
You are a marketing manager. Your company has developed a face cream for women in their 40s. It moisturizes the skin, protects against the sun, and helps to prevent wrinkles forming. Because women in their 40s want to keep looking young, you want the ads to feature a beautiful, fair-skinned, single young model in her 30s, a universal image of beauty. It will also encourage men to buy the product for their wives. Beauty sells, as far as you are concerned.

UNIT 7c Exercise 9, page 86

Student B
Read the facts. The underlined words give a clue.

1   Fact: Henry VIII of England (1491–1547) had six wives because he desperately wanted a son and <u>strong male</u> successor. But his successor…

Irony: Edward, his only son, was sickly and died at fifteen. Henry's greatest successor was his daughter, Elizabeth I, who ruled for 45 years.
2   Fact: Einstein had one of the most <u>brilliant</u> minds of the twentieth century. Yet at 17, he…
Irony: failed his university entrance exam.

UNIT 7d Exercise 7, page 88

Student A
Studies have shown that high temperatures can make people more aggressive. Many riots and violent protests have taken place in the northern hemisphere during warm or hot weather. In the UK, summer riots took place in 1981 and 2011. In France, student riots happened in May 1968, and the hot summer of 1967 sparked protests across the US. The worst of these was the five-day riot in Detroit, which resulted in 7,300 arrests and property damage of $60 million.

UNIT 8c Exercise 10, page 98

Student B
You are an Internet security consultant. Prepare to ask questions about how the owner (Student A) protects the small business's sensitive information. Ask:

*   how they use computers and the Internet
*   how they use external sites, such as social networking sites
*   whether they use the Internet for financial transactions

Give advice about security areas like passwords, public computers, financial information, etc.

UNIT 8d Exercise 6, page 100

Group B: Why do people yawn?
People yawn not to show they are sleepy, but to try to stay awake. Research says that people yawn to cool the brain so it can operate better. That explains why others yawn when they see us yawning. It is part of ancient behavior that helps groups to stay awake and be alert to danger.

UNIT 10c Exercise 11, page 122

Student B
You are a local politician. While in principle you respect the Hadza way of life, you think they present an image of Tanzania as a primitive country. You would like to encourage them to move into farming settlements. They will still be able to hunt, but as a hobby more than as a way of life.

UNIT 5d Exercise 5, page 64

Student B: Passage 2

"In the morning, I got up early and went for a long walk through the sleeping streets. I love to watch cities wake up, and Paris wakes up more abruptly, more startlingly, than any place I know. One minute you have the city to yourself: it's just you and a guy delivering crates of bread, and a couple of droning street-cleaning machines. Then all at once it's frantic: cars and buses swishing past in sudden abundance, cafés and kiosks opening, people flying out of Metro stations like flocks of startled birds, movement everywhere, thousands and thousands of pairs of hurrying legs.

"By half past eight, Paris is a terrible place for walking. There's too much traffic. A blue haze of uncombusted diesel hangs over every boulevard. I know Baron Haussmann made Paris a grand place to look at, but the man had no concept of traffic flow."

UNIT 6c Exercise 8, page 74

Student B

You are a sales manager. Your company has developed a face cream for women in their 40s. It moisturizes the skin, protects against the sun, and helps to prevent wrinkles. You think that women don't want to see an impossibly beautiful model in the ads, but someone they can identify with: average, with some wrinkles and blemishes, and representing different ethnic backgrounds. You think you could even use members of the public.

UNIT 7c Exercise 9, page 86

Student C

Read these facts. The underlined words give a clue.

1   Fact: In the American Civil War, General John Sedgwick said to his soldiers, "Don't worry. The enemy <u>couldn't hit</u> an elephant at this distance." However, …
    Irony: he was shot by an enemy bullet.

2   Fact: Alexander Bell worked hard at creating new inventions. He is often said to have invented the <u>telephone</u>, for example. But he…
    Irony: refused to have one in his own study because he said that it got in the way of his work.

UNIT 7d Exercise 7, page 88

Student B

The Stradivarius is the world's most famous violin, producing a quality of sound that no other violinmaker has ever managed to achieve. For years, musicians and scientists have proposed different theories about what makes these instruments so special. Some said it was the varnish that Stradivari used; others that it was the design. But more recently, two scientists have suggested that it's the quality of the wood. They claim that the drop in temperatures during the Little Ice Age changed the nature of the wood in the trees that the violins were made from, producing an exceptional wood that the world has not seen since.

UNIT 10b Exercise 10, page 121

Student B

As honey bees travel from flower to flower pollen collects on their legs. Some of this pollen is then deposited on the next flower they visit, pollinating it. Human beings have long depended on wild honey bees to pollinate plants. In fact, about 75 percent of the crops we grow depend on bees for pollination. We also depend on bees for honey, which they use to feed themselves during the winter months when flowers are not in bloom. Humans can use the honey because bees make far too much for their own consumption.

UNIT 10c Exercise 11, page 122

Student C

You are a property developer. You believe that no one can fight progress, including the Hadza. You would like to build eco-lodges around the national park where the Hadza live so tourists could go on safaris. The Hadza could be employed as guides and workers on the site, exchanging their way of life for a more modern, reliable, and profitable existence.

UNIT 1

Time phrases
Form and use

Certain time phrases are often, but not always, used with certain tenses.

Simple present
every week, frequently, from time to time, generally, never, nowadays, often, time and again

Present continuous
at present, at the moment, at this moment in time, currently, now, this week

Simple past
at the time, in the past, in 2006, last week, previously, prior to, three days ago

Past continuous
as, at the same time as, at the time, while

Present perfect
already, ever, for, how long, in recent times/years, just, lately, never, only just, over the last two years, recently, since, so far, up to now, yet

Present perfect continuous
for, how long, lately, recently, since, up to now

Past perfect and past perfect continuous
already, before that, by then, for some time, previously, prior to that time, until then, up to then

will, going to, present continuous for future, and future continuous
next week, in three days' (time), soon, on Friday, in a while, in the coming days/months/years, in the long term, sooner or later, this weekend

Practice

1 Choose the correct time phrase.

1 It's been ten years *since* / *before* we moved.
2 Nelson Mandela became president of South Africa in 1994. *Prior to that time,* / *Since then,* he had spent 27 years in prison.
3 When I was younger, I used to fight with people a lot. *Nowadays* / *Until then* I avoid confrontation at all costs.
4 *Over the last few decades,* / *In a few decades' time,* businesses have become more concerned about the environment.
5 China is *currently* / *previously* experiencing an economic boom.
6 Forecasters are warning that temperatures will rocket *in the coming days.* / *lately.*

2 Complete the sentences. Put the verbs given in the correct tense.

1 Nobody ___*has had*___ (have) any contact with Pedro since he arrived in Mexico.

2 Our car broke down on the highway yesterday. It _____ (run) perfectly up to then.
3 My grandparents met in 1940. They _____ (live) in Cairo at the time.
4 I've worked hard to get this degree but I'm sure in the long term it _____ (be) worth it.
5 He _____ (save) money since he got his new job.
6 Ignore his calls. Sooner or later he _____ (realize) that you're not interested.

The perfect aspect
Form

The perfect aspect has three structures: present perfect, past perfect, and future perfect. These can be combined with the continuous aspect to form present perfect continuous, past perfect continuous, and future perfect continuous.

Name	Example
Present perfect	I have worked
Present perfect continuous	I have been working
Past perfect	I had worked
Past perfect continuous	I had been working
Future perfect	I will have worked
Future perfect continuous	I will have been working

Use

English tenses contain two kinds of meaning: time (past, present, or future) and aspect (the speaker's viewpoint). There are two aspects: the perfect aspect and the continuous aspect (for the continuous aspect, see Unit 2).

The perfect aspect always looks back from one point in time to an earlier time. The exact time of the action or situation is not specified.

Present perfect
The present perfect looks back from now to actions or situations in the past that are in some way connected to the present. We use the present perfect:
• to talk about completed actions that are connected to the present.
  The movie has started. (the movie is on now)
  I've filled the tires. (they've got air now)
• with time expressions that mean up to now (*today, this week*): Have you spoken to Max today?

We also use the present perfect with *be, have, know,* and other stative verbs to talk about unfinished actions and situations that continue until now.
We've known about the problem for a while.

Present perfect continuous

We use the present perfect continuous:
- to talk about something that started in the past and is continuing now.
  He's been talking on the phone for over an hour.
- to talk about how we've been spending time recently.
  Sorry, I haven't called. I've been working really hard.

Remember that some verbs aren't used in the continuous form.
I've had this bike for six years. (Not ~~I've been having this bike for six years.~~)

Past perfect

The past perfect looks back from a point in the past to an earlier event.

We use the past perfect to talk about:
- single, completed events.
  Somebody stole her car because she had left it unlocked.
- repeated actions, when we give the number of times the action is repeated.
  I'd been to Peru once before I moved there.

Past perfect continuous

We use the past perfect continuous to talk about how long an action, or series of actions, was in progress.
He was tired because he'd been traveling for hours.

We don't usually use stative verbs (*be, have, like, love, hate, want*) in the past perfect continuous.
I'd known him for years. (Not ~~I'd been knowing him for years.~~)

Future perfect

We use the future perfect to talk about an action that is going to be completed at or before a given time in the future. We often use the future perfect with expressions with *by*.
They'll have finished repairing the bridge by next week.

Future perfect continuous

We use the future perfect continuous to talk about how long an action will have been in progress before a given time. It emphasizes the fact that the action will take place over an extended period of time.
By the end of May, I'll have been working here for 25 years.

Practice

3 Complete the sentences. Use the correct present, past, or future perfect tense of these verbs.

be	double	forget	~~have~~	miss	not do
study	work				

1 He _____'d had_____ several jobs before this one.
2 It is predicted that the world's population _____ by the end of the century.

3 The business _____ very well lately.
4 By next spring, my grandparents _____ married for 60 years!
5 Your essay is good on the whole, but you _____ some important points.
6 I sent off the contract and then I realized I _____ to sign it.
7 By the end of this year, I _____ English for six years.
8 She got sick because she _____ too hard.

UNIT 2
The continuous aspect
Form

Continuous verbs are made with *be* + *-ing*.

Name	Example
Present continuous	I**'m coming** now.
Past continuous	She called while I **was having** dinner.
Present perfect continuous	We**'ve been** driving for hours.
Past perfect continuous	They **had been waiting** a long time when I arrived.
Future continuous	I**'ll be seeing** him later.

Use

Verbs in the continuous aspect describe incomplete actions that are in progress at a specific time. The actions are temporary and of limited duration.
I'm having a hard time understanding you.
This time tomorrow we'll be relaxing by the pool.
Last year I was living in Madrid.

We also use the continuous aspect to describe repeated actions. Compare:
She knocked on the door. and *She was knocking on the door.*
He hasn't eaten. and *He hasn't been eating.*

We can use the continuous to make questions, requests, and statements less direct.
I was wondering if you could help me.
Will you be going anywhere near a post office?

Stative verbs such as *believe, know, realize, suppose, understand, agree, remember, wish*, and the like are rarely used in the continuous form. However, they can be used in the continuous form if a dynamic use is intended. Compare:
I think that's ridiculous. and *I'm thinking about resigning from my job.*

Special uses of the continuous aspect

We use the present continuous to talk about trends and changing situations.
Pollution is getting worse.

We use the future continuous to talk about what we expect people to be doing now.
I won't call her now. She'll be sleeping.

We use *always* and words with a similar meaning with the continuous to make complaints and criticisms.
She's always texting while I'm talking to her.
He's constantly losing his keys.

Practice

1 Complete the sentences with the simple or continuous form of the verbs given.

1 I didn't take a break on the weekend because I *was preparing* (prepare) my presentation.
2 I _____ (sing) while I'm working.
3 I cut myself this morning while I _____ (shave).
4 Pete sounded stressed when I spoke to him earlier. He said he _____ (try) to fix a computer issue for the past two hours.
5 We shouldn't postpone the meeting again. We _____ (push) it back twice already.
6 Do you think you _____ (still / work) here in a year?
7 I _____ (finish) this report then I'll go.
8 I _____ (have) to leave for work earlier and earlier every day… the traffic is terrible!

Present and perfect participles
Form

Present participles are formed with verb + -*ing*.
Turning the handle slowly, he opened the door.
Not being a strong swimmer, I wore a life jacket.

Perfect participles are formed with *having* + past participle.
Having graduated from college, he got a job.
Not having heard from his sister for several weeks, he decided to call her.

Use

We can use participial clauses to describe actions that happen simultaneously or consecutively.
Holding the knife firmly in his hand, the chef chopped the vegetables finely.
Backing slowly away from the bear, we turned and ran.

The main clause describes the most important event and the participial clause a secondary event. If we want to emphasize that the first action finished before the second, we use the perfect participle.
Having weighed the pros and cons, he decided against resigning.

A participial clause can express the idea of *because*.
Being a perfectionist, she sets herself very high standards.
(*Because she is a perfectionist,…*)

We can also use a participial clause to express a result.
The vase blew over in the wind, damaging the tile. (…and as a result, it damaged the tile)

Remember that the subject of a participial clause is the same as the subject of the main clause.

Practice

2 Choose the correct option.

1 *Having* / *Having had* a shower, I went downstairs for breakfast.
2 *Spending* / *Having spent* three years in Argentina, she now speaks Spanish fluently.
3 The woman slipped on the wet floor, *twisting* / *having twisted* her ankle.
4 *Not flying before,* / *Not having flown before*, I found the experience quite terrifying.
5 *Considering* / *Having considered* your application carefully, we would like to offer you the job.
6 *Being* / *Having been* the daughter of two doctors, I know a lot about medical matters.
7 I didn't understand the joke, but *not wanting* / *not having wanted* to look stupid I laughed.
8 I was nervous giving a speech, *not doing* / *not having done* it before.

UNIT 3

Intensifying adverbs
Form and use

Intensifying adverb + gradable adjective	Intensifying adverb + ungradable/limit adjective
extremely, incredibly, pretty, quite, really, so, very	absolutely, completely, entirely, quite, really, so, totally, utterly
Intensifying adverb + gradable verb	**Intensifying adverb + ungradable/limit verb**
completely, entirely, really, totally	absolutely, completely, really, utterly

Intensifying adverbs make a verb, adjective, or another adverb stronger. With adjectives and adverbs, they go directly in front of the word they intensify.
*The design was **totally** impractical.*
*The house **quite** literally shakes when a train goes by.*

Intensifying adverbs sometimes go before and sometimes after the verb they intensify.
*I agree with you **completely**.*
*I **totally** understand.*

We use different adverbs with gradable adjectives and with ungradable adjectives.

Gradable adjectives can be measured on a scale, like *small*: a room can be more or less small.

Ungradable or limit adjectives, on the other hand, are not measured on a scale. They express only extreme qualities, like *empty, wonderful*.

As with adjectives, verbs can be gradable or ungradable. For example, *agree* and *like* are gradable. You can agree with or like something to a small or large extent.

When used with an ungradable adjective or verb, *quite* means "extremely."
*The views were **quite** incredible!*

Practice

1 Choose the correct option. In one sentence, both options are correct.

1 The heating bills must be *very / absolutely* huge.
2 You'd be completely *sensible / insane* to buy that.
3 I don't agree *entirely / extremely* with his views.
4 If you could help me set up the meeting room, I'd be *absolutely / extremely* grateful.
5 You were *quite / incredibly* right to complain.
6 I've had a totally *tiring / exhausting* day at work.
7 Why is this carpet so *dirty / filthy*?
8 I'm *quite / incredibly* certain that picture wasn't on the wall last time I was here.
9 I *really / entirely* don't want to have this discussion right now.
10 Watching the way the birds built their nest was *extremely / absolutely* fascinating.

Emphatic structures

Form and use

There are several ways of adding emphasis to a sentence.

Cleft sentences (*what / it's / the thing*)
We can use *it's/it was* to highlight the part of the sentence we want to emphasize. We put the rest of the sentence into a *that* clause.
I don't like the layout of the house. (no emphasis)
***It's** the layout of the house **that** I don't like.* (with emphasis)

We can use *What* or *The thing… is/was* to put the words we want to emphasize at the end of a sentence.
I don't like the layout of the house. (no emphasis)
***What** I don't like **is** the layout of the house.* (with emphasis)
***The thing** I don't like **is** the layout of the house.* (with emphasis)

Negative inversion
Some negative adverbs can be used at the beginning of the sentence to add emphasis. In these cases we put the auxiliary verb before the subject. If there is no auxiliary verb, we use *do, does,* or *did*. These structures are often formal and literary.

You rarely see this style. (no emphasis)
***Rarely** do you see this style.* (with emphasis)

I've never seen such a messy house before. (no emphasis)
***Never before** have I seen such a messy house.* (with emphasis)

The same pattern is used with *seldom, hardly (…when), little, no sooner (…than), not once, not only, only* + time expression, *under no circumstances*.

do, does, did
We can use the auxiliary verb *do* to add emphasis to the main verb.
I like that decorated ceiling. (no emphasis)
*I **do** like that decorated ceiling.* (with emphasis)

Practice

2 Rewrite the sentences adding more emphasis.

1 This city needs more low-cost housing.
What *this city needs is more low-cost housing.*
2 I hadn't witnessed such a violent storm before.
Never _____
3 We could really do with more storage space.
What _____
4 I'm particularly concerned about the crowding.
It's _____
5 Houses rarely come up for sale in this town.
Rarely _____
6 He didn't complain once about the noise.
Not once _____
7 I won't believe a word he says ever again.
Never again _____
8 I didn't buy any pants but I bought a belt.
I didn't _____
9 I'll really miss this wonderful view.
It's _____
10 She had just arrived home when the doorbell rang.
No sooner _____

UNIT 4

Past modals
Form and use

Obligation
We use *had to* to express obligation in the past. It is the past of *must* (for obligation) and *have to*.
*I **had to** work hard to persuade people to buy the product.*

Necessity
We use *needed to* + base form to say that it was necessary to do something.
*I **needed to** come up with a new idea.*

We use *didn't need to* or *didn't have to* to say that something wasn't necessary whether we did it or not.
I **didn't need to use** my laptop, so I left it at home.

Speculation

We use *must/might/may/could/can't* + *have* + past participle to speculate about past events.

must have → you feel certain that something happened or was true
They **must have been** held up in the traffic.

may, might, could → you think it's possible something happened or was true
Their car **might have broken** down.

may not / might not have → you think it's possible something didn't happen/wasn't true
He **may not have taken** the normal route.

can't have / couldn't have → you feel certain that something didn't happen
He **couldn't have seen** the one-way sign.

Notice that the opposite of *must have done* for speculation is *can't / couldn't have done* (not ~~mustn't have done~~.)
We use *must have* and *can't have* when we know or believe something by logical deductions.
Her car's still here so she **can't have left**.
Her car isn't here so she **must have gone**.

Advisability

We use *should have* or *ought to have* + past participle to talk about the correct, advisable, or morally right thing to do in a past situation. It is often used to express regret about our own actions or criticism of others'.
I **should have brought** my camera with me. (but didn't)
She **ought to have known** better. (but didn't)

Other uses of past modals

We use *might have* and *could have* + past participle to criticize people for not doing things. *Might*, used in this way, is more formal than *could*.
You **could have cleaned** up the mess you made!
You **might have told** me you'd be an hour late!

We can also use *should have* + past participle to talk about something that we expect to have happened.
They left an hour ago. They **should have arrived** by now.

Practice

1 Rewrite the sentences in italics using past modals.

1 "I went to a technology exhibition on the weekend."
   "I bet that was interesting."
   That must have been interesting.

2 "The microwave seems to be working again."
   "Maybe Andy fixed it."

3 "Zhang's given that watch away to a friend."
   "Clearly he didn't like it then."

4 "The electricity's gone off."
   "Maybe there's been a power outage."

5 "Our Internet connection was down yesterday."
   "I'm sure that was frustrating."

6 "I got lost on my way here."
   "It would have been a good idea to use your GPS."

7 "Look! The movie theater's completely empty."
   "So buying our tickets online was a waste of time."

8 "James wasn't at the meeting."
   "It's possible he didn't know it was happening."

Probability

Form and use

We can express probability in a number of ways.

Modal verbs: *may, might, could, should*
We use *may*, *might*, and *could* to talk about the probability that something is true now or will happen in the future. Their meaning is essentially the same.
It **may / could / might** snow later.

We use *may well, might well, could well* to say that something is quite probable.
If sales continue to fall, the company **may well** close.

Might not and *may not* express future possibility but we don't use *could not* in this way.
The rumors **could be** true, but they **might not be**.

Should describes a situation we expect to happen.
The roads are clear so we **should arrive** on time.
They've fixed the printer so we **shouldn't have** any more problems with it.

We only use *should* to talk about the probability of something good happening.
We don't say ~~The traffic's bad so we should be late~~.

Adverbs: *perhaps, maybe, probably, almost certainly, almost definitely*
Perhaps and *maybe* go at the beginning of a sentence.
Maybe one day they'll invent fully automated cars.

Other adverbs of certainty go before a main verb and after the auxiliary in affirmative sentences and before the auxiliary verb in negative sentences.
The batteries **will probably need** to be replaced soon.
He **definitely won't** pass the test.

(un)likely

We can use subject + *be* + *likely* / *unlikely* or *it is likely* / *unlikely* + *that* + clause.
*The new tablet **is (un)likely to** be launched soon.*
***It's (un)likely that** the new tablet will be launched soon.*

Be likely to and *will probably* have the same meaning but *be likely to* is more formal.

Other common adjectives of probability are *bound* and *sure*. We use *be bound* + *to* + base form and *be sure* + *to* + base form to say that you think something is certain to happen or to be true.
*The truth is **bound to come** out sooner or later.*
*She's **sure to be** on time.*

Noun phrases

Noun phrases such as *The likelihood is, The chances are, There's a good chance,* and *There's no doubt* are followed by *that* + a clause.
*The **likelihood is that** this software will sell well.*

Practice

2 Rewrite the sentences using the words given.

1 I don't think you'll get a phone signal here. (probably)
You *probably won't get a phone signal* here.

2 The company probably won't upgrade its computers this year. (unlikely)
It's _____ this year.

3 We might be living abroad next year. (chances)
The _____ next year.

4 There's a good chance that the president will be re-elected. (might well)
The president _____ .

5 If we don't insure the washing machine, I bet it'll break down. (bound)
If we don't insure the washing machine, _____ down.

6 Are you sure the DVD player isn't working? (definitely)
_____ working?

7 I'm not sure that we need to buy a new printer. (may)
We _____ a new printer.

8 I'll be surprised if you don't get a call from him shortly. (should)
You _____ from him shortly.

9 There's no doubt that she'll find an excuse for her behavior. (likelihood)
The _____ for her behavior.

UNIT 5
Substitution
Form and use

In English, there are a number of ways to avoid repeating words or phrases, like **substitution** (replacing one word or phrase with another) and **ellipsis** (omitting something completely).

Substituting words

We can use synonyms to avoid repeating words.
*I thought he was **blunt**. I'm not used to people being that **direct**.*
*"I thought she looked pretty **stressed**." "Yes, she did seem a little **tense**, didn't she?"*

Substituting nouns

We can use pronouns to refer back to previous nouns.
*It was a simple **solution**, but an effective **one**.*

If two nouns are mentioned, we use *the former* to refer to the first one and *the latter* to refer to the second.
*We could take the highway or the scenic route. **The former** would get us there more quickly than **the latter**.*

Substituting verbs and verb phrases

We often use just the auxiliary of a verb phrase to avoid repeating verbs or verb phrases.
*I love **going trekking**, but my girlfriend **doesn't**.*
*I didn't **go scuba diving** last year, but I **did** this year.*

The expressions *do so* and *doing so* can replace a verb phrase.
*I'd love to **go on an around-the-world trip**, but to **do so/doing so** would be extremely expensive.*

When we respond to another person's comment, we can use a different auxiliary.
*"I'd like to take a boat trip around the glaciers in Southern Argentina." "Yes, you **should**."*
*"You should have taken the train." "Well, we **didn't**."*

When there is more than one auxiliary, we can use one or more than one auxiliary when we respond.
"It would have been better to come here off-season." "Yes, it would / would have / would have been."

Substituting clauses

We can substitute an entire clause with *that, so,* or *not*.
"Do you think it'll rain?" "I hope not."
"It'll be hard to find a hotel because there's a conference that week." "Oh, I wasn't aware of that."

Ellipsis

Ellipsis means omitting words completely. We can use *to* instead of repeating a complete infinitive phrase.
"Will you see Machu Picchu when you're in Peru?" "We hope to." (= we hope to see it)

Practice

1 Delete the unnecessary words in the sentences and make substitutions where appropriate.

1 We took some insect repellent, but we didn't have to use ~~the insect repellent~~. _____it_____

2 This line is for e-passport holders only. You don't have an e-passport so you need to join the longer line. _____

3 If I can take time off work next month, I will take time off work next month. _____

4 The hotel rooms were very expensive, but ours was one of the cheaper rooms. _____

5 You could rent a car when you go abroad, but to rent a car when you go abroad you need to have held a license for a year. _____

6 "Did you book the flights?" "I meant to book the flights but I didn't get a moment." _____

7 Hindi and English are both spoken in New Delhi. Hindi is the principal spoken language and English is the principal written language. _____

8 This train goes to the airport but that one doesn't go to the airport. _____

9 "Did you remember to bring the map?" "I'm afraid I didn't remember to bring the map." _____

Nominalization
Form and use

Forming nouns from other parts of speech, especially from verbs and adjectives is called "nominalization." We often use it in more formal situations (such as formal emails or reports).

Verb → noun nominalization

We complained about our accommodation.
→ *We made **a complaint** about our accommodation.*
Please acknowledge that you have received this email.
→ *Please acknowledge **receipt** of this email.*

We sometimes form nouns from a different verb with a similar meaning, for example with phrasal verbs.
The cost of flights has gone up.
→ *There has been an **increase** in the cost of flights.*

Adjective → noun nominalization

I'm grateful to you for supporting me.
→ *I would like to express **my gratitude** for all your support.*
Thank you for being so generous.
→ *Thank you for **your generosity**.*

Nominalizations are often followed by a preposition like *in recognition of*, *on arrival at*, and *on receipt of*.

Other types of nominalization

We can use nouns to replace relative pronouns such as *who, when, why, what, where.*
I don't know why they went on strike.
→ *I don't know the reason for the strike.*
Can you show me where it is on the map?
→ *Can you show me the location on the map?*
I can't remember when it was.
→ *I can't remember the occasion.*
Do the police know who the culprit was?
→ *Do the police know the identity of the culprit?*
I don't know what the lecture will be about.
→ *I don't know the subject of the lecture.*

Practice

2 Rewrite the sentences using a noun in place of the words in italics.

1 Why do you think Hergé's books are *successful*? What do you think is the reason _for the success of Hergé's books?_

2 I don't know *where the* hotel *is* exactly.
I don't know _____

3 We said *we would prefer* an earlier start date.
We expressed _____

4 She was impressed by *how much I knew.*
She was impressed _____

5 I *tried* to contact you several times.
I made _____

6 The weather conditions have *improved.*
There has _____

7 We were surprised that we *recovered* so quickly.
We were surprised _____

8 We will confirm your reservation *when we receive* your deposit.
Your reservation will be confirmed _____

9 Thank you for *assisting* me in this matter.
Thank you for _____

10 Everyone was relieved *when he arrived* early.
Everyone was relieved by _____

UNIT 6

Phrasal verbs
Form and use

A phrasal verb is a verb + particle (preposition or adverb). The same verb may be used with a number of different particles and the meaning of the verb changes each time. The meaning of the phrasal verb is sometimes idiomatic: the meaning is different from the meanings of the verb and particle.

There are four kinds of phrasal verb:

1 Intransitive phrasal verbs: verb + adverb (no object)

Intransitive phrasal verbs don't have objects.
Sit down!   *This situation can't go on.*

2 Separable phrasal verbs: verb + adverb + object

Many phrasal verbs are transitive and need an object. Transitive verbs can be separable or inseparable. With separable phrasal verbs, the object can come before or after the particle.
Can you turn down the volume?
Can you turn the volume down?

If the object is a pronoun, it must go between the verb and the particle.
Can you turn it down? (Not *Can you ~~turn down it~~?*)

If the object is a long noun phrase, the particle comes immediately after the verb.
She gave up going to the gym. (Not *She gave ~~going to the gym up~~.*)

3 Inseparable phrasal verbs: verb + preposition + object

With inseparable phrasal verbs, the object must go after the particle.
It took him a long time to get over his leg injury.

4 Three-part phrasal verbs: verb + adverb + preposition + object(s)

Some phrasal verbs have three parts: a verb and two particles. The object must come after the particles.
We're looking forward to seeing the play.

Most three-part verbs have one object.
It's hard to get down to work in this heat.
He always comes up with innovative ideas.

A few three-part phrasal verbs have an object after the verb and a second object after the two particles.
I'll take you up on your offer to make dinner tonight.

Practice

1 Rewrite the sentences substituting a pronoun for the words in italics.

1 I need to print out *some copies of this report.*
   I *need to print them out.*
2 Who will look after *the cats* while you're gone?
   Who _____ while you're gone?
3 Let me run though *the rules of the game* again.
   Let me _____ .
4 He admitted that he'd made up *the whole story.*
   He admitted _____ .
5 I'm sorry. I take back *what I said.*
   I'm sorry. I _____ .
6 Don't put off *doing your chores.*
   Don't _____ .

2 Write the words in italics in the correct order.

1 I won't be coming to the yoga class tonight because I've *down / come / the flu / with.*
   come down with the flu
2 I think it's too late to *talk / out / of / her* resigning.
3 I think we should *with / do / fast food / away.*
4 Could I take / up / your offer / on / you of a ride?
5 It didn't quite live / our expectations / up / to.

Verb patterns
Form and use

After certain verbs, we use infinitive.
*The player **pretended to be** injured.*

Common verbs which are followed by infinitive include: *afford, expect, fail, seem, tend, want.*

Some verbs are followed by an object + infinitive.
*The doctor **advised her to rest** her ankle.*

Common verbs which are followed by an object + infinitive include: *force, encourage, require, want, warn.*

Some verbs are followed by an object + base form (without *to*): *I **saw him pass** out.*

Common verbs which are followed by an object + base form (without *to*) include: *help, let see, hear, make.*

Some verbs are followed by the *-ing* form.
*I **suggest leaving** before the rush hour begins.*

Common verbs which are followed by the *-ing* form include: *avoid, dislike, mention, miss, recommend, risk.*

Some verbs are followed by both an infinitive or an *-ing* form with little or no change in their meaning, like *begin, continue, like, love, hate, prefer, start.*
*It **started to pour.***
*It **started pouring.***

Some verbs are followed by both an infinitive or an *-ing* form with a change in their meaning, like *forget, regret, remember, stop, try.*
*Winning this point would **mean winning** the match.*
*I **meant to call** her but I forgot.*

Some verbs are followed by a preposition + *-ing* form.
*He finally **succeeded in giving** up smoking.*

Other verbs which are followed by a preposition + *-ing* include: *complain about, insist on, rely on, think about, worry about.*

Some verbs are followed by an object + preposition + -ing form.
*The judge **accused her of lying**.*

Other verbs which are followed by an object + preposition + -ing include: *criticize/blame (someone) for; discourage/prevent (someone) from.*

Verbs + *that* + clause
Sometimes a *that*-clause can be used instead of the infinitive or -ing form. *That* can be omitted.
*The player **pretended to be injured**.*
*= The player **pretended (that) he was injured**.*

However, it is not always possible, for example:
He wanted me to come. (Not *He wanted ~~that I come~~.*)

Perfect and passive forms
The gerund and -ing forms also have perfect and passive forms.
*I wanted **to be given** another chance.*
*I didn't like **being made** to wait.*
*I regret **having lost** my temper.*

Practice

3 Complete the sentences with the verbs given in the correct form. You need to use a preposition in some of the sentences.

1 If you fail ___to arrive___ (arrive) on time, you won't be let in.
2 The high cost of parking discourages people _____ (bring) cars into the city.
3 Police warned the public _____ (not / approach) the escaped prisoner.
4 The government was criticized _____ (violate) human rights.
5 Anyone who doesn't abide by the rules risks _____ (be) disqualified.
6 He put antiseptic on the wound to prevent it _____ (become) infected.

UNIT 7

Linking words
Form and use

Additional point

and + clause		The Aztecs founded the city of Tenochtitlán **and** stayed there many years.
as well as in addition to not to mention	+ noun or gerund	She studied ancient history **as well as** Latin in college. **In addition to** writing an essay, we have to give a presentation.
moreover furthermore in addition	+ new sentence	Julius Caesar was a general and a historian. **Moreover**, he was a talented mathematician.

Reason

because since as	+ clause	He repeated the instructions **since** nobody heard them the first time.
because of on account of owing to due to as a result of	+ noun	The Greeks expected to lose the battle **owing to** the size of the Persian army.

Contrast

although but even though	+ clause	**Although** the Romans didn't invent the arch, they were the first to use them in bridges.
despite in spite of notwithstanding	+ noun or gerund	**Despite** living to the age of only 33, Alexander the Great built a huge empire.
however nevertheless	+ new sentence	It is often believed that Columbus discovered America. **However**, this is disputed by some.

Time

after, as, before, when, since, as soon as, until, while	+ clause	The Middle Ages began **after** the Roman Empire collapsed.
after since	+ noun or gerund	**After** visiting the Valley of the Kings, we cruised the Nile River.
following	+ noun	The Great Fire of London broke out **following** a fire in a bakery in 1666.
subsequently	+ new sentence	The remains of the palace were uncovered in 2001. **Subsequently**, archaeologists discovered many more artifacts.

There are a number of different kinds of linking words.

Conjunctions: *when, although, because*
Conjunctions are followed by a clause.
Although I had slept for several hours, I felt exhausted.

Some can be followed by a noun or gerund.
Since retiring, we rarely travel anymore.

Adverbs: *however, moreover, nevertheless*
It rained my whole vacation. However, it didn't spoil it for us.

Adverbs usually go at the beginning of the sentence. They can, however, go in the middle.
Today, however, it didn't rain.

Prepositional words or phrases: *in spite of, owing to*
These are followed by a noun (or pronoun), a gerund or *the fact that* + clause.
She accepted the job in spite of the low salary.
She quit, owing to the fact that it was too hard.

Practice

1 Combine the sentences using the linking words.

1   Her father died in 1952. Queen Elizabeth II came to the throne. (following)
    Queen Elizabeth II came to the throne following the death of her father in 1952.

2   History is an enjoyable subject to study. It can help us understand the present. (in addition to)

3   The event was canceled. There was not enough funding for it. (owing to)

4   We hadn't heard from you. We assumed you weren't coming. (since)

5   The pharaohs of ancient Egypt were seen as kings and gods. (as well as)

6   Herodotus was a very famous historian. Little is known about the man himself. (although)

7   I've lived in this apartment since July 2010. I moved to Madrid in July 2010. (since)

8   The Spartans lost. They were brave. (despite)

Subordinate clauses
Form and use

Sentences are made up of one or two clauses. Sometimes these are two main clauses, joined by a conjunction such as *and, but,* or *or.*
The lecture finished and the students went home.

The two clauses are called main clauses because they can both make sense on their own:
The lecture finished. The students went home.

Other sentences are made up of a main clause and a subordinate clause, joined by a conjunction such as *when, if, although, because.*
When you get a moment, *have a look at this website.*

The main clause makes sense on its own, but the subordinate clause (in bold) does not make sense without the main clause. Also, the subordinate clause and the main clause can have different subjects.

Subordinate clauses add meaning to the main clause by giving more information about, for example, cause, comparison, or time.

cause/reason	*as, because, considering (that), given (that), in view of the fact that, since*
condition	*as long as, assuming (that), if, provided that, supposing (that), unless*
contrast	*although, even though, having said that, in spite of the fact that, regardless of the fact that*
time	*as, before, when, while*
precaution	*in case, in the event of*
comparison	*compared to, contrary to, relative to*
other	*as far as… is concerned, thinking about it, insofar as*

Practice

2 Choose the correct option.

1   I have a jacket *unless /* (*in case*) */ if* it gets cold.

2   *Contrary to / Compared to* earlier belief, medieval children had toys.

3   *In spite of the fact that / Given that* we're trying to save money, I don't think we should go abroad this summer.

4   He was offered the job *given / in view of / regardless of* the fact that he had no experience.

5   You are allowed to organize a dig *provided that / in case / even though* you have a license.

6   In the Middle Ages, most children didn't know their grandparents *although / since / in case* they had died before they were born.

7   Let's take some cash with us *if / considering / in case* the store doesn't accept credit cards.

8   The meeting was scheduled to begin at 2 p.m. *in spite of / in view of / assuming* the fact that people had a long way to travel.

9   Temperatures, *insofar as / while / provided that* we can tell, will be mild.

UNIT 8

Passive reporting verbs
Form

We can report actions and events using the passive in two ways:
A: *It* + passive verb + *that* clause
It is believed that *the company* **was sold** *yesterday.*
B: subject + passive verb + *to* + infinitive
The company **is believed to have been sold** *yesterday.*

A: *It* + passive verb + *that* clause
Reporting verbs that commonly follow this pattern are: *agree, allege, announce, assume, believe, claim, consider, decide, estimate, expect, fear, hope, know, presume, report, say, suggest, think, understand.*

Present

It is thought that the pictures are real.
It is believed that the pictures are real.

Past

It is estimated that 10,000 people **were rescued**.
It was alleged that the boy **hacked** into his school's computer.

Future

It is expected that the new stadium **will open** in May.

B: Subject + passive verb + *to* + infinitive

Reporting verbs that commonly follow this pattern are: *allege, assume, believe, consider, estimate, expect, know, report, say, think, understand.*

Present

The eyespots on butterfly wings **are thought to startle** their enemies.
The senator **is believed to be considering** resignation following the scandal.

Past

Ten thousand people are estimated **to have taken part**.
The boy **was alleged to have hacked** into his school's computer.

Future

The new stadium **is expected to open** in May.

Infinitives		
	affirmative	**negative**
active		
simple	to sell	not to sell
continuous	to be selling	not to be selling
perfect	to have sold	not to have sold
perfect continuous	to have been selling	not to have been selling
passive		
simple	to be sold	not to be sold
perfect	to have been sold	not to have been sold

Notice how we use passive reporting verbs with *there*.
It is known that there are small traces of mercury in fish.
There are known to be small traces of mercury in fish.

Use

We use reporting verbs in the passive when:
- we cannot verify the source of the information.
- we assume that the reader or listener is not interested in who the agent or source is.
- the agent or source is obvious from the context.

This structure is very common in formal writing like newspaper articles, academic essays, and business documents, as well as in formal speaking contexts, such as academic discussions and business presentations.

Practice

1 Rewrite the sentences using passive reporting verbs.

1 Conservationists fear that polar bears may soon become extinct.
It *is feared that polar bears may soon become extinct.*
2 Journalists reported an oil spill in Mexico.
An oil spill _____
3 Detectives know the robbery took place in the early hours of this morning.
The robbery _____
4 Insider sources say that the player has not been selected for the Olympic team.
The player _____
5 Scientists think that dinosaurs were wiped out when an asteroid hit Earth.
Dinosaurs _____
6 Doctors say a climber who fell 100 feet down a steep ridge is recovering well.
A climber who _____
7 The president is expected to announce a tax increase tomorrow.
It _____
8 The police believe there weren't any witnesses.
There are _____

Expressions with *no*

Form and use

Only certain nouns are used in these expressions. Here are some of the most common.

no + noun + *-ing*
There's no point (in) worrying.
I had no difficulty (in) finding the venue.
There's no harm (in) trying.
There's no sense (in) waiting.
It's no use arguing.
It's no good complaining.

no + noun + *of* + *-ing*
There's no way of finding out.
He had no intention of leaving.
There was no mention of having to pay.
We had no means of getting there.
I've got no chance of winning.
There's no hope of finishing the project on time.

no + noun + *that*
There's no question that it'll work.
There's no doubt that she's right.
There was no suggestion that we would have to attend.
There was no expectation that he would pay.

no ... except/but to + infinitive

I had no choice but to resign.
We have no alternative except to sell the house.
He had no option but to report the matter to the police.

no matter + relative pronoun

No matter what I say, he won't believe me.
No matter how hard I try, I can't forget what happened.

Practice

2 Rewrite the sentences using an expression with **no** and the words given.

1 You've got nothing to lose by trying. (harm)
   There's _____

2 The ad has been effective. (doubt)
   There's _____

3 Why buy it if you don't need it? (point)
   There's _____

4 The reality is, however many possessions we have, we always want more. (matter)
   The reality is, _____

5 Calling him is a waste of time since he never answers his phone. (use)
   It's _____

6 Pilots say that they will be forced to go on strike if an agreement isn't reached. (alternative)
   Pilots say _____

7 You can't access it without a password. (way)
   There's _____

8 I assure you I don't intend to leave before this matter is resolved. (intention)
   I assure you _____

UNIT 9

The adverb *just*

Form and use

The adverb *just* can appear in several positions within a sentence. It is placed before the word it emphasizes.

- before the main verb: *They've **just** released a new CD.*
- before a preposition: *The band split up **just** over a year ago.*
- before a noun: *It's **just** a suggestion.*
- before an adjective: *Her voice is **just** amazing.*
- before a conjunction: *I'll be with you **just** as soon as I've finished this call.*

Just is often used in spoken English and has a number of different meanings.

very recently	*She's just left the office.*
simply	*It's just a matter of luck.*
only	*He just sings; he doesn't write the music.*
exactly	*It's just the kind of music I love.*
a little	*They were on stage for just over two hours.*

In some cases, *just* has no particular meaning but is used for emphasis:

*I **just** love this track!*   *That's **just** not acceptable!*
*It's **just** amazing!*   ***Just** taste this pizza!*

Other uses of *just*

We use *just* when something almost doesn't happen.
*I can **just** hear you.* (with difficulty)
*We **just** made it on time.* (but we nearly didn't)

Just about means *almost.*
*I've **just about** had enough of this.*
*The program's **just about** over.*

Just as is used to emphasize that something is equal to something else.
*The view is **just as** good from here.*

Practice

1 Put the words in the correct order.

1 to / I / for / can't / just / wait / come out / the new album
   I *just can't wait for the new album to come out.*

2 just / we / stood / of / the stage / in front
   We _____

3 the new single / raving / about / were / the reviews / just
   The reviews _____

4 bought / came out / after / just / I / it / the CD
   I _____

5 just / one day / sell out / tickets / for / often / in / the music festival
   Tickets _____

6 an hour / been / just / for / over / we've / waiting
   We've _____

7 I / you / were / wondering / just / where / was
   I _____

8 my essay / about / finished / I've / just
   I've _____

9 as / just / her / sister / talented / she's / as
   She's _____

10 misunderstanding / was / it / just / a
   It _____

Expressing purpose

Form and use

We can use several structures to express the reason why we do something.

Infinitive of purpose

We can use infinitive on its own.
*I went to the post office **to get** a package.*
***To get** the best deal, we'll need to order well in advance.*

Or we can use *in order to* or *so as to* + base form. *In order to* is more formal than *so as to*.
*We need to increase sales **in order to make** a profit.*
*We moved forward **so as to get** a better view.*

It is common to use *in order not to* or *so as not to* before a negative
Handle the CD carefully **so as not to / in order not to** *damage it.*
(Not *Handle the CD carefully* **not to damage it**.)

for + noun
I'm learning English **for pleasure**, *not for work.*

avoid + -ing or avoid + noun + -ing
I keep my guitar in a case to avoid scratching it.
I keep my guitar in a case to avoid it getting scratched.

so that / in order that + clause
So that and *in order that* are conjunctions and are followed by clauses. The subject of the clause may be different from the subject of the main clause. When we talk about the present or the future, *so that / in order that* are often followed by *can* or *will*.
I'm starting early **so that I won't need** *to rush.*
I'm leaving now **so that I can get there** *sooner.*

We sometimes use the present tense to talk about the future.
I'm going to take some sun screen **so that I don't / won't** *get sunburn.*

In sentences about the past we usually use *would, could* or *should* after *so that / in order that*.
The concert tickets were free **in order that everyone could have an opportunity to go**.

So that is more common than *in order that*, especially in informal English. In informal English, we can omit *that* after *so*.
I'll practice now so (that) I don't have to later.

Practice

2 Rewrite the words in italics using the words given.

1   The band went on tour *because they wanted to promote their new album.* (to)
    to promote their new album.

2   I often wear headphones while working *because I like to block out the surrounding noise.* (order)

3   I took some painkillers *because I wanted to get rid of my headache.* (to)

4   He didn't complain to the noisy neighbors *because he didn't want to cause a scene.* (avoid)

5   I went to bed early *because I wanted to feel fresh on the day of my exam.* (so that)

6   The burglar wore gloves *because he didn't want to leave fingerprints.* (so as)

7   He took his laptop with him *because he wanted to be able to work on the train.* (in order that)

8   I'll send him the concert tickets *because I want him to get them by Friday.* (so that)

UNIT 10
Tag questions
Form
To form tag questions, we use the auxiliary of the verb in the main sentence. When the main verb in the sentence is affirmative, the tag question is negative. When the main verb in the sentence is negative (including sentences with words with a negative meaning like *no one, never, hardly*), the tag question is affirmative.
***You're Evie, aren't you**?*

Note that when the subject is a noun, we use an appropriate pronoun in the tag question.

Verb or verb form (+ auxiliary)	Examples
to be (is, are, was, were)	*It's interesting, isn't it?* *I'm right, aren't I?* (With *I am…*, we don't say *I'm right, am not I?*) *You were at the festival, weren't you?*
Simple present (do, does)	*You live in Manila, don't you?* *She doesn't work here, does she?*
Simple past (did)	*He worked for NBC, didn't he?* *She didn't explain it clearly, did she?*
Perfect and continuous (the same auxiliary verb)	*They haven't voted before, have they?* *You aren't paying attention, are you?*
Modal verbs (the same modal auxiliary verb)	*It should be here by now, shouldn't it?*
Imperative (will, won't, would)	*Send me some photos, would you?* *Don't forget to reply, will you?*
Let's (shall, OK)	*Let's take a break, shall we?* *Let's not be late, shall we?* *Let's stop for a moment, OK?* *Let's leave early, OK?*

Use
We use tag questions in speech or in informal writing to check that something is true or to request agreement. The meaning is shown by the intonation we use. If the tag is a real question to check something is true, we use rising intonation.

We're meeting at three, aren't we?

If we are just requesting agreement, we use falling intonation.

That was a very productive meeting, wasn't it?

We can also request agreement with the word *surely*. *Surely he's made a mistake?* means the same as *He's made a mistake, hasn't he?*

It is possible to have an affirmative question tag after an affirmative sentence. We use this structure to express interest, surprise or concern.

*So your mother's from Guatemala, **is she?***

If the subject of the sentence is *no one, someone,* or *anyone,* the pronoun in the question tag is *they*. *Someone will meet us at the airport, **won't they?***

We can also use a rising intonation with the word "right" as an affirmative tag question.

*Someone will meet us at the airport, **right?***
*We're meeting at three, **right?***

Practice

1 Add question tags to these sentences.

1 It's been a long day, *hasn't it* ?
2 There hasn't been a phone call for me,
   _____ ?
3 Hardly anyone turned up to the meeting,
   _____ ?
4 He never takes responsibility for his actions,
   _____ ?
5 I'm going to be late, _____ ?
6 You gave this to me, _____ ?
7 She should ask for help, _____ ?
8 We had great fun at the carnival, _____ ?
9 Let's meet up again next week, _____ ?
10 You didn't tell anybody what I said, _____ ?

Adverbs
Form and use

Adverb + verb
Adverbs of manner describe how something is done. They often, but not always, end in *-ly* (*quickly, carefully, quietly, well*).
*Ants depend **primarily** on pheromones.*

Adverbs of manner usually come after the verb they describe. If the verb has an object, the adverb goes after the object. Placing the adverb before the verb adds emphasis.
*The ants attacked their prey **fearlessly**.*
*The ants **fearlessly** attacked their prey.*

They can also come in the middle of the sentence, between the subject and the main verb. When there is an auxiliary verb, the adverb comes after the auxiliary and before the main verb.
*The ants were **busily** searching for food.*

They can also come at the beginning of the sentence.
***Carefully,** the ants carried the crumbs back to their nest.*

We don't usually use adverbs of manner between the subject and verb or at the beginning of the sentence, when no other additional information is given after the verb, like an object or a prepositional phrase.
*They behave **fearlessly**.* (Not ~~Fearlessly, they behave.~~)

Adverb + adjective
We can use adverbs of manner to add information or comment on an adjective or another adverb.
*Ants are **remarkably** strong.*

Adverbs with the same form as the adjective
Some adverbs have the same form as the adjective.
*Ants work **hard**.*   *This is **hard** work.*
*He's a **fast** runner.*   *He can run **fast**.*

Other such words include: *direct, easy, fine, free, high, late, long, pretty, straight, tight, well, wide.*

Adverbs meaning *almost ... not*
The adverbs *hardly, barely,* and *scarcely* mean "almost not." They are often used with words like *any* or *anyone* and with adjectives and verbs.
*There was **barely/scarcely/hardly** anywhere to sit.*
*Some ants are so tiny that they are **barely/scarcely/hardly** visible.*

These words have a negative meaning and aren't used with *not* or other negatives: ~~I couldn't hardly see.~~

Adverbs not formed with the *-ly* suffix.
When an adjective ends in *-ly, (friendly, lively),* it is not possible to make them into adverbs with an *-ly* suffix. They need to be expressed in a different way, for example, with an adverbial phrase such as *In a ... manner / way / fashion.*
They spoke to me in a friendly way. Not ~~He spoke to me friendly.~~ or ~~He spoke to me friendlily.~~

Other adjectives ending in *-ly* include: *cowardly, daily, deadly, early, likely, lively, lonely, lovely, orderly, ugly, worldly.*

Some adjectives ending in *-ed* cannot be made into adverbs by adding the *-ly* suffix.
They communicate in a civilized way. Not ~~They communicate civilizedly.~~

Practice

2 Rewrite the sentences, adding an adverb or adverbial phrase formed from the adjectives given. It may be necessary to make other changes to the sentence.

1 He explained what we had to do. (complicated)
   He explained what we had to do in a complicated way.
2 I was speechless when I heard the news. (complete)
   _____
3 It was so airless in the room that I couldn't breathe. (bare)
   _____
4 The best way to get rid of ants is to go to the source: the nest. (straight)
   _____

5   He devoured everything on his plate. (hungry)

6   She pushed him aside. (unfriendly)

7   It solved the problem. (instant)

8   He agreed to let me pay for the taxi. (reluctant)

UNIT 11
Unreal past
Form and use

There are a number of structures in English that are followed by past tenses which have a present or future meaning. We use these structures to express unreal or hypothetical situations.

would rather / would just as soon

We use *would rather* or *would just as soon* + subject + past tense to express a preference.
I'd rather they didn't visit us this weekend.
I'd just as soon you didn't mention this to anyone else.

It is also possible to use *I'd rather* and *I'd just as soon* + base form when there is no change of subject: *I'd rather not see him.* However, if the subject changes, we use the past tense. *I'd rather he didn't see me.* (Not *I'd rather he not see me.*)

I wish / if only

We use *I wish* and *if only* to express regrets and wishes for things that are unlikely to happen. *If only* has a more emphatic meaning than *I wish*.
I wish / If only you didn't live so far away.

We use the past perfect to express regrets about the past.
I wish I'd spent more time preparing. (but I didn't)
If only I had trusted my instincts. (but I hadn't)

We use *wish* + *would* to express a wish for action: for someone to do something about a situation or for the situation/action to stop.
I wish you would stop making that noise.

We also use *would* + *wish* to talk about another person's annoying habits or unwillingness over something.
I wish / If only she would listen to my advice.
I wish he wouldn't interrupt me while I'm speaking.

Notice that we don't use *would* if the subjects in both clauses are the same.
I wish I didn't live here. (Not *I wish I wouldn't live here.*)

what if / supposing / suppose

We can use *what if, supposing,* and *suppose* at the beginning of a question to ask about consequences.
What if I wasn't here to help you; what would you do?

We can also use these structures to make suggestions.
Suppose we were to offer you a raise; would you stay?

What if is more informal than *suppose* and *supposing*.

it's time

We use *it's time* + subject + past tense to say that something needs to be done very soon. We can use *high* before *time* to add emphasis.
It's time I had a vacation.

Note that we can use *were* instead of *was* with these structures, especially in a formal style.
I wish I was/were somewhere else.
Suppose I was/were fired; what would we do?

It is occasionally possible when we talk about a hypothetical situation to use the present instead of the past tense: *What if nobody comes/came?*

Practice
1 Rewrite the sentences using the words given.

1   He ought to take a break. (time)
    It's time he took a break.

2   I'd prefer it if you would break the news to her. (rather)

3   She might leave him. Then he'd be devastated. (what if)

4   Why does he have to be so critical about everything? (wish)

5   The government really needs to change the laws on gun ownership. (high)

6   Would it help if we hired someone to clean the apartment? (supposing)

7   It would be so good to have more free time. (only)

8   I'd be as happy for you to drive as for James. (soon)

Inversion in conditionals
Form and use

In more formal speech and writing we can make conditional sentences by putting an auxiliary verb before a subject instead of using *if*. This structure is most common after *should, were,* and *had*.
Had we known there were tickets left, we'd have bought some. (= If we had known there were tickets left, we'd have bought some.)

should

Should you have any questions, please don't hesitate to contact me. (= *If you have any questions, please don't hesitate to contact me.*)
Should you ever need a place to stay, you'll always be welcome here. (= *If you ever need a place to stay, you'll always be welcome here.*)

Second conditional

Were we in a stronger financial position, we'd offer to lend you the money. (= *If we were in a stronger financial position, we'd offer to lend you money.*)

We can use *were + subject + to* to talk about future possibilities, but not about unreal situations.
Were my parents to approve, I'd be able to go. (= *If my parents approved, I'd be able to go.*)

We can use the structure *were it not for (the fact that)* to say that without something, things would be different. We use this structure in more formal speech.
If she hadn't helped me, I wouldn't be a doctor. → Were it not for her help, I wouldn't be a doctor.
If my friends didn't live here, I would move to a different town. → Were it not for the fact that my friends live here, I would move to a different town.

Third and mixed conditional

If I'd read the reviews, I wouldn't have bought the book. → Had I read the reviews, I wouldn't have bought the book.
If I hadn't had the operation, I'd still be in a lot of pain. → Had I not had the operation, I'd still be in a lot of pain.

We can use the structure *had it not been for (the fact that)* to say that without something, things would have been different.
If she hadn't been so persistent, she wouldn't have found such a good job. → Had it not been for her persistence, she wouldn't have found such a good job.

Note that negative auxiliaries are not contracted in inversion sentences.
Had you not come, I would have left. (Not ~~Hadn't you come…~~)

Practice

2 Put the words in the correct order to make conditional sentences with inversion.

1 the police / acting / you / should / please / suspiciously / notice / contact / anyone
   Should you notice anyone acting suspiciously,
   please contact the police.

2 not / into / cold / so / town / were / we / could / it / walk
   ....
   ....

3 you / should / know / our plans / I'll / change / let
   ....
   ....

4 you / the helpline / any / experience / technical problems / please / call / should
   ....
   ....

5 offered / I / to be / a promotion / were / stay / the company / I / would / at
   ....
   ....

6 would / have / the weather / had / better / been / we / longer / stayed
   ....
   ....

7 your help / I / known / wouldn't / what / have / it / not / for / to / do / were
   ....
   ....

8 be asleep / my alarm / I / had / would / still / not gone off
   ....
   ....

UNIT 12

Approximation
Form and use

It is common in spoken and informal written English to use approximate language when you don't know or need to give exact details.

Numbers

*30-**odd** people; two hundred **or so** trees*
***some** fifty books*
***around, about, roughly, approximately, in the region of, something like** ten properties*
*500 dollars, **more or less***
dozens of** jobs, **hundreds of** birds, **loads of** time, **in a** month **or two
***(well) under, above, below** zero*

-odd can mean "about" or "a little more than." *Some* before a number suggests a large number.

Adjectives

We use *kind of* when we can't think of a better adjective to describe something.
It's kind of rubbery.

The suffix *-ish* makes an adjective less exact and is usually added to words describing physical features (like size, color) or time.
It's reddish, it's brownish, it's longish, it's roundish.
"What time are we meeting?" "One-ish."

some

We use *some* plus a singular noun to refer to a person, thing, or time that is unknown to us.
*We'll arrive **some** time in the afternoon.*
*I read about it in **some** newspaper article.*
***Some** idiot backed into my car.*

Vague words

We use vague words like *stuff* and *things* to refer to something when we don't know the name, the name is not important, or it's obvious what we're talking about. *Stuff* is more colloquial than *things*.

*What's that green **stuff** in the water?*
*Leave your **things** in the locker.*

Practice

1 Complete the sentences with these words.

around	-ish	kind of	or so
~~some~~	stuff	things	well

1 I hope to see you ___*some*___ time soon.
2 Life has been _____ tough recently.
3 The leaves had turned a yellow _____ color.
4 None of this _____ is urgent.
5 It takes an hour _____ to get there.
6 My swimming _____ are in this bag.
7 Its history spans _____ over 1,500 years.
8 The village stands _____ 5,000 feet above sea level.

Qualifiers

Form and use

A qualifier is a word or phrase that intensifies or softens the meaning of the words that follow it.

quite, pretty, really, and *fairly*

We use *fairly* to modify the meaning of adjectives and adverbs. It means "to a limited degree."
*It was **fairly** easy to understand.* (pretty easy, but not very easy)
*I'm **fairly** certain this will work, but I wouldn't bet on it.*

Quite often suggests a higher degree than *fairly*.
*His explanation was **quite** confusing. None of us understood what he meant.*

Quite can also qualify nouns and verbs.
*I **quite** like reading poetry.*
*It was **quite** a difficult assignment.*

When modifying an adjective + noun, *quite* comes before *a/an*.
*The story had **quite** an unexpected ending.*

Really and *pretty* can only modify adjectives and adverbs. They suggest a higher degree than *fairly*. They can also suggest "more than usual or expected" and are slightly more informal than *quite* or *fairly*.
*It's **pretty** unlikely that things will change.*
*The tickets were **really** expensive.*

rather

Rather is an intensifier that can modify adjectives, adverbs, nouns, or verbs. It can express disappointment, criticism, or surprise.
*It's **rather** spicy.*   *It was **rather** a disaster.*

slightly, a little, a bit

Slightly, a little, and *a bit* soften the meaning of the words they qualify. They can qualify adjectives, adverbs, and verbs. We often use these words to make a criticism sound less direct.
*It seems **slightly / a little / a bit** unnecessary.*
*She drives **slightly / a little / a bit** fast.*
*His attitude surprised me **slightly**. / His attitude **slightly** surprised me.*

Slightly, a little, and *a bit* can be used before comparative adjectives whereas *quite, fairly,* and *pretty* cannot.
*The view is **slightly** better from this window.* (Not ~~The view is quite better from this window.~~)

When we use *a bit* or *a little* before a non-comparative adjective, the meaning is usually negative.
*He's **a little** spoiled.* (Not ~~He's a bit intelligent.~~)

We can use *a bit of a/an* before a noun.
*He can be **a bit of a** pain.*
*I've got **a bit of a** headache.*

Practice

2 Cross out the qualifier or qualifiers which do NOT fit in each sentence.

1 It was *quite / ~~a bit~~ / ~~fairly~~* a steep drop.
2 He told a *rather / quite / bit* long-winded story.
3 The meadows look *slightly / quite / a little* more lush than last time I was here.
4 It was *rather / quite / fairly* an uncomfortable journey.
5 The mountain views are *pretty / a bit / rather* stunning.
6 My legs were beginning to ache *rather / slightly / quite*.
7 The landscape was a *bit of / bit / bit of a* bleak for my liking.
8 It's *a bit of / pretty / quite* an unspoiled beach.

Unit 1

🔘 **1**

So let's start by considering these descriptions of people.

"Oh, Carlos—he's a family man"; "Sayah's an anthropologist—she's spent most of her life studying apes in Africa"; "Frank's a serious coin collector—he's been collecting coins since he was a boy"; "Jae is one of life's drifters—he will have been just about everywhere by the time he's 60"; "Ana's a committed animal rights activist—that came as a shock to her friends because she had never even owned a pet before she joined the Animal Defense League!"

We define each person by a different criterion: their interests, their profession, their outlook on life; or by their values—like the importance of family for Carlos—and their beliefs. So which of these things is it that really defines a person?

What if we asked the same question about a six-year-old child? Well, you'd probably say that what defined them first and foremost are the common factors that make them a child—being curious about the world, often playful, a little vulnerable maybe. In ten years, that child will have become a teenager and teenagers, of course, share certain defining characteristics too. They tend to be quite self-centered and moody. Often they're angry at the world. And because they're not sure of what their identity is, they define themselves by what they are not and by the things they dislike: "But Mom, I don't want to go to a college. I hate school."

Now let's look again at the adults we described at first. Carlos, our family man, has a job as a carpet salesman, which is OK. It's a job and it keeps him and his family comfortable. He had had an opportunity to run his own business at one point, but he decided job security was more important.

His real passion is his family and spending time with his two boys. Sayah, the anthropologist, on the other hand, lives for her work. She's visited Central Africa many times to study bonobo apes and is fascinated by their social behavior. Jae—the drifter—has been doing bits and pieces of carpentry and building work. He loves traveling and experiencing different environments, so he picks up work as and when he can. He fell in love when he was 25, but the relationship ended and he hasn't committed to anyone else since.

So, we can see that what defines each of these people in the end is their life experiences. It could be within their job or interests or relationships that these occurred, but it's the experiences themselves that shape each of us as individuals. So when someone asks you what you do, they are…

🔘 **2**

M: OK, Kia, so tell me about yourself.
K: OK, so I'm Kia. I'm 24 years old and I'm a very active person. I don't just mean that I play a lot of sports, although I do run and go to the gym several times a week. What I mean is that I'm a person who likes to get involved in things. I've organized a lot of social events in my life and I've been part of a lot of campaigns, um… A recent one was campaigning against the building of a new parking lot in the center of my hometown. And that was successful. We got it stopped or at least delayed so, um… Excuse me, I'll just take a sip of water… Yes, so, as I was saying, I'm a firm believer in taking action. I don't think it's enough to want to change things and to say the right things, I think you have to act—to get out of your chair and do something that makes a difference.
M: And your current situation?
K: Well, I graduated from college two years ago with a degree in journalism, but I haven't been able to find a job that really suited me. To be honest, newspapers aren't an easy world to break into, unless you have the right contacts. So instead, I decided on a fresh approach, which was to seek out companies I admire; basically any company or organization that's working for some positive good in society. And that's how I found you. And my hope is that when I find the right company, they'll see that I have the right attitude and the right skills, so that we can both benefit from working together, um, yeah…

🔘 **3**

K: OK, so I'm **Kia**. I'm **24** years old and I'm a very **active person**. I **don't** just mean that I **play** a lot of **sports**, although I **do run** and **go** to the **gym several times** a **week**. What I **mean** is that I'm a **person** who **likes** to **get involved** in things.

Unit 2

🔘 **4**

P: We'd all like to jump into a fire, right? Uh, I don't think so, but that was how smokejumper Kerry Franklin explained her career choice to me earlier when I interviewed her for GBC. For those of you who don't know, smokejumpers are firefighters who are dropped into remote and inaccessible areas to combat forest fires. Here's what Kerry told me.
K: Women firefighters are well-suited to this kind of work. Weighing on average 150 to 180 pounds, we're the right weight for it. If you're a lot heavier than that, you descend too fast and hit the ground hard, risking serious injury. And if you're a lot lighter and there's a strong wind, it can take your parachute and leave you a long way from your intended landing point.
P: You mean like in the middle of the fire itself?
K: Yeah, that's been known to happen. But we wear a lot of protective gear. Of course we're aware of our personal safety, but it's not the first thing on our minds.
P: No, I imagine not. So, having landed near the fire, what do you do then? I mean, not having a fire engine or a fire hydrant nearby, you can't exactly start fighting the fire in the conventional way, can you?
K: You see, we're like the initial line of attack. We get dropped in with tools—chainsaws, axes, chemicals for fighting fires—we get water pumps too, portable ones. But first we need to assess how bad the fire is—how we think it's going to develop—and get that news back to base. If it's cooking pretty good, we've got to look for a way to try and contain it. Usually that means finding a natural firebreak.
P: What's that?
K: It's something like a road, or an area of rock, or thinner vegetation that the fire's going to have to cross before it continues on its path of destruction. So having located a firebreak, we do our best to make sure it's going to be effective, getting anything that could burn easily out of the way, sometimes using controlled burning to burn back to the main fire as it approaches the break.
P: And what's it like being a woman in this world, because firefighting is traditionally a male-dominated domain?
K: Fire doesn't distinguish between men and women, nor do the trainers at smokejumping school for that matter. You either make the grade or you don't. Having faced the same challenges together in training, those who make it have a natural respect for each other. Sure, during my training I met a few guys who had a different attitude, but I haven't met any who didn't just end up thinking a smokejumper's a smokejumper.

5

Hello, everyone. I hope you're enjoying your first day. I imagine you're feeling pretty overwhelmed by everything you've had to take in, and I don't want to keep you long. I've been brought back as someone who's been through the system and come out the other side, so the college asked me to talk to you as one of you and give you a student's side of the story.

So with that in mind, I'd just like to say one thing really, which is: get involved in something other than your major as soon as you can. You'll be amazed at how quickly time goes by here. Before you know it, you'll be in your third year and you'll be thinking, "What now?" How many of you actually know what you're going to do when you leave? I'm sure there will be some people who know what career they'd like to embark on, but there will be an awful lot of you—and I was definitely one of them—who don't.

That's where clubs, societies, and volunteer groups come in. I remember when I first came here to study history, I had no idea what job I'd end up doing. But in my first year, I joined the college radio station. I was interested in reporting, so I used to go out and find interesting stories about college life, and then come back and present them—when they were interesting enough to everyone else, that is. I did that once a week. Then in my second year, I got a summer job helping out as a researcher at the local PBS radio station, and it all followed from there, because first of all I was clear about what I wanted to do—which was to work in broadcasting—and second, I had some contacts I could call, which in this line of work is a key thing.

So that's really my message to you today. Don't delay, get out there, join some clubs and societies and start developing your interests. This college has so many terrific opportunities to do that, and you won't get another chance in life like it. So, thanks for your time. Oh, and come talk to me afterwards if you'd like to… I'll be in the lounge.

 6

Hello, everyone. I hope you're enjoying your first day. I imagine you're feeling pretty overwhelmed by everything you've had to take in, and I don't want to keep you long. I've been brought back as someone who's been through the system and come out the other side, so the college asked me to talk to you as one of you and give you a student's side of the story.

 7

Hello, everyone. First of all, let me extend a warm welcome from myself and all the staff. My name's Sarah Curtain, and I'm the principal here at State College. I'm very happy to see, once again, such a large and diverse range of nationalities at the college. This year we have over

60 different nationalities, speaking 33 different languages. It's that diversity and international perspective that makes State a unique place to study.

I'm afraid I have to mention a few administrative matters first, but then I'll give you some more general advice about how to make the most of your time here.

So, immediately after this session, there will be coffee in the students' union where you can meet and talk to the staff and other students. That's from 11 to 12:30 p.m.

Course registration takes place on Monday morning. It's mandatory that everyone attend and it'll be in the main college hall—this room—between 10 a.m. and 2 p.m. You must attend to officially register for the courses you are going to take this year.

Also, during the next week, I'd ask those of you who haven't done so already, to bring copies of all your documents to the Admissions office—Room 301—so that we can keep them on file. That's all official documents—high school transcripts, student visas, bank account details—to Room 301 by the end of next week. This applies to all overseas students, that is everyone except those from the US. Even if you don't think you have all of these, please come and see us anyway—that's very important.

Now, as for your orientation here at State College…

8

OK, everyone, I'd just like to say a few words about reading—something you're going to be doing a lot of here. At the end of this session, I'll give you your reading list for this particular course. Your other instructors will do the same. There'll be 30 or so books on each list, but please don't think that means you have to read every page of every book. There are three or four key books highlighted at the top of each list, which we do recommend that you read in full, but the others will mainly be for reference—that's to say, there'll be one or two chapters in them that are relevant to a particular essay or piece of work.

So, most importantly, when I give you the list, please don't go out to the nearest bookstore and buy them all. If you do that, you'll leave yourself no money for food or anything else. All these books are, in principle, available at the library— some may be out on loan, of course, when you want them. You'll probably want to buy some of the more important ones. My advice to you is first to look online and see if you can pick up any used copies there. There's also a second-hand section in the campus bookstore, where you might find what you're looking for.

What about strategies for reading? As I said at the beginning, you'll have a big volume of reading to do, so it's important that you get faster at it. Is there a secret to

that? Well, I'm afraid the answer is, not really. What I would say, though, is that the more you read, the faster you will get. So don't worry too much if it seems like it's taking forever at first—everyone feels that…

Unit 3

9

P: Welcome to *Grand Architecture*. We're changing focus completely today and looking at small homes. I'm very pleased to welcome Swedish architect Jonas Wilfstrand, who specializes in the design of compact living spaces. I've been looking at some of these on your website, and I must say some of them are absolutely stunning. I really liked the timber and glass vacation house with the built-in sauna. Is this a trend we're seeing, Jonas, for smaller homes?

J: I don't think it's really a trend in the sense that lots of people are wanting smaller homes, but I think there *is* definitely more interest in them. In a lot of places, dwellings are small out of necessity—people are either incredibly short on space or they simply can't afford a bigger house.

P: And where do you get your inspiration? Where did you look for ideas?

J: Well, there were two homes in particular that got me interested in this. One was the houses of the Dolgan people in central north Russia, who live a lot of the year in freezing temperatures, as low as minus 40 degrees. Their houses are shaped like a sugar cube and extremely basic—just a single room with two or three beds, a table, and a stove. They're constructed from wooden frames and reindeer skin, which is a great insulator. The Dolgan are nomadic people who tend reindeer, and when it's time to find new feeding grounds, they move houses, quite literally. Their houses are on sleds and they get pulled along by the reindeer to the next stop.

P: Why did these Dolgan houses impress you so much?

J: Well, several reasons: their mobility, the way the Dolgan use only readily available materials, and the fact that they're just so simple. They were what got me thinking about the whole concept of more compact living.

P: And you mentioned another home that inspired you.

J: Ah yes, that's not at all simple. It's the apartment of an architect in Hong Kong. As you probably know, space is at a premium in Hong Kong. It's a really overcrowded city. Gary Chang lives in a tall apartment block in an apartment that's only 340 square feet. And he used sliding walls—partitions—within the apartment to be able to transform it into a living room, a kitchen, a library, a bedroom; in fact, he claims he can have 24 different rooms in all. He entirely rethought the way we arrange living space. I thought it was wonderfully innovative. There are some great photos of it on his website. Here's one…

P: It looks distinctly cramped to me, but very stylish.

10

1 You're absolutely right.
2 That's really kind of you.
3 I'd be very grateful.
4 It's completely out of the question.
5 Yes, I'm quite certain.
6 That's so typical.

 11

I have to say, I really like this piece. It has several things to recommend it. First of all, as a work of art, it seems very accessible. What I mean is, it's not too intellectual or difficult to understand, like a lot of modern art pieces. So in that way, I think everyone—children and adults—should be able to relate to it. Also, the fact that it's in the shape of an open book will give it popular appeal. It reflects the long tradition of our city as a place of learning very well. It's a clever touch, I think.

Third, and I don't think we should underestimate this, it's just good fun. The quotes and jokes that appear on the pages will attract a lot of attention. People will be able to sit on benches and watch as the different messages roll across the screen. So it becomes an interactive work of art, and I think this is important, given its central location in the city. And the idea that it could become a tourist destination also really appeals to me.

Well, that more or less sums up my position. What does everyone else think?

 12

1 "What I mean is, it's not too intellectual…"
2 "The idea that it could be a tourist destination…"
3 "The water and the area in front of the fountain…"

Unit 4

13

P = Presenter (male), M = Martha Kay

P: It's difficult to imagine what life must have been like before the invention of certain things. If you're in your teens or twenties, you might never have wondered how people searched for information before the Internet existed. The electric light is another thing that we all take for granted. But how do such inventions come about? Is it necessity that drives innovation? Or commercial profit? Or something else? Here to discuss these questions is business historian Martha Kay. Martha, there are a lot of things around us that we clearly could live without, so the necessity argument is not the whole answer, is it?

M: Hello, Evan. No, of course it isn't. History is littered with inventions that people thought they didn't need at the time. In 1878, a British parliamentary committee, which had to comment on the usefulness of Alexander Graham Bell's telephone, said, "…it is good enough for our transatlantic friends, but unworthy of the attention of practical men."

P: Well, maybe they should have been more open-minded. But in 1878, people didn't need to have phones, did they? You could conduct your daily business and daily life perfectly well without one. But now it's become a necessity, a need has been created, if you like.

M: Well, people in the nineteenth century needed a way to communicate at a distance more effectively; they just hadn't envisaged the telephone. Of course, there are some inventions which fill an urgent need—like vaccines against particular diseases. But most innovations aren't like that. Entrepreneurs have often come up with ideas to make our lives a little more convenient or comfortable and then, over time, we come to rely on them. Television is a case in point. Remote shopping—that is, mail-order, or these days, online shopping—is another. It was dismissed by *Time* magazine in the 1960s because they said, "women like to get out of the house and like to be able to change their minds."

P: I'm sure they did—like to get out of the house, that is. That certainly was a different era…

M: Another form of innovation is to take something that's at first expensive to produce and therefore exclusive to rich people, and make it available to many. There are quite a few things that we now see as everyday necessities that have come to us this way—where an entrepreneur has found a way to produce something more cheaply, like the cell phone or the computer. Another example: in the 1890s, the automobile was thought to be a luxury for the wealthy. *Literary Digest* predicted that it would never "of course, come into common use."

P: I see, so in that sense what it comes down to is wants rather than needs. But what about all those things that we don't really need? How do you explain…?

 14

1 You should have told me.
2 Did you have to wait?
3 He must have forgotten.
4 You shouldn't have worried.
5 She may have left already.
6 I didn't need to be there.

 15

1 a You might have <u>told</u> me.
  b You <u>might</u> have told me.
2 a You shouldn't have <u>waited</u>.
  b Flowers? Oh, you <u>shouldn't</u> have!

 16

We have an idea to encourage volunteering. It's a new phone app called "Volunteer Planner." What is it? It's an interactive calendar that links volunteers to organizations looking for help. Why is it necessary? Because there are a lot of people out there who'd like to give their time to help others in the community—helping the disabled or the elderly. But they never come forward because their time's limited and it's too complicated to plan. So what does Volunteer Planner do exactly? The app allows organizations to show when they need volunteer help; it allows volunteers to communicate their availability; and it allows both parties to make changes to the schedule in real time. What's our ambition for Volunteer Planner? Ultimately, it means more people giving a little of their time rather than a few people giving a lot. So it encourages and spreads the practice of volunteering.

 17

What is it?

How does it work?

Why is it necessary?

What does it do exactly?

"So what?" I hear you say.

Isn't it going to be expensive?

So, how do we achieve this?

What's our ambition for…?

Unit 5

🔊 18

P = Presenter, S = Shyla

P: ...to places you and I would probably never think of visiting. And Shyla, what's your book?

S: My choice is *Where the Indus Is Young* by the Irish writer Dervla Murphy. It's about a trip that she took with her daughter up the Indus River valley—a region called Baltistan—into the heart of the Himalayas when the girl was only six years old. This was in the 1970s.

P: And why have you chosen this one in particular?

S: Well, traveling in this region is dangerous enough at the best of times, but to do so with a six-year-old girl is just incredible. They encounter raging rivers, falling rocks, steep rocky ascents. Murphy herself says in the book that the extremeness of the landscape in this region cannot be exaggerated. In fact, Rachel—that's her daughter's name—became the hero for me, because where many kids would be complaining constantly, she never does. Her mother takes advantage of this, and so keeps pressing on, along narrow paths next to deep ravines. I'd like to read a short extract if I may, where they're coming down a track on horseback next to the side of a mountain:

We found ourselves looking into a ravine so profound that one's first reaction was incredulity. The shadowy chasm was very narrow and perhaps half a mile long. It lay between the brown mountain we now stood on and the white mountain ahead, and at a conservative estimate it was 1,500 feet deep, with absolutely sheer sides. This scene was the very quintessence of Himalayan drama—vast, beautiful, cruel—belonging to a landscape that has no time for the paltry endeavours of men.

P: I've heard critics say that Murphy can be political. Would you agree with that?

S: Well, maybe. She does mention a few times in this book and in others, how unspoiled places like this are being ruined by "technological progress" and Western ideas. An example of the former is when she talks about modern transportation bringing diseases to areas that hadn't suffered these before. Other writers of course have said the same thing, and I'm always a little suspicious of people who want to enjoy unspoiled parts of the world and then return home to the comforts of their own Western lives. But you can't say that the point of this book is to send a political message. It's not. It's just a wonderful description of an amazing journey, and the ability of a young child to overcome fear and a completely different environment. I found it absolutely gripping.

🔊 19

1 A: You have to be careful not to get lost.
  B: Yes, I know that.

2 A: Would you like to drive?
  B: No, I'd rather you did.

3 A: Did he take warm clothes with him?
  B: I hope so.

4 A: Do you mind traveling alone?
  B: No, I actually prefer it.

5 A: Are there guidebooks about La Paz?
  B: Well, there are some.

6 A: Do you have an up-to-date map of Russia?
  B: No, but I have an old one.

🔊 20

I'd like to read from *The Third Man*, a thriller by Graham Greene. The context for this story is post-Second World War Vienna, around 1948. A writer, Rolly Martins, has come to Vienna to find his old friend, Harry Lime, but he discovers that Harry has died under suspicious circumstances. At this point in the story, Martins is walking back through the deserted streets of Vienna at night. It's a great example of how to build suspense.

"Passing by the end of the street he happened to turn and there, just around the corner, pressed against a wall to escape notice, was a thick, stocky figure. Martins stopped and stared. There was something familiar about that figure. Perhaps, he thought, I have grown unconsciously used to him during these last twenty-four hours; perhaps he is one of those who have so assiduously checked my movements. Martins stood there, twenty yards away, staring at the silent motionless figure in the dark side-street who stared back at him. A police spy, perhaps, or an agent of those other men, those men who had corrupted Harry first and then killed him; even possibly the third man? It was not the face that was familiar, for he could not make out so much as the angle of the jaw, nor a movement, for the body was so still that he began to believe that the whole thing was an illusion caused by shadow. He called sharply. 'Do you want anything?' and there was no reply. He called again. 'Answer, can't you?' and an answer came, for a window curtain was drawn petulantly back by some sleeper he had awakened and the light fell straight across the narrow street and lit up the features ...of Harry Lime."

🔊 21

"...for the body was so still that ..."

"... he began to believe that the whole thing was an illusion caused by shadow. He called sharply. 'Do you want anything?' *[pause]* and there was no reply. He called again. 'Answer, can't you?' *[express urgency]* and an answer came, for a window curtain was drawn petulantly back by some sleeper he had awakened and *[build volume here]* the light fell straight across the narrow street and lit up the features... *[pause]* of Harry Lime."

Unit 6

🔊 22

P = Presenter, B = Ben

P: ... thanks for those comments, Sarah. I'd like to turn now to someone who should know more about sports injuries than most, and that's ultrarunner Ben Newborn. Ben, before we get into the question of injuries, can you just explain for our listeners what ultrarunning is?

B: Sure, basically ultrarunning is running distances beyond a usual marathon distance. So, it could mean running 60 miles in a single day, or it could involve running several marathons on consecutive days.

P: And how did you get into it?

B: I was a runner anyway and I just wanted to take it to another level—to really test myself physically and mentally. So in 2008, I registered for the Ultra-Trail race in the Alps which requires runners to run 100 miles around Mont Blanc.

P: Didn't you worry about doing yourself real damage?

B: Actually, I wasn't so concerned about regular running injuries. I was more worried about failure. And I knew that to succeed in overcoming exhaustion and the things that make you feel nauseous, I had to get my diet and nutrition right. That's ultimately what would let me run in relative comfort.

P: Comfort's not a word I'd automatically associate with a 100-mile run, but anyway... What about injuries? This must put intense strain on your body.

B: I think the most important thing in any sport is to recognize when your body's in pain. A lot of athletes try to go through the pain. If they have a small muscle strain or a twinge in a joint—an ankle, for example—they tend to take some painkillers or put on some kind of support and just keep going. Because they feel they can't afford to rest. But that of course is completely wrong. Pain is your body warning you to be careful—to stop often—because minor problems will inevitably develop into more severe injuries. So that's the first thing: to listen to your body.

P: Yes, but we all get aches and pains. Surely that shouldn't discourage us from doing things like exercise?

B: Well, my point really is that if you do the right kind of preparation, you can avoid getting injuries in the first place. I follow a method developed by a sports physiologist, which is a series of stretches and gentle exercises that strengthen the key muscles and ligaments. It's definitely prevented me from getting ankle sprains and helped with other things I used to suffer from: lower back pain, runner's knee and so on...

🔵 23

A: So, everyone, this is an initial brainstorming session to come up with some concrete ideas for promoting health and fitness among employees. As you're probably aware, health is an issue that's very topical at the moment and our own chairman and CEO want us, as a company, to take the lead on it. Of course, there's also an obvious benefit to us in terms of productivity and days not lost to sick time. So, I'd like to hear any ideas you have. Yes, Jen…

B: Well, as I see it, there are two routes we could take: one is just promoting the idea of health and fitness at work by encouraging people to do simple things like walking to work, not spending long periods sitting at their computers, that kind of thing. Or we could spend some serious money on the problem and do something like installing a gym or fitness center on site that people can use on their breaks or after work. But I realize that there may not be a budget for that.

A: Hmm, OK. Yes, Ben…

C: I don't know what others think, but for me the key is getting people to enjoy exercise. If you offer activities that employees think are fun, you'll get much better participation.

A: Such as…?

C: Such as team sports—baseball, basketball, and so on—and we can arrange competitions. Also dance classes. Admittedly, a lot of people may do these things anyway in their free time, but I bet there are a lot more who'd like to but never get around to it.

A: Thanks, Ben. And what about the idea of group exercises in the mornings? The kind of collective warm-up routine you used to see in companies fifty years ago. It's not a particularly original idea, I'll grant you, but it might be fun and also build team spirit.

B: I think you have to be careful there. People may think that you're trying to coerce them into some kind of forced exercise regime. I know that isn't the intention, but it could look that way. I think it'd be much better to give people incentives to do things on their own. So, for example, if we had a "bike to work" program where we offered to pay part of the cost of, say, a new bicycle to encourage people to cycle to work. I haven't thought through exactly what proportion of the cost, but I think that that kind of individual incentive probably works much better.

A: Mmm, I like that…

B: Of course, it wouldn't be so easy to monitor whether they used the bike to commute to work or for leisure, but you'd probably just have to accept that risk.

C: Yeah, I definitely think that idea could work and it wouldn't really matter if…

🔵 24

1 It's not a particularly original idea.
2 It wouldn't be so easy to monitor…

🔵 25

1 I know it's not a very practical solution.
2 It wouldn't be that simple to convince people.
3 I'm not actually sure of the exact numbers.

Unit 7

🔵 26

P: A recent archaeological dig on the banks of the River Thames in London has uncovered evidence about the lives of children in the Middle Ages. Archaeologist James Newman is here to tell us more about it. James, correct me if I'm wrong, but compared to children today, I imagine children in medieval times didn't have much of a childhood!

J: Well, as far as historians are concerned, that is—or certainly *was*—the accepted view of it. In the 1960s, a French social historian, Philippe Ariès, claimed that parents in the Middle Ages didn't really form emotional attachments to their children, but instead sent them off to work as soon as they could to be economic providers for the household. According to Ariès, the idea of a childhood didn't really appear until the sixteenth or seventeenth century. Up until then, children were just little adults, expected to do what adults did. If you look at paintings of children in medieval and Renaissance times, in fact, they do appear as small versions of grown-ups.

P: But considering people had much shorter working lives, you can understand why they'd want to get their children working earlier. Having said that, it does seem a pretty harsh view of human nature: to assume that people in the Middle Ages had no emotional bond with their children. But you think you've found some evidence to show this wasn't actually the case.

J: Yes. I was working on a dig, retrieving objects from mud banks by the River Thames. We found various items dating back to the thirteenth century: little cannons and guns, metal figurines, and miniature household objects such as chairs, jugs, and even frying pans complete with little fish. And insofar as the objects have great historical value, you could say we struck gold! Also, assuming that these *are* all medieval toys—and they look just like doll's house furniture—they paint a different picture of childhood in the Middle Ages.

P: You mean that perhaps children *were* allowed to be children, more than people thought anyway.

J: Yes, exactly. Someone clearly went to the trouble of making toys for them so they could play. The other interesting thing is that, regardless of what they tell us about children at the time, some of these objects are things we didn't know existed in medieval households, like a birdcage and a three-legged stool.

P: Mmm, sounds fascinating. Now, in case any listeners want to see these items, the collection will be going on tour around the country and a list of…

🔵 27

1 Insofar as the objects have great historical value, you could say we struck gold!
2 Assuming that these *are* all medieval toys, they paint a different picture of childhood in the Middle Ages.
3 Regardless of what they tell us about children at the time, some of these objects are things we didn't know existed in medieval households.
4 In case any listeners want to see these items, the collection will be going on tour around the country.

🔵 28

L: Yes, you in the third row.

A: Yes, hello. Thanks for a very interesting talk. Uh, I'd just like to make sure I understood what you said about the plague that affected the Roman Empire so badly. Am I right in thinking that the drought in Africa caused an increase in the number of rats?

L: Well, not exactly. The drought actually caused a lot of animals to die—rats and mice and also those animals that *hunted* rats and mice. But when the rains returned, the numbers of mice and rats grew much more quickly than the number of the animals that hunted them, so they quickly spread everywhere and so did the plague. Yes…?

B: I always understood that there were a lot of different reasons for the decline of the Roman Empire, but the logical conclusion of your argument is that it just wouldn't have happened without the drought. No drought, no decline. Is that what you're saying?

L: Well, I don't know—and I don't think anyone knows precisely, but climate change certainly set off a chain of events: the plague was caused by changes in the weather, and in turn, a lot of people within the Roman Empire died in the plague, and so the world order was changed. And, girl at the back…

C: Yes, I have a question. You mentioned the Little Ice Age. Can you explain what you meant by that? Was it really that bad?

L: No, the term "little" really describes both the fact that it was quite short and that it wasn't as intense as a regular Ice Age, but it certainly had an effect—on northern countries in particular. Crops failed and animals died. When people don't have enough food, of course, this has political and social consequences. You can see that throughout history. Yes, you in the blue shirt…

D: Umm, maybe I missed something, but how do punishments fit in with the Little Ice Age?

L: Ah, people always look for someone to blame when things go wrong, even if it's something out of our control like cold weather. So they found people that they thought were troublemakers anyway and punished them.

29

1 Am I right in thinking that the drought in Africa caused an increase in the number of rats?
2 Is that what you're saying?
3 Can you explain what you meant by that?
4 How do punishments fit in with the Little Ice Age?

Unit 8

30

P = Presenter, S = Sarah Palmer

P: OK, we hear about companies being customer-focused all the time these days, but there's no point being focused on your customers if *they* aren't focused on *you*. Sarah Palmer from the e-marketing consulting firm Excite is here to tell us how organizations can generate that kind of interest. Sarah…

S: Thanks, Sanjay. The key to good marketing is being able to turn your customers into fans, in other words, people who want to share a passion for what you do with others. These days, a company has no hope of doing that unless they use social media, not just to sell their products and services, but to really involve people in what they're doing. Basically, customers want to know your story, and they want to learn something. And *you*, the company, want to get them to buy into your story. There's no doubt that a straight sell can work occasionally; for example, if a customer happens to be looking for a particular thing at a particular time and an ad pops up on their screen. Companies are getting much better at engineering that kind of event, but creating a loyal following is far more effective.

P: So, can you give us some examples of organizations that use social media effectively, in the way that you're describing?

S: Yes, we've been looking at examples of best practices in social media marketing and a good one is National Geographic. They actively encourage fan interaction, inviting users to share travel stories, or to do surveys on how ecologically they live, and then compare their scores with their friends. You can enter competitions, and there are also links to different causes you can support—like helping to protect an endangered species.

P: OK. That all sounds great, but is there no mention of selling at all?

S: Yes, there is… there are offers of discounts for magazine subscribers, coupons you can use for National Geographic products. It's a business, too.

P: And I see how this fan-building works for an organization with a worthy mission. But what about a company that's just trying to sell a regular product, like bathroom cleaner? They have no alternative but to present the product in an ordinary way.

S: No, it's really no different—the same principles apply. Try to tell a story or engage customers in a way that's fun. No matter what you're selling, if you can involve people, you'll find an audience. I was recently looking at a company that sells tea, and their website had this great widget that gave you an interactive tour of the teas of China. It was really fun, and you wouldn't believe the number of varieties and how much some of them cost. It's a whole other world out there.

31

P = Presenter, M = Martin Roddick

P: Hello, and welcome to the *Nature Today* podcast. Today we're going to look at some new evidence about what is arguably one of the most spectacular sights in nature: the phenomenon of waves glowing at night and mirroring the stars with lots of tiny, blue lights. It's been known for some time that the source of this light is organisms called phytoplankton. But how they produce the strange blue light has been a mystery—until now. Here's Martin Roddick of the Oceanographic Institute.

M: Hi. There are a number of different bioluminescent sea creatures, in other words, that are able to glow in the dark. The creatures which have this ability tend to spend most of their lives in deep ocean waters, which suggests that being able to light yourself up, so to speak, is useful for finding food or scaring away predators, or perhaps just lighting your way as you move around. But the most common bioluminescent organisms—phytoplankton—live near the surface. And it's these that create this strange, blue light that people see on beaches and in waves.

P: And how do they do it?

M: It seems that electrical signals in the phytoplankton cause a chemical reaction to take place, producing a blue light. The light is usually emitted in waves, so it's reasonable to assume that the electrical signal is generated by motion in the water.

P: Thank you, Martin. And if you'd like to know more about this research, you can read details of the study on the OI website…

32

Today we're going to look at some new evidence about what is arguably one of the most spectacular sights in nature: the phenomenon of waves glowing at night and mirroring the stars with lots of tiny, blue lights.

Unit 9

33

1 Just a minute.
2 Phew! Just in time.
3 I'm sorry, I just don't get it.
4 Thanks, I just had one.
5 Thanks, I'm just looking.
6 Hi, did you just call?
7 We're just friends.
8 I just wondered.

34

The study of the effects of music on the brain is still a work in progress, but exciting things are coming to light all the time. We know that music activates many different parts of the brain—there's no one music center. We also know that music has the power to release endorphins. As you're probably aware, endorphins are chemicals that are vital to our well-being, released at times of stress to help us deal with pain, but also used by the body to produce feelings of happiness, elation even. So when we listen to music, we're rewarded with this boost of feel-good chemicals. Hospitals now use music to calm people before surgery, or for pain relief after an operation.

But what I'm particularly interested in is another recent finding: that of the close relationship between music and language. If you're someone who has to strain so as to hear what people are saying in a noisy room, the chances are that you're not musically trained. That's because we use the same parts of the brain to process both music and language. So those people with musical training have improved their brain's ability to distinguish specific sounds, whether musical or simply spoken.

What are the implications of this? Well, I'm not saying you should take up the violin so that you can hear people better at parties, or in order to be a better linguist—though that's not a bad idea. There are some important medical applications here. This relationship between music and language means we could use music to help people overcome conditions like dyslexia, or other learning disabilities. At Harvard, a neuroscientist called Dr. Gottfried Schlaug has had amazing results using music therapy with people who have suffered strokes. He conducted experiments with people in whom the stroke had affected the left side of their brain—the side that principally deals with language. Before the music therapy, these patients responded to questions with incoherent sounds and phrases, but when taught to sing phrases or to speak in time to the rhythm of the music, within minutes they were able to recite their addresses, say their names, and even sing parts of songs. The results were really remarkable.

Similar positive results have been recorded with patients with dementia and memory loss. This news should be music to our ears, if you'll pardon the pun. Degenerative memory function is going to become more of a problem for all of us as we live longer, and we clearly need to find a way to lessen the impact of this on people's lives. Music may just hold the key.

35

P: Today's castaway is a disc jockey who's been hosting his own radio show for over 30 years. Where most disc jockeys come and go with the changing trends in music, he has managed to maintain a loyal following of listeners over the last 35 years, and to attract new ones from each new generation. He is Frank Steel. Frank, what's the secret of your continuing success?

F: That's a good question, but it isn't something I've thought a lot about. I don't think it's a secret, really. I take an interest in what's happening now in the music world, and I look out for new trends. People do that in other fields, like science or art. It's just that with pop music, you're not supposed to stay trendy after you're 30. But I don't agree with that.

P: So you still get excited by new music. What, for you, makes a good record?

F: I honestly don't know. What makes a particular piece of music move you is something that can't really be described or identified. I'd rather not think too much about why I like a particular song or record.

P: And what's your first record?

F: This is a song by John Etheridge, a blues and jazz guitarist. I think it was the first blues record I ever heard and it opened up a whole new world to me. I also associate it with the summer of 1976, which was a really hot summer. I was supposed to be studying for exams, but I spent most of my time hanging out in the park. It was too hot to work.

P: 'Crossroad Blues' by John Etheridge. Your taste in music is very wide—eclectic, some would say. How did that happen?

F: That's hard to say. It wasn't planned, if that's what you mean. I just keep my ears open for anything interesting, and I don't confine myself to any particular source for that. It's a question of staying curious, I guess.

36

That's a good question.

That's an interesting question.

I've never really thought about it.

It's not something I've thought a lot about.

It isn't something I've thought a lot about.

I don't really look at it like that.

I honestly don't know.

I couldn't really tell you.

That's hard to say.

Frankly, I've got no idea.

37

1　perhaps
2　maybe
3　I'm not sure
4　I can't say

Unit 10

38

P: Citizenship education is a hot topic at the moment and we're seeing more countries introduce it into the curriculum in schools. But many people wonder if the approach of teaching children about the country's laws and political institutions and so on actually helps them to be better citizens. Here to discuss this is sociologist Zhang Wei. Wei, surely any training is better than none, isn't it?

W: Well, I'd like to say yes and I know the intentions are good, but I think this kind of citizenship education is missing the point.

P: And what *is* the point?

W: Of course, teaching people about the way institutions function is important, but what's far more important is to get people to think about what their duties and responsibilities to society are.

P: And in your view, young people don't know what those are.

W: Well, I don't think there are any clear-cut answers. That's why I said "get them to *think* about" these things. It's a question of noticing others in your community. There was an interesting survey done, a few years ago now, by the ISSP— that's the International Social Survey Program—which asked people from all around the world what they thought the duties of a good citizen were. People were asked to rate the importance of various duties, for example: "to be active in social organizations," or "always to obey laws and regulations." But there were some duties on a more human level, like "to try to help people who are worse off than you," and "to try to understand the reasoning of people with other opinions."

P: And you think that kind of duty is closer to the spirit of good citizenship, do you?

W: Yes, I don't think the starting point should be how we relate to state institutions, but how we relate to each other, at a more basic level.

P: And how did people rate these duties? I imagine there wasn't that much difference in the way different nationalities responded, was there?

W: Actually, there was—huge variation. For example, 60 percent of Filipinos thought it was very important to be involved in social organizations, whereas only 15 percent of Japanese did. There were also some unexpected findings. In Switzerland, only half the people surveyed thought always obeying laws and regulations was very important.

P: That *is* surprising, isn't it?

W: It is. And there were great differences too when it came to feelings of duty to one another. Eighty percent of Mexicans thought it was very important to help people worse off than you. In some other countries, it was as low as 30 percent.

P: So you'd like to see more discussion in schools about our duties to each other then?

W: Yes, I think we need to get children thinking about the basic things they can do to help a community function better: taking care of their environment, helping poorer people in the community, being open-minded and tolerant of differences. If you get those things right, the other elements will naturally follow.

39

1 Surely any training is better than none, isn't it?
2 And what is the point?
3 And you think that kind of duty is closer to the spirit of good citizenship, do you?
4 And how did people rate these duties?
5 I imagine there wasn't that much difference in the way different nationalities responded, was there?
6 That is surprising, isn't it?

40

1 You couldn't give me a hand, could you?
2 He would say that, wouldn't he?
3 You think I'm overreacting, do you?
4 Surely the answer is four, isn't it?
5 She didn't give a great performance, did she?
6 Let's go, shall we?
7 Nobody noticed I wasn't there, did they?

41

A: Hi, Jorge! Do you have time for a game of tennis this afternoon?
B: Oh hi, Rosario! 'Fraid not—I'm too busy.
A: Why? What are you doing?
B: Working. I have to get that sociology essay in by tomorrow afternoon.
A: Oh, yes. I've done mine already. What are you writing about?
B: Um, I've been researching a model society set up in the 1880s in Chicago by George Pullman, the guy who made restaurant and sleeping cars for trains.
A: Really? Sounds interesting.
B: It *is*, actually. What's odd is that he based his society on capitalist principles, thinking that capitalism was the best way for a society to fulfill its material and spiritual needs.
A: Unusual idea.
B: Yes, isn't it? 'Cuz usually utopian societies are based on some kind of communal living ideal—principles of sharing and equality and being unmaterialistic and that kind of thing. As you probably found out yourself.
A: So how did Pullman's society work?
B: Well, I'm still reading about it, but as far as I can see it was basically a purpose-built town with his factory at the center. It had a very rigid class structure with everyone knowing his place—manual workers, skilled workers, managers—with Pullman at the top, of course, living in a grand house while his workers lived in small tenements. He owned all the buildings and rented them to the workers.
A: Doesn't sound very utopian.
B: No, it doesn't, does it? And I think the workers weren't very happy. They weren't allowed unions; there was only one bar in the town and it was for visitors.
A: So I suppose it probably failed in the end then.
B: Probably—these things often do. But I haven't gotten to that part yet. I'll let you know.
A: Yeah, please do. No, seriously, I'd be very interested to know because it's a really unusual story. The one I chose was a farming community in Oklahoma. Anyway, good luck and let me know if you want a break from it. I'd love to play tennis sometime.

B: Yeah, me too. See you soon, anyway.
A: Yeah, hope so.

Unit 11

42

I: Now, does modern life stress you out? Do you wish that you felt more in control of things? If so, perhaps it's time you looked into "emotional intelligence training," a fast-growing area in the field of practical psychology. Our guest today is Naomi Myers, from the EIQ Institute, EIQ being Emotional Intelligence Quotient. Naomi, can you tell us a little more about how this works?
N: Sure. Simply put, emotional intelligence is about two things. One is understanding your own feelings so that you can recognize which are constructive and which are harmful emotions; when to follow your gut feeling and when to follow your head. The other's about understanding how others around you are feeling, and that can be particularly useful in work relationships.
I: And why do people need this training? We've gotten along without it up to now.
N: Well, as you said, modern life is stressful and confusing. And it's led to an increase in anxiety disorders across the world. In Japan right now there are nearly one million hikikomori: young people who have withdrawn totally from society and stay shut up in their bedrooms at home. We're able to help people understand their fears and overcome them. Suppose you were someone who felt very on edge when speaking in public—we have techniques for helping you deal with that.
I: Such as?
N: Well, I'd rather your listeners took one of our courses than got advice free over the radio! But, for example, we help people to eliminate negative predictions about how they're going to perform.
I: Huh, and what about reading other people's emotions? How do you help people do that?
N: Well, one thing we do is train people to read micro-expressions.
I: And what are they?
N: Well, most facial expressions remain on the face for several seconds, but micro-expressions—and we all make them—appear for only a fraction of a second. They're so short because they're a glimpse of a concealed emotion or an emotion that's been very rapidly processed. What if I were to tell you that you'd already made one of these during our discussion?
I: I'd be a little alarmed.
N: No need to be—it was just a momentary look of shock when I said I wasn't going to tell you about our training techniques. The point is that an ability to read these micro-expressions is very useful—in a business negotiation, for example, or when deciding whether to trust someone. A doctor came to me recently and said, "If only I were better at building rapport with my patients, I'd be so much better at my job," and we were able to help by training him to read people's emotions better.

43

1 a Was that a deliberate mistake?
  b Don't deliberate for too long.
2 a We need to separate the groups.
  b That's a separate issue.
3 a He's very articulate.
  b He couldn't articulate what he meant.
4 a Let's not duplicate the work.
  b I have a duplicate copy.

44

Conversation 1
A: Hi there, Phil, good to see you. How are you? Do we have time for coffee before we go into the meeting?
B: Actually, we're already late—we really need to go in right away. Do you have the report and other papers with you?
A: Yes, I have all that. You look a little upset, though. Is everything OK?
B: Do you know, Fernando, it's just that perhaps you had a different attitude toward time-keeping in your previous company. Punctuality is very important here, particularly for people like Jeff Kravitz, whom we're about to see, and I'm very anxious to start this meeting on the right note.
B: Oh, sorry, Phil. Honestly, I didn't realize. You're right, it wasn't such a big deal in my last company—the attitude toward time was much more laid back. I'll definitely try to be more punctual in the future. And don't worry—I'm very well prepared for this meeting. It's going to be good.

Conversation 2
C: Becky, have you got a minute to talk about your design for the new ad? I don't think it's quite there yet and we need to send it over to the web designer tomorrow.
D: Oh, I'm surprised. I included all your suggestions from our last meeting. I thought it was looking OK. Uh, perhaps you should get another person to look at it.
C: I'm sorry, I didn't mean to offend you. These things are always subjective, but please don't take it personally.
D: No, I'm sorry, Alicia, that came out wrong. I'm not offended. I genuinely meant it would be a good idea to get a third opinion. But whatever you want. I'm very happy to work with you to get it looking right.
C: Thanks. I appreciate that. I'll call Stacey and see if we can arrange a meeting with all three of us to look at it this afternoon.

Conversation 3
F: Hi, Megumi. I haven't seen you for a long time. How are you? Jen said you'd gotten a new job with an American company in Tokyo.
E: That's right. With Disney. I'm going to be in charge of all the merchandise for classic storybook characters, like Winnie the Pooh, Alice in Wonderland, Pinocchio. I'm very excited. Why are you smiling? Did I say something funny?
F: Oh, I'm sorry, please don't think I'm rude—I wasn't laughing at you. It was just the idea of being in charge of all those characters, like a playgroup leader or something. It conjured up a funny mental picture. But it sounds great. When do you start?

45

alarmed

concerned

distressed

embarrassed

insulted

offended

shocked

surprised

worried

Unit 12

 46

I: Sophie Huxter, you're best known for writing travel guides, but recently you've been writing about the Japanese poet Matsuo Basho. Can you tell us what attracted you to him?

B: Yes, it was the subject of observing nature, especially its little details—the brilliant color of a particular flower, or the way light catches the spray from a waterfall and makes a rainbow. When I started to look into it, it really struck me how much I took the natural world for granted. And I think that's probably true for most of us: that observing nature is either a bit of a luxury, or just something that gets forgotten, because we all get too caught up in our own busy lives.

I: And how does that relate to Basho?

B: Yeah, well, that's quite interesting, because as a poet, one of his preoccupations was observing nature and writing down his thoughts. But fairly late in life, he decided he needed to get away from it all and get closer to nature. You see, Basho was already quite a well-known poet in his lifetime and he wanted to escape his celebrity and live a more simple life. So at the age of 46, he set off on a journey across the island of Honshu. That journey was the background to his masterpiece in poetry, *Narrow Road to a Far Province*.

I: Ah, yes, I know it… at least parts of it.

B: So, he traveled on foot through Japan's backcountry—a distance of slightly less than 1,200 miles—and he kept a kind of diary of the things he saw in poem form as he went. So he would stop along the way to observe nature's modest dramas: a leaf floating through reflections in a crystal clear stream, the splash of a frog as it hopped from a leaf into the water, the sunlight on an avenue of trees on an autumn evening.

I: That's a lovely way of putting it— nature's modest dramas.

B: Well, what I love about the poems is that the language he uses is rather plain and simple, but the overall effect is very profound. Each haiku is like a polished stone; it captures the beauty and simplicity of nature in just a few words. I'll read you an example of one which pretty much sums this up. At one point, he came across an old ruined military fort, overgrown with grass, and it kind of upset him. He wrote: "Mound of summer grass / Are soldiers' heroic deeds / Only dreams that pass?"

 47

A: OK, so we'd like to hear your views about two possible ways of relieving traffic congestion downtown. Craig is just going to summarize the two main proposals before we open up the discussion. Craig…

B: Thank you. The first proposal is a congestion toll, that's to say creating a zone downtown which vehicles have to pay a fixed fee to enter. The exact limits of the zone haven't been defined yet, nor has the exact amount of the fee. The second proposal involves simply banning all private cars from downtown and providing a park-and-ride bus service from various points on the outskirts of the city into the downtown.

A: Thanks, Craig. So now we'll open the discussion to the floor. Please try and keep your comments reasonably short so that everyone gets a chance to speak.

C: Well, I don't see how we can really comment on the first proposal without knowing what the scope of the zone is and how much it's going to cost: those really are key issues. I mean, if it's going to mean that local residents have to pay to get downtown, then that's not really fair, is it?

I live on Charles Street, which is…

D: Excuse me, can I just say something in answer to that? We had a similar plan where I used to live and people who lived within the zone were exempted from paying the fee.

B: Yes, I think that's absolutely right, and you can also give a discount to people who work downtown so that it doesn't discriminate against them, either. Otherwise a lot of people who really need their cars…

D: No, hang on a minute. If you keep making exceptions for different groups of people, you're going to end up with a system that costs a lot of money and doesn't provide much benefit. I think you have to be strict about this…

C: Yes, but how much is the fee going to be? No one's given us any…

D: Excuse me, can I just finish what I was saying? The point is that unless you're strict about it, the plan won't bring in enough revenue to pay for itself, and so those who do pay will question the whole thing.

 48

Excuse me, can I just interrupt you there?

Can I just say something in answer to that?

No, hang on a minute…

No, I'm sorry I have to stop you there…

Yes, but…

Excuse me, can I just finish what I was saying?

Just a moment, please…

OK, you can make your point in a minute.